TRANSFORMING DISPLACED WOMEN IN SUDAN

TRANSFORMING DISPLACED WOMEN IN SUDAN

Politics and the Body in a Squatter Settlement

ROGAIA MUSTAFA ABUSHARAF

THE UNIVERSITY OF CHICAGO PRESS • *Chicago and London*

Rogaia Mustafa Abusharaf is associate professor of anthropology at Qatar University and visiting scholar in the Human Rights Program at Harvard Law School. She is the author of *Wanderings: Sudanese Migrants and Exiles in North America* and editor of *Female Circumcision: Multicultural Perspectives,* as well as special issues of the *Ahfad Journal* and the *South Atlantic Quarterly.*

The University of Chicago Press, Chicago 60637
The University of Chicago Press, Ltd., London
© 2009 by The University of Chicago
All rights reserved. Published 2009
Printed in the United States of America
17 16 15 14 13 12 11 10 09   1 2 3 4 5

ISBN-13: 978-0-226-00199-9 (cloth)
ISBN-10: 0-226-00199-7 (cloth)
ISBN-13: 978-0-226-00200-2 (paper)
ISBN-10: 0-226-00200-4 (paper)

Library of Congress Cataloging-in-Publication Data

Abusharaf, Rogaia Mustafa.
   Transforming displaced women in Sudan : politics and the body in a squatter settlement / Rogaia Mustafa Abusharaf.
       p.   cm.
   Includes bibliographical references and index.
   ISBN-13: 978-0-226-00199-9 (cloth: alk. paper)
   ISBN-10: 0-226-00199-7 (cloth: alk. paper)
   ISBN-13: 978-0-226-00200-2 (pbk.: alk. paper)
   ISBN-10: 0-226-00200-4 (pbk.: alk. paper)   1. Squatter settlements—Sudan—Khartoum.   2. Squatters—Sudan—Khartoum.   3. Internally displaced persons—Sudan—Khartoum.   4. Women—Sudan—Khartoum—Social conditions.
5. Khartoum (Sudan)—Social conditions.   I. Title.
   HD7287.96.S732K437   2009
   305.48'96914096262—dc22

                                                   2008043528

In loving memory of Abdel Khaliq Mahgoub,
who first conceived of the promise of the New Sudan,
and of Mustafa Abusharaf,
who devoted his life to its fulfillment

CONTENTS

A gallery of photographs appears following page 110.

ACKNOWLEDGMENTS

The powerful voices of women in Khartoum's shantytowns provided inestimable help in posing crucial questions, explaining the predicaments of displacement, exploring innovations, probing mysteries, and articulating the imaginings of southerners who have been forced by civil war to live in the northern capital of our native Sudan. On countless occasions, southern Sudanese women, despite being desperately bereft, tolerated my inquiring presence with patient good humor and opened up to me about their intimate worries and hopes for restoration. I salute their struggle, courage, and forbearance. In particular, Cecilia Joseph, Haboba, Silas Jojo, and Chaplain Moi were instrumental throughout my research; without their friendship and cooperation, conducting this ethnography would have been difficult, perhaps impossible. To David Brent at the University of Chicago Press, I convey my utmost gratitude for his remarkable insight and consistent support of this project. I am thankful to Grey Osterud, who helped me organize this unruly mass of material and streamline its presentation, and to three anonymous reviewers, whose critiques enabled me to clarify and sharpen my arguments.

Several institutions and foundations made it possible for me to embark on a long ethnographic journey that extended from 2000 to 2008 in the Sudan, the United Kingdom, and the United States. I wish particularly to acknowledge financial support from the United Kingdom's Royal Anthropological Institute, the Harry Frank Guggenheim Foundation, and the Andrew Mellon–MIT Center for International Studies. Fellowships at Brown, Durham, and Harvard universities offered stimulating intellectual exchange. I am especially indebted to Michael Ignatieff of the Carr Center for Human Rights Policy at Harvard University's Kennedy School of Government, who has since become leader of the Liberal Party in Canada; Ignatieff read my work attentively, asked perceptive questions, and gave me constructive commentary throughout this project.

Also at Harvard, Henry Louis Gates Jr., Jennifer Leaning, David Little, and Larry Sullivan were extremely supportive; Samira Khan provided excellent research assistance. At MIT, Sharon Stanton-Russell was especially helpful. At Brown, Elizabeth Weed has been an invaluable resource during the years I have been working on these issues. At Durham, Robert Layton and Paul Sant-Cassia conducted significant discussions about the theoretical and empirical framework of urgent anthropology within which I situated this project. I also thank my advanced students at Durham, particularly Tom Newmark and Loveday Silence Redgate. I received equally constructive comments from my students at Brown, Tufts, and Wellesley. Most recently, my students at Qatar University in Doha raised pointed questions about culture and politics; I am especially grateful to Abdel Rahman Al-Thani, Najla Al-Shammari, Aljazi Al-Gahtani, Zowayna Al-Kalbani, Woddouh Al-Marri, and Looloa Al-Thani.

Colleagues invited me to speak about this project at Barnard, Brandeis, Cornell, Dartmouth, Franklin and Marshall, Middlebury, Northwestern, Temple, Yale, and John Moore Liverpool University; special thanks to Mark Auslander, Misty Bastian, Elizabeth Castelli, Lewis Gordon, Maggie O'Donnell, Rosalind Shaw, Leni Silverstein, and Eiman Zein. Michael Steinberg invited me to deliver one of the inaugural lectures for the Cogut Center for the Humanities at Brown University, where I received very valuable comments. The "Future of Minority Studies" symposium, convened at Cornell University by Satya Mohanty of Cornell and Chandra Mohanty of Syracuse University, was especially stimulating. I am particularly grateful to Salah Hassan of Africana Studies at Cornell, a fellow Sudanese who shares my concerns about reconciliatory practices in Khartoum's communities of displaced southerners, for helping me understand the localized enactment of peace at the level of the everyday. I also benefited from discussion of this project as part of the "Migratory Aesthetics: Thinking Mobility Two Ways" panel in Murcia, Spain, in 2007; I especially appreciate Mieke Bal's enthusiasm for my arguments.

My father, Mustafa Abusharaf, did not live to see this book in print, but his support and example were essential throughout this project. He offered invaluable assistance by speaking to my southern friends in their local language; many of them described him as the nicest Arab man they had ever met. His affection and affinity for the people of the South, as well as his memories of working and living in the region, inspired my respectful interest in displaced southerners' stories. His dedication to a multiethnic Sudan was at the foundation of his progressive vision for the country. My uncle, Mohamed Mahgoub Osman, also discussed this project with me over the years. Both men recognized this work's complementarity with my previous research on Sudanese exiles and stressed the deeper quandaries of the tearing apart of communities that the overwhelming experience of *alshatat* or dispersal has visited upon Sudanese citizens both within and beyond the nation's borders. To my Sudanese friends, Fahima Abdel Hafiz Hashim, Somia Kardash, and Father William Deng of Saints Patrick and Paul Cathedral in Khartoum, who provided much-needed assistance every step of the way, I extend my deepest appreciation.

Finally, I express my thanks to the Rift Valley Institute. John Ryle and Justin Willis invited me to join them in Rumbek, Southern Sudan, for conversations that proved critical in expanding the scope of my queries about voluntary return to the South after the Comprehensive Peace Agreement. Ambassador Swanee Hunt gave me an invaluable opportunity to serve as rapporteur for one of the most important peace initiatives organized by Inclusive Security: Women Waging Peace in Washington, D.C., where I was able to follow exchanges on international peacemaking vis-à-vis my home country. In this context, I had the good fortune to deliver presentations to the Woodrow Wilson Center for International Scholars, the U.S. Institute of Peace, and the United Nations. Hunt also facilitated my speaking about displacement and peacemaking with International Alert, an NGO based in London. I owe Ambassador Hunt a great debt for broadening the horizons of my commitment to public anthropology.

When all is said and done, any shortcomings that remain in this book are mine alone.

I am grateful to the editors and publishers of journals where portions of the material in this study previously appeared in different forms:

"Life in Khartoum: Forced Migration and Cultural Change among Displaced Women." 2004. Rosemary Rogers Working Papers Series, no. 30. Cambridge, MA: MIT Center for International Studies.

"Narrating Feminism: The Woman Question in the Thinking of an African Radical." *Differences* 5, no. 2 (2004): 152–71.

"'The Shadow of a Man Is *Not* Better Than the Shadow of a Wall': The Uses of Anthropology in Understanding Women's Human Rights and Struggles in the Sudan." *Oriental Anthropologist* 4, no. 1 (2004): 1–19.

"Smoke Bath: Renegotiating Self and the World in a Sudanese Shantytown." *Anthropology and Humanism* 30, no. 1 (2005): 1–22.

"Sudanese Women Waging Peace." *Forced Migration Review* 24 (2005): 44–46.

"Virtuous Cuts: Female Genital Excision in an African Ontology." *Differences* 12, no. 1 (2001): 112–40. Reprinted in *Going Public: Feminism and the Shifting Boundaries of Public and Private,* ed. Joan Wallach Scott and Debra Keates, 201–25. Urbana: University of Illinois Press, 2004.

INTRODUCTION

Through the Eyes of the Displaced

Transforming Displaced Women in Sudan: Politics and the Body in a Squatter Settlement begins and ends in medias res, in an unstable present poised between a violent past and an unknowable future. It looks back to women's lost homes from the vantage point of their traumatic sundering and forward toward their prospects as they themselves envision them. This community of southern Sudanese women was forged in a shantytown on the outskirts of Khartoum, the largely Muslim, heavily Arabized capital city of Sudan. The internally displaced persons (IDPs) at the center of this ethnography had already been there for some time in 2000; most still remain in this makeshift settlement today.

Positioned within urgent anthropological and feminist ethnographic frames, this book is based on personal interviews with displaced women and careful observation of the strategies they adopt to reconstruct their lives and livelihoods. Their voices and viewpoints are presented alongside an analysis of the problems they confront on a daily basis. Exploring gender, the body, political violence, and social transformation, it describes the interweaving of culture and politics in ordinary life and interrogates discourses on Arabism and Africanism in a nation that perceives itself as a link between Africans and Arabs. Building on the peace they make among the diverse residents of the camps and shantytowns and translating their victimization into activism, displaced women's groups speak out to ensure that the internationally mediated agreements intended to resolve conflict encompass gender equity, cultural difference, and national citizenship.

In presenting the experiences of women in Khartoum who were displaced from villages in Southern Sudan, I demonstrate that when everything is unsettled, space can be opened for positive changes as well as irretrievable losses, provided that women are able to summon the resources necessary to resume their lives. The gendered self is transformed through the experience of displacement and through women's encounters with the rituals of bodily modification prevalent in their host communities. I explore why they adopt, alter, and/or reject such practices as henna, the smoke bath, and female circumcision in the process of negotiating identities and relationships with others. Understanding sociality among IDPs is of paramount importance given the extent of forced migration in a country that has been described as "the cradle of displacement" (Ruiz 1998).[1] Squatter settlements are not necessarily chaotic localities whose residents are utterly abject and subject to sadistic deeds, as prevailing images suggest. This ethnography shows that these shantytowns are sites of cultural production where questions about multiple, mutually reinforcing marginalities are constantly being raised in ways that promise radical changes in society at large. Speaking directly about the consequences of African civil wars and gender inequality, this book uncovers fundamental quandaries of displacement: the struggle for subsistence on the fringe of cities by women without kin, property, or rights; the renegotiation of identities and relationships; and the connections among women's informal interactions, their exclusion from state politics, and their organizing to overcome differences among themselves and to make peace in their country.

In this shantytown, I discovered potential resources for progressive politics akin to those I encountered in my earlier research on political life in the context of transnational migration, discussed in *Wanderings: Sudanese Migrants and Exiles in North America* (Abusharaf 2002). While the exile community in the United States and Canada was described then as a "nation in absentia," this work explores displaced communities within Sudan as nations in microcosm. In both settings, in spite of the ocean between them, the bridging of gaps between people who have come from diverse backgrounds generates powerful stories of hope for a society grappling with infinite turmoil and obstinate antagonisms. The displaced are initiating new forms of dialogue with their hosts as each becomes keenly aware of the miseries of the other within the milieu they share. In these shantytowns, displaced women meet women from diverse cultural groups in the South and West and impoverished women from northern Sudan who are also struggling to eke out a living. In large measure, they confront the Sudanese state together, not separately. To shed light on the complex dimensions of displacement and selective adjustment, I address subjects that range from "zones of taboo" (Das 1997), such as women's intimate bodily practices, to social conflict and state politics. In excavating the effects of forced migration on subjectivity and collectivity, ever-shifting notions of home, loss, and recovery are germinal to uncovering women's efforts to mitigate massive violence by engaging in local diplomacy and day-by-day strategies of truth and reconciliation.

An ethnography that locates promises of healing does not require a recitation of the fraught history of the Sudan from the colonial period to the present. Not only would a capsule history be redundant, given the extensive coverage of the topic elsewhere, but it would vastly oversimplify a complex, contentious past that has been written, read, and interpreted differently by Sudanese people themselves. Instead of taking readers on a long detour through a "background" whose trajectory and relevance to the present are debatable, this book begins with what is happening in the foreground of the Sudanese political scene and explores how the many pasts of southern women in the northern capital figure in the present. Most important, careful scrutiny of this conflict within the context of Sudanese history reveals that the polarities of Arabs versus Africans, nomads versus villagers, and ethnic secessionists versus centralizing state that dominate current international discourse are woefully misleading. This ethnography interrogates false dichotomies and misplaced assumptions about conflict between North and South, viewing questions of identity and polity through the eyes of the displaced.

This book does not attempt a longitudinal study that would focus on a few specific groups and trace the dynamic processes of transformation that occurred under stressful conditions through their multiple displacements. No anthropologist who encounters the dilemmas of social and cultural analysis in conflict-ridden societies could undertake such a project, except perhaps by generalizing about the past from studies of different people living under conditions that diverged markedly from those of the subjects at hand. In the Sudan there is no static "before," no golden era of peace and stability that was suddenly interrupted by armed conflict, as many analyses of the impact of war on civilian populations assume. Indeed, that model is singularly inapplicable to the African continent, whose history of conflict extends nearly uninterrupted from generations of resistance to colonial regimes through the power struggles that mark so many postcolonial states. Instead, this ethnography starts from the premise that the gender relations that prevailed before these women's forced migration were neither uniform nor fixed and documents the specific forms in which those whose lives were disrupted by political violence communicate their responses to the atrocities that beleaguered them for decades. It is impossible to trace individuals and kin groups through the chaotic, dreadful terrain they traversed on the way to Khartoum; indeed, that so many became lost to one another is the single most salient fact of their present lives. The problems that displaced women face are so daunting that they would crush anyone who had not already survived the violent destruction of her family, home, and way of life. Some women I interviewed were still so afflicted by their losses that they wondered aloud whether they might be better off dead. The reunions that they had hoped for with the loved ones from whom they had been forcibly separated seemed more and more impossible as the years wore on, and everything that sustained them receded into the irretrievable past. These women's existential question arose from their sense that the continuation of their existence was merely a condemnation to suffering. Their eloquent utterances were followed by silence; there was no possible reply.

The effects of displacement on gender relations can only be assessed within the particularities of these multiple and various statements, because conditions that prevailed in Sudan since its independence militate against any homogenization of southern women's experiences. This ethnography—located at the vital intersections of social, economic, political, and cultural processes—shows the fortitude and purpose of women whose lives have been shattered and reinvented strategically in resistance and explores how they moved forward in situations of extreme violence and despair.

Urgent Anthropology

I began doing fieldwork in the government-run camps and squatter settlements in the vicinity of Khartoum in 2000,[2] when some southern women had been there for a decade and others had just arrived (Abusharaf 2004a). In the shantytown I call Izzbba,[3] I conducted a systematic survey of residents and intensive interviews with a cross-section of women forced by civil war to flee their homes. I have continued to visit these places regularly ever since, following my subjects through the closure of camps, the eviction of squatters, and their makeshift resettlements. As some women have established a more stable existence, newly displaced women have arrived from Darfur. In Rumbek, a former garrison town in the South, I participated in conversations focused on questions of repatriation and return following the signing of the Comprehensive Peace Agreement (CPA) in 2005. I also served as an international rapporteur on initiatives aimed at putting gender at the center of peace negotiations. My own perspectives have been shaped by the triangulation of ethnographic material and civic dialogue in the North and the South, as well as Europe and America. Taken together, these multifarious fieldwork sites have yielded extraordinary insights into women's ever-shifting ideas about self and the world. As a Sudanese woman, I seek to bring their most desperate problems to international attention by presenting the gendered impact of political violence on women. My inquiries were welcomed by displaced women, who always gave me the benefit of the doubt: not only was I an outsider delving into their intimate lives, but I was a northerner, albeit a displaced one, a daughter of what is perceived as the educated elite in Sudanese society who has gone to America but not forgotten her homeland.

Urgent anthropology is an essential tool for narrating the experiences and perspectives of people living with the unspeakable consequences of mass atrocities. It provides the basis not only for increasing others' knowledge of communities undergoing extreme brutality but also for articulating displaced people's own views about their rights and entitlements and developing public policy that facilitates the rehabilitation of their fractured lives. Anthropology's growing recognition of the significance of human rights supplies essential resources for addressing key questions regarding its efficacy. In a theoretical and methodological commentary on urgent anthropology, Russell Bernard pointed out the most obvious problem with this approach: "We [anthropologists] surely have no way of knowing or testing urgency." He concluded, "I think we should continue to follow our interests in selecting our research" (1973, 330). The crucial question, however, is not how to define urgency, as if making the term more precise would make the enterprise more scientific, but rather who gets to define urgency and whose material as well as intellectual interests should set our priorities. Although it is perhaps counterintuitive to suggest that anthropologists should take into account the relevance of ethnography to the subjects in question, it is ultimately they who inform our understanding. To me, urgency lies in the glaring glossing over of the experiences of displaced women as gendered bodies besieged by war and who, some presume, are without reflexive self-consciousness or social and political perspectives of their own. Urgent anthropology creates conditions of possibility for a cross-cultural conversation in which both parties have equal speaking parts.

Like other participants in ethnographies documenting the devastating long-term effects of massive violence, these women were anxious to tell their stories in the hope of reaching a wider audience (see Bell 2001). When I explained to Angelina Bortolo Odengala, the housekeeper at a Catholic parish in Khartoum, that it is a common practice to hold the names of people and places in confidence so as to safeguard their rights to privacy, she replied unequivocally: "I don't want my name changed. I don't want to be unknown. You can keep my name as is. What if someone reads the story and decides to help me out of this misery?" Speaking in their own names rather than anonymously helps women affected by war to verbalize their desire for an acknowledgment of their grievances and suffering. Most important, urgent anthropology holds researchers accountable to those whose lives we expose to critical examination. Although it makes public their victimization and suffering, it enables these women to emerge as agents of change rather than naive objects whose lives are to be interpreted by experts.

Christina Dudu, who is active in the Sudan Council of Churches and owns a tailoring shop in Khartoum, has demonstrated that although southern Sudanese women have varying opinions about the problems they encounter in the capital, they recognize common losses and gains (1999). Losses include the disintegration of kin networks, child sexual abuse, ill health and reproductive difficulties, lack of food security, destruction and deprivation of economic resources, unemployment, and limited access to education. The stories of these women remain hidden from public view, yet similar experiences were prevalent across the South, as they are now in Darfur in the West and in the disputed regions of the East. Breaking the silence about breaches of human rights is one of the priorities of urgent anthropology that guided my research.

Urgent anthropology dovetails with its public anthropology counterpart in highlighting anthropologists' burgeoning role in a world in flux, when accountability to those whose lives are central to our scholarship is of utmost ethical import (see Bourgeois 1997; Harrison 1997). It departs from salvage anthropology, its predecessor, whose preoccupation with rapidly vanishing cultures has long been called into question. *Transforming Displaced Women in Sudan* is not aimed at documenting linguistic and cultural groups that are threatened with extinction or merely compiling testimonies by persons in distressful social situations. In framing this work within urgent anthropology, I ask: Can ethnography promote public understanding of displaced women's predicament? Can it be of material help in fostering their interests and advancing their welfare by relying heavily on their views as individuals whose lives and communities have been disrupted by political violence? Urgent anthropology responds to these queries by placing victims front and center in the analysis of the institutionalized power of the state over citizens.

It also sheds light on the potential for sound human rights policies, given the chronic instability that pervades Sudan. As I write, the threat of the resumption of conflict between the ruling party and its partners in the Sudan People's Liberation Movement, which together formed the coalition Government of National Unity, looms on the horizon. As the crisis in Darfur has unfolded since 2003, the country has gained wide notoriety in the media; both scholarly attention and international humanitarian concern have focused on these seemingly interminable and intractable political disputes. This conflict took a new twist as a massive attack against civilians was launched in Omdurman, just north of the capital, by the armed forces of the Justice and Equality Movement in May 2008.

Descriptions that come from both the displaced and their hosts demonstrate the volatility of these communities, making this research project an example of what Carol Greenhouse, Elizabeth Mertz, and Kay Warren call "ethnography in unstable places" (2002; see also Nordstrom 1997). Amid this constant fluidity, the stories of women in Izzbba striving to find their own inner rhythms offer compelling examples of tenacity and resilience. These women's narratives of change in their everyday lives provide powerful commentaries on how identities have been produced on a daily basis within and beyond the shantytown. I pay particular attention to the effects of forced migration on subjectivity, foregrounding the difficulties women face as gendered and embodied beings.

Urgent anthropology explicates the intricacies of complex emergencies and examines the woefully inadequate public responses to refugees and IDPs. When the topic of protection of civilians comes to the fore, as it does on many occasions as the centenary of the first International Peace Conference at The Hague approaches, various topics occupy top priority: "evolving norms and laws, international organizations and their strategies, the interests and behavior of belligerents, and case reviews of the local contexts in which violence against civilians occurs" (Jones and Cater 2001, 237). Women's concerns remain largely invisible. Unlike many other IDPs, who fled to places under the precarious control of the Southern Sudanese opposition forces, these women had to take refuge in the territory ruled by the regime that figured in their home communities as the oppressor, both because it sought to impose Islamic law on non-Muslims and because it attempted to appropriate the South's rich energy resources. Southern Sudanese women living on the margins of the sprawling capital city faced daunting challenges: victimized by war, bereft of their families and kin, uprooted from their lands and villages, and stripped of resources, they were plunged into an urban milieu that had no place for them and, when it noticed them at all, met them with hostility.

Displaced women have long experience in coping with neglect, gendered violence, and political conflict and have much to contribute to the foundation of a just and lasting peace in the country. By engaging their concerns, this ethnography affords them the opportunity to articulate their views on the politics of war, as well as offering them ownership and recognizing their agency. In bringing together displaced women's stories, this book interprets their experiences in the context of Sudanese society and places their perspectives on war, displacement, and resettlement in the broad framework of human rights and grassroots, as well as international, approaches to peacemaking.

Feminist Ethnography

In mapping out the shifting terrain on which IDPs are reformulating their lives, I rely on women's testimony and ethnographic observation as the authoritative sources on their forced migration and the reconfiguration of their lives in northern Sudan. Long quotations from these interviews, which I conducted in Arabic and have translated into English, are central to this work.[4] Through feminist ethnography,[5] I explore the ways in which women reposition themselves in situations of war and social upheaval and the microeconomy of cultural exchange through which they reconstruct their identities and communities.

The wedding of urgent anthropology to feminist ethnography is critical for the interpretation of displaced women's subjectivities, revealing major transformations in gender relations, generational positions, ethnocultural identities, religious affiliations, and political orientations. I do not portray these women as passive victims. Instead, this ethnography is committed to illuminating their creativity and agency by delineating the complex reshaping of ideas about self and society that takes place during the profound upheaval wrought by war (see Abusharaf 2005a). Southern women's responses to the overwhelming experience of displacement varied widely. Not only did they come from different cultural backgrounds, socioeconomic situations, and family positions, but they were able to make a living, re-create family and kinship ties, and orient themselves to an alien urban society to differing degrees. Without erasing the wide variations in displaced women's responses to their predicament, I analyze key elements of their adaptations, including their ways of securing livelihoods, reconfiguring family and kinship ties, establishing new friendships and social networks, adopting or refusing to adopt bodily practices from their new neighbors, shifting religious affiliations, and taking political action in forms that range from unruly crowds to peace organizations. Finally, I consider their common and divergent responses to the question of repatriation to the South.

The overwhelming majority of women in this study now live without adult men, though many have sons growing up in Khartoum and a few are in contact with older kinsmen. They can still be studied as gendered beings, in large part because women's relationships with other women are enacted on gendered ground. Visitors to camps and shantytowns observe immediately that adult men are singularly absent. Those who were not killed in the war or by the diseases, accidents, and unexplained disappearances that displacement entailed tended to depart for the armed forces, gather in places closer to home, or become refugees across international boundaries. While women with small children in tow undertook painfully long journeys across treacherous and increasingly unfamiliar terrain to end up in Khartoum, those adult men who survived the destruction of their home villages circled more locally, moving in and out of the armed forces, finding and fleeing areas temporarily under the control of the resistance, and crossing and recrossing nearby borders, often all of these in succession. The war zone was so fatal that displaced women cannot hope to be reunited with the husbands, brothers, fathers, and sons who initially fled in other directions; family members who have not found one another during the intervening years are, with good reason, presumed to be dead. A considerable number of young men from the South who had witnessed the killing of their parents and been separated from their surviving relatives fled to other nations and sought refuge in North America, where this orphaned remnant has become widely known as "the lost boys of the Sudan." Their harrowing treks and more or less successful adaptations to American life are chronicled in leading newspapers, television programs, and autobiographical novels. Attention has focused on these few young men who journeyed across deserts and oceans, but not on the many mature women who brought younger children and other dependents from the South to the capital city in the North a thousand or more miles away. Women have not received commensurate attention despite their bleak situations and the myriad problems they face.[6]

Within feminist ethnography, first-person narratives have considerable appeal as a methodology for retelling and interpreting experience (Abu Lughod 1990). However, this project is not intended to add yet another collection of tales of woe to the vast body of testimony on human suffering around the globe by presenting unmediated, decontextualized, and depoliticized narratives. I seek to bring the narrators' desperate problems to international attention by presenting the tremendous impact of political violence on women as gendered, classed, raced, and embodied beings (cf. Cooke 1996; Williams 1991). In bringing the voices of southern Sudanese IDPs to larger audiences, my utilization of feminist ethnography highlights the gender-specific ways in which women suffer during and after massive violence. It shows how squatter settlements can become zones of cooperation and reparation rather than extended zones of conflict, unlike many camps for IDPs and refugees in other conflict regions.

Narratives of change in women's everyday lives provide powerful commentaries on how identities have been reproduced and renegotiated. Most elements of social organization are revisited as women cope with traumatic memories and adapt to their new circumstances. With respect to cultural change and adjustment, I do not hold a static notion of identity, for that is entirely inappropriate, especially to the Sudanese context. If identity is "the way in which we more or less self-consciously locate ourselves in our social world" (Preston 1997, 43), we might even conclude that it is a brilliant masquerade. The peoples of Southern Sudan are remarkably diverse, not only culturally but also in their specific encounters with the northern-dominated state and in their involvement in various movements and moments of political and armed resistance. "Southern Sudanese" comprises people from a wide variety of ethnocultural and linguistic groups, and any meaningful discussion of cultural traditions must refer to more specific groups. For example, though some are Christian, many hold what Sudan's constitution calls "Noble Spiritual Beliefs," indigenous faith practices that are unique to specific locales. Yet, these women themselves declared, the conditions of displacement make it impossible for them to continue the cultural traditions that they practiced at home. In the disjunction between past and present, the unbridgeable gap between the locally grounded faith traditions of their southern villages and the world religions that exercise hegemony in their northern urban environment, women find both loss and opportunity. While some cling to memories they can no longer enact as rituals, many turn to the churches and mosques that welcome them. Their shifting religious affiliations exemplify their forging of new identities and affiliations.

Displacement and bereavement necessitate the reconfiguration of selves and of relationships with others. When this process occurs in an environment as diverse and dynamic as a Khartoum shantytown, cultural specificities and differences are revisited as social networks are rebuilt. After the destruction of support systems, especially marital ties and kinship networks, and amid exposure to the plethora of particular ethnocultural and linguistic groups and the multiple and simultaneous religious affiliations of other women from across southern Sudan, new, flexible, and often plural self-identifications arise among IDPs. Over time, through communication and cooperation with other southerners, sister IDPs, and native-born, poverty-stricken shantytown dwellers, as well as through more or less conflictual contacts with well-off residents of Khartoum, organized Muslims, and the state, collective identities emerge as Southern Sudanese, as IDPs, and as women citizens of a multicultural nation.

Both within and outside of Sudan, where polarizations dominate discourse among the national elite and international bodies, identities cannot be treated in a singular and narrow fashion. What becomes audible at the grass roots are the ways in which difference has been revisited through the reconfiguration of selves in new locations. Southern Sudanese is neither an oppositional category ascribed or imposed by northern Sudanese nor a category constituted solely by political formations such as the Sudanese People's Liberation Movement and Army (SPLM/A). Rather, in the camps and shantytowns, IDPs from a range of diverse groups have developed a sense of common identity. Some think of themselves as southerners, and thus different not only from the host society, especially the Islamic fundamentalist state, but also from their previous identities as members of specific groups, such as Balanda, Dinka, or Fujulu. This emergent identity might be called pan-Southern, parallel to the "pan-Indian" identity that developed among some Native American groups in the 1960s after they mixed and mingled in urban areas and joined in political coalitions. Some displaced southern Sudanese women identify with others as IDPs, and thus share experiences with Darfurians and others, many of whom are Muslims. Some, perhaps those with the most prolonged and frequent contact with the surrounding neighborhoods and the rest of the city, think of themselves as belonging to the urban poor who live on the fringes of the Sudanese capital. Those emergent identities are emic, developing inside this culture, rather than imposed by the ethnographer or the government. The contemporary scene is in too much flux and disarray to yield a singular answer to the predicament of identity.

As displaced women have reconstructed their livelihoods, identities, and relationships, many appreciate the gains they felt came with dramatic shifts in gender politics. Women attained more autonomy and were able to think and act independently when they migrated alone or became heads of household. A social worker in the camps who also comes from the South told me: "In Khartoum, the woman is the mother, the father, the worker, the provider. She is everything. When a man sits home all day when his wife is working, he starts to become very hateful and resentful. He can turn into a nasty beast, as happened to me with my husband, whom I kicked out not so long ago. But this doesn't change the fact that there are improvements for women in the process." Whether relationships ended because of warfare or the alienation consequent on displacement, women have gained self-respect and the power to demand respect from others. An Izzbba resident, L.K., remarked that she gave her husband a book about the rights of women, but when she takes power he becomes depressed. Displacement entails a surprising, yet necessary, degree of empowerment. Women confronting impoverishment and social marginality exhibit amazing resourcefulness, improvising new ways of earning a subsistence and adopting new modes of living as they adjust to the urban environment. In order to form new social ties with their hosts, the majority of displaced women strive to "compose a life"—to borrow a phrase from Mary Catherine Bateson (1989).

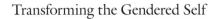

Transforming the Gendered Self

To contend that displaced women have succeeded to a great extent in cultivating and nurturing social networks that encompass other segments of the urban poor is not to romanticize life in squatter settlements and IDP camps or to portray the complex, unstable relationships generated there as entirely amicable. Conflicts develop under conditions of extreme scarcity of resources, and antagonisms are sharpened as persistent governmental neglect exacerbates poverty and powerlessness. Adjustment and discord should be seen as a continuum in which conflict is resolved as life proceeds and people become more aware of the root causes of their misery and deprivation. These ideas were set out with abundant clarity in IDPs' accounts of social life as they attempt to eke out a subsistence by relying chiefly on their wits. Although these shifts can be considered as conscious tactics for self-empowerment, I do not treat women's responses as homogenous forms of social action. No one can pronounce what is feminist and what is not. Rather, I develop a notion of feminist praxis that explicitly builds on these women's voices, viewpoints, and visions of the future by articulating their most intimate worries and recounting not only their difficulties and discontents but also their prospects and aspirations for improving their lives and regenerating their communities.

The chapters that follow show the tenacity and resilience of women who have managed to reconstitute their lives through selective adaptations and strategic decisions. When urgent anthropology is linked to feminist ethnography, with their common focus on heightening women's abilities to narrate their concerns in concrete political terms, a new picture of transformative politics appears. These narratives trace displaced women's emergent identities as southern Sudanese and IDPs, as they move from their specific ethnocultural, linguistic, and religious groups through the destruction of support systems for those identities in the process of displacement to the formation of new self-identifications, relationships, and solidarities. What lessons can we draw from the story of displaced communities whose lives have been shattered by political violence? On the outskirts of Khartoum, powerful voices from Izzbba challenge essentialist concepts of self and identity. These discursively created elements of personhood are contingent upon everyday existential realities as displaced women remake home in extraordinarily imaginative ways.

Women's experiences in Izzbba as well as in other sprawling urban slums illuminate the constant renegotiation of ideas about self, gender, and community as they forge new political positionings. Julie Peteet describes the intricacies of existence in Palestinian refugee camps in a rare ethnography, *Landscape of Hope and Despair*. "The camps could be seen as a built environment, as everyday abodes, and as places where possibilities for the future emerged" (2005, 131). This observation applies to Sudanese IDP camps and shantytowns as well. Here life is marked by resourcefulness and innovation; new links between self and space are fashioned through networks of association and mutual attachments. As circumstances shift, so do previously held focuses and frames of reference. Both identity and home are becoming borderless and mobile as they are actively altered to facilitate the negotiation of new worlds within and beyond shantytowns. As a feminist ethnography, this study explores the ways in which women in resistance strategically reposition themselves in situations of war and social upheaval, focusing especially on the cultural exchanges through which they reconstruct their identities and communities. These mutual-aid networks are equally fundamental for understanding the process through which bodily rituals become acceptable to some of those who did not previously practice them and come to signify women's acceptance of their new localities as home.

Gendered rituals have enabled women to remake "strategies of selfhood" (see Bhabha 1994) in their new surroundings as they struggle to fashion a sense of centeredness and direction. Their selective adoption of bodily modification practices that were previously foreign is a valuable lens for understanding the alternative paths followed by displaced women in making new places for themselves and redefining culture and society. These women's acceptance of new "traditions," while not entirely a matter of free choice, is a sign of deeper ambiguities in the social organization of shantytowns. Who an IDP comes in contact with and how those relationships affect her plays a momentous part in the changes she chooses or declines to enact. This study reveals that the views of displaced southern Sudanese women in Khartoum are wide-ranging and diverse.

Consider, for example, the case of female circumcision: while some women talked about adopting it in the course of marriage and Islamization, others resisted the practice in the name of cultural continuity and bodily integrity. One Izzbba resident summarized her vehement opposition to the practice when she posed the question: "Was God foolish to create women with these parts that they decide to cut off in circumcision?" Not only did this woman interrogate the premises on which women base their adoption of new bodily modification practices, but she raised a major philosophical point that has been made by community activists to eradicate female circumcision. Conforming to specific beliefs, rituals, and value systems of their northern hosts is an adaptive strategy that some criticize and others champion. Evidence presented with respect to this practice should by no means be taken as a validation of circumcision. Both northern and southern women are upset by some IDPs' adoption of this practice and worry it is being done in response to circumstances that make it nearly involuntary. Today, women in those African societies where genital mutilation is prevalent seek to transform attitudes toward the sexual and reproductive body and to empower women and girls to make different decisions, mobilizing social and religious support for women's bodily integrity (see Abusharaf 2001, 2006). Practices such as the smoke bath, which are matters of personal decision, differ markedly in their meanings from the issue of head covering, which is imposed on women by local laws.

After examining critical dimensions of the social lives of displaced women, including the interethnic connections they forge in the shantytowns, this ethnography explores women's sustained efforts at peacemaking. In *Throwing the Stick Forward*, Mary Anne Fitzgerald, who examined internal displacement in the South, remarks: "It is an inspiring insight into the lives of women who have become peacemakers and leaders despite having to put their energies into simple survival day after day" (2002, vii). Their activities extend beyond displaced communities into feminist peace activism across Sudan. Sudanese women from different backgrounds have been making peace among themselves on a daily basis as they mix and mingle in and around Khartoum. Resolving everyday conflicts, pooling material resources, and sharing diverse customs for bodily adornment, they have developed peacemaking strategies that ameliorate the conditions of their war-torn lives. In spite of their regional, ethnocultural, linguistic, and religious differences, and drawing on their multiple identities as women and citizens, they have laid the groundwork for postconflict reconstruction and devoted their amazing energy to creating a New Sudan where all will be at home.

From Victimization by War to Participation in Peacemaking

The grave contraventions of women's rights in the context of the protracted and violent political disputes in Sudan, though profoundly damaging, had the unintended consequence of sharpening women's views about their civil, political, economic, and cultural rights. The persistence of gender-based violence has raised women's awareness of themselves as political subjects. They realize they can play momentous roles in community mobilization as well as in nation building through peace and reconciliation (cf. Hunt 2004). Because of their contributions to their communities before, during, and after the war, Sudanese women have earned the right to take part in fashioning a homegrown democratization process that challenges and overturns deeply embedded gender ideologies and practices that marginalize women in politics.

The first chapter, "Dissent Historicized," places the situation of IDPs in social and political context, exploring two incidents of resistance in which camp and shantytown residents were involved and probing the cultural challenges that displaced southern women face in the Muslim-dominated, Arabic-speaking North. Of vital importance here is the difference between IDPs' reciprocal, sometimes harmonious and sometimes conflictual, interactions with the marginalized residents of the slums surrounding the capital and their coercive treatment at the hands of the Sudanese state, with its project of Islamization and Arabization. Placing these issues in the current Sudanese context, I investigate broader political processes relating to nationalist ideology and exemplified in the so-called Civilizational Project promulgated by the state as a tool for redefining nationalism and political identities. Because this research was conducted after the enactment of sharia law in September 1983, the status of Islamic legal norms and their effects on non-Muslim Sudanese are central elements in discussions pertaining to the root causes of the civil war (Johnson 2003).

Chapter 2, "Becoming Displaced," considers the fundamental processes that result in displacement and the complex problems to which it gives rise. These women's losses can be understood in light of the work of Maurice Eisenbruch (1991) on cultural bereavement, which offers a compelling framework for grasping the intricacies of refugees' and displaced persons' experiences of and responses to loss without imposing Western categories of analysis, such as the psychiatric diagnosis of post-traumatic stress disorder, that might not be relevant to how loss is expressed. While avoiding the assumption that cultures are static, I use Eisenbruch's concept to expand our understanding of the sociocultural character of loss and suffering.

The intertwined economic, political, legal, and social forces that militate against human rights are the most important matter for reflective consideration. Displaced women display a full range of responses to these problems, from accommodation to changing circumstances to protest against the hegemonic order of things. Most women adapt selectively, simultaneously fine-tuning their survival strategies and resisting the forces that jeopardize their security. Since most displaced people arrive from villages and rural areas, exploring the effects of urbanization is especially important. I probe the characteristics of host and guests and explore their experiences regarding economic subsistence, political participation, and social mobility as residents of shantytowns in Khartoum. Although I situate cultural, political, and economic rights within the larger context of human rights, this book focuses particularly on women's rights. Since gender is a central dimension of women's identities and relationships, women's rights form an indissoluble bundle of rights, as women's own experiences make abundantly clear.

To elucidate the subtle ways in which women seek to create mutual understanding and build community, chapter 3, "Gendered Rituals," examines some extraordinary, everyday means for stimulating neighborly coexistence and mutual tolerance. Displaced women improvise ways of earning a livelihood and adopt new modes of living as they adjust to the urban environment alongside others from Darfur who were displaced in the early and mid-1980s, as well as some from the eastern region and the central Nuba Mountains. These tactics include the adoption of gendered bodily practices propagated by members of the host communities throughout shantytowns and IDP camps. The analysis goes beyond sexuality and the body in the context of forced migration to treat the espousal of new bodily practices as a material and symbolic effort to reduce the distance between hosts and displaced persons. We must dissolve essentialist concepts of community and identity to understand the remarkable versatility and plasticity of these social formations. The variety of stories women tell about life in Khartoum demonstrates that women are not conforming to these ritual practices because they feel coerced or threatened. Rather, they state that shifting circumstances have necessitated new modes of being and functioning in the world. The wide range of women's choices about these matters demonstrates that women adapt as they think best, not as others wish them to.

In chapter 4, "Negotiating Peace," I draw attention to the emergent forms of feminist subjectivity among displaced women through a careful investigation of both formal and informal strategies for effecting peace. This feminist consciousness has to be situated historically in order to appreciate its full complexity. Elsewhere (Abusharaf 2004b), I argue that to understand feminism in Sudan today, we have to come to terms with the intricacies of the past as inscribed in the sociopolitical and historical problems of the country as a whole. Feminism and peace activism go hand in hand, just as women's rights discourse was historically formulated within anticolonial struggle. Southern women's peace activism is making its mark both within Sudan and abroad.

The majority of displaced persons in the North manage to sustain peaceful coexistence with their hosts through everyday cooperation and negotiation. Displacement offers southerners, as marginalized peoples of Sudan, the opportunity to see for themselves the lived realities of northerners. They witness the impoverishment and suffering of slum dwellers in the North who are just disadvantaged as themselves. This commonality offers a unique opportunity for residents of shantytowns from all over the country to forge a "New Sudan" in microcosm, as detailed analysis of their narratives of exchange and mutual support demonstrates. Displaced southerners have learned to make clear distinctions between northern-dominated governments and ordinary northern Sudanese citizens. A Dinka priest in Khartoum explained: "The government doesn't represent the view of all northerners. This is not an elected government, so no one has a say in what it does to its citizens. Of course, there is racism toward southerners. But in actual reality it is important to understand that jihad is not waged by ordinary people. They are conscripted and forced to engage in it."

Women in Sudan have demonstrated a commitment to serve as agents of change by supporting the continuing efforts for peace. However, they have largely been excluded from the formal negotiations. Determined to make their voices heard, Sudanese women displaced within the country and in neighboring countries have established organizations and networks to raise awareness of the human costs of the conflict and to call for an inclusive approach to the implementation of the peace agreement.[8] These women are strengthening the constituency for peace throughout the country. It is essential to draw on the assets, experiences, and dedication of these women in order to set into motion a peace-building process that resolves the underlying political and economic problems, addresses ethnic cleansing in Darfur, and builds sustainable peace.

Taken together, these chapters offer unique perspectives on the renegotiation of identities and relationships among IDPs and with the host society through mutual aid and shared rituals of belonging. They illuminate the powerful connections between women's informal interactions, their exclusion from state politics, and their organizing to overcome differences among themselves and to make peace in their country. These women's voices and viewpoints shed light on homegrown democratization processes, agitation for rights, and postconflict mobilizations whose ultimate purpose is to illuminate the participants' needs and concerns and raise them as central to any future referendum on the South in light of the Comprehensive Peace Agreement (CPA).

The epilogue explores displaced women's ideas about repatriation to the South. Concepts of home have shifted dramatically over the course of their stay in Khartoum. At present, the large-scale repatriation to the South projected by the CPA is not taking place, given the uncertainties that surround the political future of the country as a whole. Most important, displaced women realize their former homes have been destroyed; for most, resettlement will mean starting over all over again. Many have adjusted to being in Khartoum and now look at their squatter settlements as home, drawing on vibrant social networks and practices of mutual aid for subsistence and support.

The determination of many displaced women to remain in the North attests to new imaginings of self, community, and nation as they make a new place for themselves in Sudanese society. Mapping identity through the peace process illuminates its fluidity. This quality has been skillfully  rendered in Kwame Anthony Appiah's philosophy of culture: "Every human identity is constructed, historical, every one has its share of false presuppositions, of the errors and inaccuracies that courtesy calls 'myth,' religion 'heresy,' and science 'magic.' Invented histories, invented biologies, invented cultural affinities come with every identity; each is a kind of role that has to be scripted, structured by conventions of narrative to which the world never manages to conform" (1992, 174). The narratives and life histories featured in this book elucidate the perceptual and emotional processes that reshape concepts of self and society. They help us to apprehend the indefinite, supple, and conditional nature of the question posed constantly by displaced people: "Who are we becoming?"

ONE

Dissent Historicized

All of you Sudanese women with tears in your eyes turned to the sky in a large and painful begging, from all parts of Sudan, from peace talks to roundtable confer ences, from Addis Ababa to Abuja, from Abuja to Nairobi, from Nairobi to Asmara, from Asmara to Cairo, from Cairo to the Intergovernmental Authority on Develop- ment in Djibouti, mobilizing only men and capitals: Why not mobilize women, children, and old people, who are always yearning for peace?

Rose Lisok Paulino, 2005

Angola, Dar El Salaam, Mandela, Mayo, Soba Aradi, and other teeming squatter settlements and camps in the Sudanese capital, Greater Khar- toum, accommodate between two and three million internally displaced persons (IDPs) who fled civil war in the southern provinces of Equatoria, Bahr El-Ghazal, and Upper Nile, as well as the Nuba Mountains and the western region of Darfur.[1] Numerous United Nations reports iden- tify the main causes of population displacement as mass evictions, forced regroupment, looting and terror, attrition, continuous harassment, and the disruption of subsistence farming.[2] Official camps established by the Sudanese government were woefully inadequate to house the swelling numbers of IDPs, so shantytowns—unofficial settlements on the out- skirts of cities where displaced persons construct their own dwellings on vacant land—grew up in the vicinity. Camps hardly provide a stable home for the displaced; the Sudanese government has demolished camps and removed some residents to more remote places in the desert, leav- ing others to fend for themselves. Unofficial shantytowns are always vul- nerable to destruction. Despite the government policy of "replanning," these squatter settlements are becoming an enduring feature of Sudanese sociopolitical and urban life (Abu Sin and Davies 1991). (For a list of camps and shantytowns, see appendix B.)

Forced migrants display amazing resilience and resourcefulness, reconstituting their lives and reinventing themselves in host communities that are linguistically, ethnically, and religiously different from their regions of origin. As they traverse spatial and cultural borders, the displaced employ imaginative strategies not only to survive but also to craft new social worlds. Unstable and unfamiliar circumstances require flexibility and reward adjustment. Despite being forced to move again and again, often without the men in their families and increasingly without property or access to resources, women have improvised, supported themselves and their children, and forged bonds with women and men from other groups in the new places they find themselves. The enormity of their continued suffering should not blind us to the significant and subtle ways in which displaced women have, individually and collectively, transformed themselves and remade their worlds. Whether they return home, resettle elsewhere, or remain in Greater Khartoum depends not only on the peace agreements and resettlement policies of all parties to recent conflicts but also on these women's choices about the lives they have reconstructed as displaced persons.

To grasp the intricate genealogies of these forced migrations, we must recognize that Sudan has a long history of social and political turbulence. Wars, political conflicts, ethnic disputes, famine, and human rights abuses have marked the landscape of this vast and diverse[3] country ever since it achieved independence from British rule in 1956. While the roots of current conflicts between regions were sown during the period of British colonial domination, they were exacerbated by the contests over resources, power, and political programs that accompanied the formation of the postcolonial state.[4] The recent Comprehensive Peace Agreement (CPA) between the Government of Sudan (GoS) and the Sudanese People's Liberation Movement and Army (SPLM/A) ended the longest-running civil war in modern African history.

Armed conflict between the North and the South over the terms of national political, economic, legal, and sociocultural integration has consumed fifty of the past sixty years. Warfare along this major fault line has continued alongside other, more episodic conflicts between and within the country's multiple regional, ethnocultural, and political groupings. The North-South conflict has proven the most intractable to political settlement, whether imposed from within or agreed with outside mediation. At issue are equitable distribution of economic resources, power sharing at the center, and national identity. Nationalism and the quest for a unified cultural identity have proven especially deadly, as northern-dominated governments have stressed Arabism and Islamism as a main frame of reference for the inculcation of national subjectivity, while southern movements have resisted the imposition of these measures. As Michael Ignatieff puts it in *Blood and Belonging,* nationalism legitimizes an appeal to blood loyalty and can call for blood sacrifice, but nationalism "can do so persuasively only if it seems to appeal to people's better natures, and not just to their worst instincts. Since killing is not a business to be taken lightly, it must be done for a reason that makes the perpetrator think well of himself. If violence is to be legitimised, it must be in the name of all that is best in a people, and what is better than their love of home" (1994, 9). This love of "home" has entailed tremendous suffering for those who oppose the ideologies of the powerful political elites in the North.[5] In the name of unifying the homeland, massive violence has been perpetrated in Sudan.

In this clash, the death and destruction experienced by Southern Sudanese communities have far exceeded the fatalities suffered in recent wars in Bosnia, Kosovo, Chechnya, Somalia, and Algeria combined (U.S. Committee for Refugees and Immigrants 1999; 2002). Millions were forced to flee their homes; some crossed the borders to neighboring African countries, while others became internally displaced within Sudan. Refugees attract international attention and assistance, but IDPs are supposed to be cared for by their own governments, so their needs are often neglected by international organizations.[6] In Sudan, the number of IDPs exceeded the number of refugees, which made international observers less aware of the scale of these conflicts. Southern IDPs' situation was made worse by the fact that most could not flee to, or remain in, areas controlled by the SPLM/A. As UN reports emphasize, IDPs usually came under control of the government of Sudan, which was originally responsible for their displacement. In the words of J.Y., a Christian Fujulu who was displaced from Juba in 1984 and arrived in Khartoum at the age of thirteen in 1993: "I have very fond memories of prewar days and before I was forced to move. I am very sad and stressed when I think about what has happened to my family back home and in Khartoum. I pray that peace will come back so that we can return to our land and enjoy life in the same way as we did before war displaced us."

To the IDPs and refugees of the Sudanese civil war who hail from villages in which Noble Spiritual Beliefs and Christianity are the primary faith traditions, the signing of the historic CPA marked the first admission of remorse as well as the remediation of historical wrongs inflicted by northern-dominated governments on the marginalized peoples of the South.[7] This measure was a marked divergence from previous policies, which had swung repeatedly between warfare and stalemate. Save for the Addis Ababa Agreement of 1972, which halted the bloodshed for a decade and guaranteed regional autonomy for the South, no major efforts were made to end the aggression. Gaafar Mohamed Nimeiri, the president whose abrogation of the Addis Ababa Agreement in 1983 provoked the formation of the SPLA, was given amnesty by the current military regime in Sudan.[8]

The new Machakos peace deal, which was signed in Kenya on May 26, 2004, established a ceasefire and numerous political changes instituted on January 9, 2005, which balanced the principles of national unity and regional difference for a transitional period.[9] The most prominent provisions of the CPA include the withdrawal of opposing military forces to their own territories and their joint presence in contested areas; a referendum on independence of the South after a six-year period; the equitable sharing of power and wealth, especially revenues from the exploitation of southern oil resources; a guarantee that sharia, Islamic law, not be imposed on non-Muslims throughout the country; and the creation of a new constitution to allow for these reforms to be converted into a lived reality.

Dissent has long been a galvanizing force in Sudanese political topography. Recently, two conspicuous cases of communal violence erupted in Khartoum and other cities despite the signing of the CPA. The collective resistance of southern IDPs in the North feature prominently in both incidents. These violent conflicts exemplify the enduring entanglements of the politics of war and peace and illuminate the role of memory as the ultimate source for locally based articulations of historical, ethnocultural, and racial scripts in Sudanese society. In such a diverse society, with hundreds of cultural and linguistic groups with distinctive outlooks on life, cosmologies, faith traditions, and localized experiential knowledge, the impossibility of reaching consensus about national identity has entailed untold miseries and intractable disputes, especially for the peoples of Southern Sudan and Darfur. These two incidents of communal violence share a common ancestry in guarded wariness toward the Arab-dominated regime.

The Massacre at Soba Aradi

On May 18, 2005, more than five months after the historic peace agreement was implemented, violent altercations arose in Soba Aradi, one of the largest shantytowns in Khartoum, which houses tens of thousands of displaced people from Southern Sudan, the Nuba Mountains, and Darfur. Residents who resisted forced removal to an undisclosed location found themselves in an altercation with local police. This version of events was told to me by a Soba Aradi resident who witnessed the dreadful episode and gathered reports about it from others:

> A total of thirty-seven people (seventeen IDPs, six children, and fourteen policemen) were killed yesterday, the eighteenth of May 2005, during a violent clash between the police and the displaced people of Soba Aradi, fifteen kilometers south of Khartoum. According to the report, when the displaced people woke up in the morning, they found the whole area surrounded by armed policemen and vehicles ready to relocate the displaced people in the area to an unknown desert area. When the community members wanted to ask the policemen about the plans for the relocation, the policemen reacted by shooting the IDPs, killing a number of them, which angered the IDPs and sparked more violence. The angry IDPs demonstrated at the police station, where six children were shot by the police, and that angered the civilians more. As a result, they retaliated by killing fourteen policemen and burning the police station and the office of the government popular committee in the area. When the governor of Khartoum State was asked, he responded that the police were on the defensive side because the civilians first attacked the police. He further stated that it was their plan to rezone the IDP camps in Khartoum State. The governor and the police commissioner claimed that guns were stolen from the police station, and they are mobilizing to search for the stolen guns. Although the situation was quiet in the afternoon, shooting was heard all around Soba Aradi at around 6:30 p.m., and the whole area was again full of tear gas. It was reported that there were no disturbances during the night, but tension is still high between the police and the civilians, and the IDPs are staying without going to work.

By the time the violence ended, fifty people, including the fourteen policemen, had been killed, and many others were seriously wounded. Reports about the incident stated that many more Soba Aradi residents had been killed, including women and children who constitute the overwhelming majority of displaced people. This incident was received with horror in Khartoum.

These atrocious events summoned this response from Philip Alston, special rapporteur on extrajudicial, summary or arbitrary executions of the United Nations Commission on Human Rights, and Walter Kälin, representative of the United Nations secretary-general on the human rights of IDPs:

> We were greatly disturbed to hear the violent clashes recently sparked when Sudanese security forces sought to relocate displaced persons living in the Soba Aradi IDP area south of Khartoum on 18 May. According to media and United Nations reports, Sudanese officials, accompanied by police, sought to relocate the 23,000 residents of the camp, who are among the over two million internally displaced persons from various parts of Sudan living in and around Khartoum. Residents reportedly resisted the relocation and a conflict ensued in which a number of civilians and police were killed or injured, and several buildings in the camp were set afire, including the police station. Conflicting versions have been offered concerning who commenced the violence, whether the police used firearms against a crowd, and the precise numbers of death[s] and injuries on both sides. While it is clear that the Government of Sudan is entitled to plan the locations at which it provides shelter and other vital services to displaced persons, it is obliged to make every effort to avoid new displacement to this already impoverished, traumatized and vulnerable population, as pointed out by the Guiding Principles on Internal Displacement. Where this is not possible, any relocation should be carried out in full consultation with the affected persons. Moreover, relocation sites must be suitable for habitation, with adequate access to shelter, water, food, employment and vital services. Most importantly, relocation should not be undertaken in an atmosphere conducive to violence. Seeking the voluntary and fully informed consent of persons subject to relocation is one important means to ensure this. Another is for police and security forces to apply non-violent means to the degree possible before resorting to the use of force, in accordance with pertinent international norms, such as the United Nations Basic Principles on the Use of Force and Firearms by Law Enforcement Officials. We call on the Sudanese authorities to ensure that a thorough investigation of this incident take place as soon as possible and to take all appropriate steps to prevent similar incidents in the future. (May 20, 2005)

The Soba Aradi massacre also received significant attention from the Sudan Organization Against Torture (SOAT), which provided a list of names of people who were taken into custody, detailing their punishments and sentences. SOAT urged respect for human rights and basic freedoms in accordance with national norms and international human rights conventions (SOAT 2005).

The conflict demonstrates the collective anxiety of a population that continued to face displacement after arriving in the capital city.[10] The IDPs' defense of Soba Aradi is emblematic of their resolve to protect their new homes at all costs. The conflict dismayed residents of other shanty-towns. In the words of a social worker in Mandela: "What happened to the people of Soba Aradi is a sobering reminder that it can happen to people living here and in other shanties. The government rezoning and distribution of land to wealthy people does not account for the lives of displaced people who started after years of displacement to feel at home."[11] In the camps and shantytowns, daily sociability gives rise to solidarity. Displaced residents turn into active agents in organizing "space over time, and the allocation of resources in space and over time" (Rappaport and Overing 2000, 157). Shantytowns are makeshift settlements, and at first people still think of their place of origin as home, but over time they become reoriented to the place they live. Within the camps and shanty-towns, a shared IDP identity emerges. This new collective spirit infused the resistance at Soba Aradi. It continues the insurrection against the hegemonic ideologies that relegated the South to the fringes of Sudanese society, but it does so at the center rather than from the periphery.

Black Monday

Sudanese citizens are adept at overthrowing repressive regimes by non-violent means. The first revolution took place on October 21, 1964, when the people terminated the military rule of General Ibrahim Abboud. The second, and most trying, was the April 1985 uprising against the regime of the military commander Gaafar Mohamed Nimeiri, one of the most brutal dictatorships that Sudanese society has ever witnessed. A third, but unfortunately abortive, popular revolution began on July 8, 2005, with the arrival at Khartoum airport of Dr. John Garang De Mabior, the leader of the southern-based Sudan People's Liberation Movement (SPLM) and of the National Democratic Alliance (NDA), a broader coalition. Under the CPA, Garang was named first vice president of Sudan. The celebration the next day exemplified the Sudanese people's thirst for tranquility. The long-awaited coming of this freedom fighter was brimming over with symbols and metaphors highlighting nation building and democratic transformation. As Garang joined the central government after more than twenty-five years of coordinated political and armed struggle, his message of creating a New Sudan[12] based on ethnic tolerance and political pluralism was announced with crystal clarity.

July 9, 2005, marked a historic day in the political theater of Sudanese revolution making. The streets of Khartoum were adorned with posters welcoming Dr. Garang to the capital. One of most powerful and eye-catching featured Garang and Ali Abdul Latif, the leader of the 1924 rising against the British in Sudan—both men of Dinka origin whose part in furthering the causes of self-determination and pride for all Sudanese is etched in the collective memory of Sudanese people today. Throughout the struggle, Garang stressed his vision of the New Sudan as a country in which people from all regions would enjoy fundamental human rights and equal opportunity as citizens, regardless of their political inclination, religious affiliation, ethnic identification, and cultural outlook. Bestowing peace on "the people of Sudan, from Halfa in the upper north to Nimoli in the far south," as Garang put it in his speech that day, was never a component of the political repertoire of the successive governments of Sudan, which sought from their stronghold at the center to impose an Arabist, Islamic hegemony on the multiplicity of lifeworlds across this vast territory.

More than four million people, mostly supporters of the Sudan People's Liberation Movement, along with progressives from the north and west who joined the National Democratic Alliance, gathered in Al-Saha al-Khadra (Green Square) in Khartoum to greet Garang with open arms. A week before, President Omer El Bashir had delivered an address celebrating the sixteenth anniversary of the National Salvation government in the same central place; now he grasped Garang's hand and greeted him as "our brother." To his supporters, John Garang's long-anticipated return to Khartoum for the first time in more than twenty years marked the unfolding of the New Sudan. His subsequent installation as first vice president and the anticipated formation of the National Unity government provided assurance to millions who aspired to democratic change.

Three weeks after his appointment, on July 30, 2005, Garang was killed in a helicopter crash while returning from Uganda. His death, which was immediately regarded as suspicious, ignited the fires of communal violence that came to be known as Black Monday. Hours after news of the crash broke, displaced southerners and other marginalized people in Khartoum rioted, attacking shops in the city center and working-class neighborhoods on the periphery near the shantytowns.[13] Many northerners were killed and injured; northern-owned shops were set ablaze, and houses were looted and burned. Despite appeals for calm by the Khartoum government and SPLM leaders, including the widowed Rebecca N. Garang De Mabior, who insisted that the crash was a tragic accident,

rioting convulsed the capital city for three days. According to the official
police report, at least 90 people were killed and 967 seriously wounded.
Property damage was estimated at 16.5 billion Sudanese pounds, about
US$6.5 million.

The riots incited a strong backlash by northerners when news of the
death and devastation wrought by southerners became known. According to an Associated Press article on August 22, 2005, Khartoum criminal
police chief Kamal Eddin Jaafar defended his department against allega-
tions that repression was directed at Southern Sudanese: "The current
police crackdowns are not targeting certain ethnic or religious groups
but are being launched in accordance with confirmed information."[14] At
least 3,347 people were arrested during and after the riots. Those who
participated—who were not all southerners, despite northerners' percep
tion that they were the primary instigators of the violence—acted out
their distrust of the government and their discontent with the horrific
demise of their hopes for peace. It is one of the profound ironies of recent
Sudanese politics that so soon after the historic CPA, southerners and
northerners rapidly lost confidence in each other's intentions. The crim-
inalization of displaced people from the South was a lamentable effect
of these somber events. Newspapers quoted eyewitnesses who described
random raids and arrests of innocent displaced persons in shantytowns
and camps around Khartoum.[15] At least five children were killed when
a school for southerners in Kalalaka was burned; the imam of the local
mosque died as well. Northerners who participated in the retaliation justified their actions as self-defense.

Throughout this period of unrest, GoS and SPLM/A leaders appealed
to people's fragile sense of the possibility of peace and national unity.
Salva Kiir Mayardit, who succeeded Garang as vice president of the Sudan and president of Southern Sudan, released a statement on August 1,
2005, seeking to restore confidence: "I take this opportunity to assure
the Southern Sudanese in particular and the Sudanese people in general
that we in the SPLM/A leadership will continue the vision and objectives
of the movement that Dr. John Garang De Mabior has articulated and
hoped to implement. We also want to assure everyone that the leadership
and all cadres of the SPLM/A will remain united and strive to faithfully
implement the Comprehensive Peace Agreement. . . . I call upon all members of the SPLM and the entire Sudanese nation to remain calm and
vigilant." The powerful appeals for self-restraint by the SPLM and GoS
were important symbols of a restoration of faith in the CPA. Neverthe-
less, the riots had grave consequences, driving a wedge between southern

and northern communities. In an AFP feature article titled "Khartoum Residents Say They Can Live Together in Peace but Prepare for a Return of Violence," many northerners and southerners voiced their mutual distrust after the death of Garang and the riots.[16]

Despite the presence of between two and three million IDPs in Greater Khartoum, the capital had never before been a site of conflict. The communal violence that followed Garang's death represented a serious departure from the peaceful coexistence among local residents and the displaced that had registered, yet did not replicate, the dislocation and devastation of war elsewhere. This violence cannot be understood without an examination of the root causes of the war, including the state's propagation of Arabization and Islamization anchored in *El-Mashru El-Hadari,* "the Civilizational Project," which emphasized the adoption of sharia, Islamic law, as a main source of governance. The religious basis of the law has been contested over the years, not only by non-Muslims but also by secular Muslims who believe firmly in separation between religion and the state in a pluralistic society. Examining the divergent articulations of Arabism and Islamism places southern dissent in its proper historical and sociocultural contexts. Situated knowledge of Arabism and Islamism is especially useful in understanding the IDPs' experiences and perspectives, because responses to this project have differed historically and continue to vary in the present. During their prolonged residence in northern Sudanese towns, including the capital city, some southerners continued to resist these processes as emblems of their perpetual subalternity. Others, however, intermarried with host populations, adopted new northern cultural practices, and manufactured identities anew.

Articulations of Arabism and Islamism, Enslavement and Exploitation

The Sudan is often seen as a bridge between Arabic-speaking Africa and sub-Saharan Africa. According to Ali Mazrui (1968, 240), the Sudan can also be seen as a bridge between Muslim and Christian Africa, and between a future Africa of homogenized nation-states and present-day Africa with deep ethnic cleavages within states. The history of Arabization and Islamization in Sudanese society reveals more about ethnic antagonism than about cohesion, since these twin processes were experienced differently by various communities. Nor did Arabization and Islamization always occur together. Indeed, Arabization and Islamization have played a paramount role in producing multiple and complex permutations in Sudanese political and cultural identities. These processes began as early as the tenth century CE, as Arab traders and nomadic cattle grazers migrated south and intermarried with local Sudanese peoples, introducing Islam and the Arabic language. By the fifteenth century CE, a "Black Kingdom" of African Muslims had emerged, and by the turn of the nineteenth century the Funj-Abdallab state extended into Kordofan and the Nuba Mountains. According to historian Justin Willis, "The southern expansion of the Arabs was halted in the water divide. This event coincided with a counter northerly expansion of the Nilotes, especially the Shilluk, which succeeded in stopping the Arab penetration and the spread of Islam. At this water divide a cultural frontier was created between what came to be known as the north and southern Sudan. This 'frontier' was not static; it was not infrequently shifting over a wide zone" (2004, 3). Interaction took place across the frontier, especially trade in ivory and slaves. Many of these interactions, however, reinforced differences and asymmetries between North and South.

Willis argues that "the existence of this frontier has prejudiced our analysis of modern Sudanese history. The Southern Sudanese tended to portray the relations between the 'North' and the south in terms of aggression and economic exploitation from the . . . [northern] states. From the Northern Sudanese perspective, political, economic and social developments were generally explained in terms of Muslim and Arab movements. By the twentieth century the North is portrayed as Arab and Muslim and the south as African (or Negroid) or 'pagan' (or animist) and progressively as Christian. Such an image was largely promoted by the writings of [British] colonial administrators and anthropologists. The historical reality . . . is more complex: political, economic and cultural contacts existed" between the two regions (2004, 4). The contradiction between the two regions' frequent interactions and the prevailing image of a bifurcated Sudan is not the only contradiction in play here. The ways in which advocates of the two regions imagine the conflict between them are also contradictory: northerners think of their differences from southerners in cultural, religious, and linguistic terms, while southerners (perhaps because they are less homogeneous themselves) feel exploited economically and dominated politically and militarily by northerners.

While the majority of northerners assert Arab genealogies, southerners think of themselves as indigenous Africans and of northerners as "Arab bastards."[17] Ali Mazrui argues that both Arabic speakers of the North and southerners exaggerate the ethnic chasm that separates northerners from the people of the South (1968, 243); Arabs in the Sudan became thoroughly indigenized.[18] In the North, Arab immigrants' assimilation into Sudanese host communities through marriage practices and religious conversion took place with amazing alacrity. The South, by contrast, remained for the most part untouched by the newcomers' influence, as environmental and epidemiological factors as well as population and political pressures militated against the incursion of immigrants. It is clear, however, that Arabs' acquisition of power and privilege in the Sudan was furthered to the detriment of non-Arab populations. Ethnic and religious contestations produced vagueness and uncertainty about Sudan's national identity, a situation that brought claims to Arabism under substantial scrutiny.

The infiltration of Arab traders in Southern Sudan and their heavy involvement in slavery added injury to insult, as it were, by making Arab exploitation and enslavement of southerners part of popular memory. As Susan Slymovics demonstrates in her ethnography *The Object of Memory: Arab and Jew Narrate the Palestinian Village* (1998), people reconstruct their past in light of their present and interpret their present in light of their past. Reenacting in the present the legacies of a chaotic past has proven to be one of the most tenacious problems in Sudanese political life, as well as a formidable obstacle to nation building. Stories of resistance to Arabization circulate widely and fuel continued resistance. "In the vast swamp world of the Sudd in South Sudan, a Negro rebel army fights an unquenchable war against the Islamic rulers of Sudan using dugout canoes for transport and crocodile for food," wrote Tom Stacey about the Anya-Nya, the armed force of rebellious southerners that preceded the SPLA.[19] The kaleidoscope of events surrounding the enslavement of southerners is the most frequently remembered atrocity etched in the collective consciousness of Southern Sudanese communities.

Mistrust of all that is Arab and northern pervades the nationalistic views of some southerners. The Anya-Nya contended that Arabs would never succeed in dominating Sudan. A statement the rebels issued at a particularly fraught moment during the conflict typifies this perspective:

> The Arabs in Sudan might lose nothing from antagonizing the Africans in the South. They could continue their flirtations with the other Arab States. But they should bear in mind the notion many Africans hold that if the Arabs had been as strong as the Europeans during the scramble for Africa, they would also have colonized Africa. There is evidence that they wanted to colonize the Nyamwezi Africans of Central Africa. They set up city-states like Ujiji and Tabora to rival the traditional authority

of the Nyamwezi. But under the leadership of Mirambo, the Nyamwezi defeated the Arabs and sent them away from their soil. Is it a similar situation in Sudan in the twentieth century?[20]

This statement, which posits Arabs as would-be colonizers who were defeated by Africans, is more mythic than historical in its appeal to a proud past before recent defeats.[21]

Southerners recount incidents from recent Sudanese history that, in their eyes, demonstrate the untrustworthiness and brutality of Arabs. The act of remembering, rather than history as such, is at play in the process of constructing the Arab as a contemptible enemy; the past matters only because it echoes recent conflicts, not because it evokes "ancient" antagonisms. Retelling fuels dissent and resistance, leading to more war and the dislocation of millions of Southern Sudanese civilians. A notorious 1970 incident in which Christians were massacred by soldiers from the North who had come to fight the Anya-Nya illustrates the process through which this cycle of remembering occurs. This report, based on the testimony of surviving witnesses, was published by the Southern Sudan Association a month after the event:

> On Thursday July 23, 1970, at midday, Christians of the indigenous Barakole Church had gathered in a converted prayer center to intercede for a sick child who had been confined to bed in the house of a certain Christian named Kandolo. The prayer center is situated on the Congo-Sudan border between Yei and Aba. The Arab soldiers of the North found themselves assembled there. Some months ago the same Arabs reached the same camp and told the people not to be frightened, as they were only after the Anya-Nya; for that reason these refugees did not escape when the Arabs arrived on July 23. The troops then tied the lay reader with liana ropes, together with all the men and women, led them back into the chapel and fastened them against the pews—children seated in front of their parents. They then shot the people and set the chapel on fire. Some of the children who were only wounded tried to escape from under the blazing chapel, but were caught and thrown back into the flames. The Arabs were shouting, according to the survivors [and] witnesses, "we shall kill you inside your chapel and your God will come and save you."[22]

The September *Church Times* reported on the incident in Banja, in which some sixty worshippers were killed by forty-one soldiers, along with other "shocking" instances of "the brutality of the Arabs" toward unarmed civilians, including women, children, elders, and the disabled. A member of the Norwegian television team that was taken by Anya-Nya soldiers to document the scene reported: "I am convinced that the Arabs are committing what we call genocide in the Southern Sudan."[23] The outrage this incident provoked not only reinforced the commitment of the resistance but also contributed to constructing the conflict in religious terms. In April 1971, the Anya-Nya issued this statement:

> There is really nothing more to say for the hundreds whom the Arab soldier [has] murdered this way and cannot be remembered, except by their families and relatives. . . . [T]he Arab soldier has made life so cheap that when we hear so and so has been killed by the enemy and his body thrown into his blazing house, a very common practice, we commend his soul to God and go about our own business waiting for our turn. And yet, we find the strength to laugh, and rejoice and live and fight for our freedom for as long as the war takes.[24]

At the same time, Mario C-Lye-Labu of the Anya-Nya detailed the crimes committed by Nimeiri, who ruled the Sudan from 1969 to 1985, during his previous army service in the southern region. As garrison commander in Eastern Equatoria, he had ordered the burning of eight villages inhabited by a total of about 9,700 people.[25]

These events, compounded by deep-seated memories of slavery, solidified southerners' fears and doubts about the North. "Faced with the assimilative excesses of the ruling classes in the North," writes Mansour Khalid, "the South has experimented with the entire spectrum of resistance, from political crusade to be recognized having their own authenticity and rights as citizens of the Sudan, to carrying arms" (2003, 308).

A major and continuing cause of conflict is the propagation of *El-Mashru El-Hadari*, "the Civilizational Project," which promotes the Arabization and Islamization of Sudanese society regardless of cultural and religious differences.[26] In the past, as Abdel Ghaffar Ahmed and Sharif Harir (1978) emphasize, the Arabic culture introduced into Sudan by migrants and traders was not a "pure" form but represented a popular version mixed with indigenous elements.[27] In contrast, contemporary Arabization and Islamization is an elite project that marginalizes indigenous identities. This program was designed not to assimilate non-Arab, non-Muslim groups but to dominate them. As Rose Lisok Paulino observed the landscaping of Khartoum for the 2005 celebration of the city as "the capital of Arab culture," she remarked that "even the simple act of planting palm trees was done for a political reason," to bring the character of the national capital in line with other Arab capital cities. The promulgation of this ideological project was fundamentally located within a jihadist discourse that justified aggression against non-Muslim communities. Historically, these processes were aggravated by the social, economic, and political subjection of Southern Sudan.

In many political circles, however, observers attributed the war to colonial policies that separated the North and the South by way of the Closed Doors Ordinance and Southern Policy and planted the seeds of disunion, pitting North against South, Muslims against Christians, and Arabs against Africans, and in the process enhancing the security of one group at the expense of another. The Closed Doors Ordinance limited northern access to the South; indeed, it forbade outsiders—except for British colonialists and missionaries—from entering the southern districts. The ordinance stipulated:

> All Sudanese (other than government officials or officials on duty, or traveling in transit) are forbidden to enter or trade in certain areas of the Sudan without special permission from the Ministry of the Interior or the Governor of the Province concerned. Sudanese may also be refused entry to trade in such areas on certain specific grounds. The districts concerned are Equatorial, Upper Nile, Bahr el Ghazal Provinces, the Nuba Mountains area, an area of Western Darfur Province, and the Southern Part of Funj district in Blue Nile Province. (*Sudan Almanac* 1961: 124–25)

British colonial administrators saw the incursion of Arabs into the South as threatening to the integrity of Southern Sudanese cultural and religious identities. Responding to a paper on Southern Sudan by Canon Warren, M. W. Parr, who had served as governor of the Equatorial Provinces from 1934 to 1942, defended the policy with extraordinary zeal:

> To me who served for 15 years in the Arab North and for 8 years in the African South, it is certain that the Gulf between North and South could not have been widened by an expatriate action. In the North the educational system was based on "education in the mother tongue," followed by education in English, the language of higher and university education. In the South precisely the same principle was followed; to have introduced that difficult language Arabic into the South would have the Southerner permanently and hopelessly behind the Northerner, educationally. It would have been an educational crime, of which the Condominium Governments were fortunately not guilty.[28]

DUBOIS - gifts.

From a British colonial vantage point, preventing the infiltration of Arab-ization and Islamization was a necessary means toward "preserving all that was good in the cultures of Southern Sudan."[29]

Southern Sudan was subject to other foreign influences, however, as the British promoted Christian missionary activity across the region. While Islamization was curbed with great success, Christianity was zealously preached among followers of indigenous faith traditions. The colonial regime encouraged missionaries, seeing Christianity as a vital pillar of citizenship and public education.[30] A memo on the progress of Christianization acknowledged, "Most of the successful missionary work in the Sudan has been done among Southern Sudan communities. Missionaries spared no effort in promoting the scrupulous study of scripture and prayer as well as to the training of evangelists," converts who would preach the Christian message in their own language.[31] Despite their divergent religious views, then, both the northern Sudanese and British governments made relentless efforts to transform the identities of southerners by way of religious conversion. The implications of missionary education were far-reaching. Missionaries, as numerous writings on the southern question make abundantly clear, used every opportunity to keep the memory of southerners' enslavement at the hands of Arabs alive (Beshir 1965; Abdel Rahim 1969). The centrality of slavery to the missionary education system shaped southern Sudanese subjectivity, as listeners began to acquire "identities from hearing their biographies" (Resnik 2003, 300).[32] Discriminatory practices within Arabic-speaking communities toward southerners furthered their sense of marginality, as southerners became increasingly aware of the role of language in their confinement to the lower ranks of society. Sayings such as "his ear is red to Adam" or "so-and-so has the bitter vein" signify the predominant racial ideologies that denigrated the Africanity of non-Arab communities in the Sudan (see Khalid 2000).

For this reason, more often than not, southerners meet the attribution of the conflict to British colonialism with protests, and even indignation. In the words of a world-renowned Egyptian journalist: "I have never met a single educated Southerner who did not express his utter outrage at Northern political parties and successive governments since 1956; as if the troubles of the South were their responsibility alone and not that of the colonizers who took complete charge of the Southern region and labored to plant contradictions and unequal development among the members of the same nation" (El-Sherif 2004, 261). There is no doubt British colonialism contributed to the creation of insurmountable obstacles to national unity. To concentrate on colonial history, however, not only conceals the agency of violators who infringed upon international conventions guaranteeing the rights of ethnolinguistic and religious minorities, but also absolves them from their responsibility in shaping policies that made Sudan's civil war the bloodiest in history.

The drive for strict enforcement of sharia and the perpetuation of jihadist ideology under political Islam contributed significantly to the perpetuation of war. The National Islamic Front has played a key role in the Bashir government, overwhelming more secular parties in the North as well as insisting on the imposition of Islamic law nationwide. In recent years, a new culture of martyrdom was propagated to conceal the gravity of dying in Southern Sudan. Northern families who lost their sons in the war were discouraged from mourning their deaths. "People are told to ululate and celebrate because as parents and siblings of martyrs they should take solace in their sons' eternal life in heaven. People were told that their sons did not die but they are alive and are getting married to *horiat el-janna,* or the virgin brides of heaven," commented an eighty-one-year-old man satirically. As ethnic and religious differences became increasingly politicized, both Arabism and Islamism emerged as powerful symbols of state totalitarianism in which contravention of minority rights became regarded as acceptable, even desirable.

The power of political Islam resonates in the courtyard of St. Peter's Catholic Church in a Khartoum suburb. This parish church, which is separated by a towering wall from the adjacent mosque, provides a discursive space in which the majority of the congregation membership can contemplate the meanings and consequences of *El-Mashru El-Hadari.* This multiethnic congregation comprises people from numerous southern groups in addition to Ethiopian and Eritrean migrants and exiles. During a lengthy conversation, the priest explained that the long arm of politics had reached the neighboring mosque, which turned overnight from a place of worship into a forum for jihadist oratory:

> I have been living here long enough to witness the radical change in our neighboring mosque with which we coexisted for years. It used to enjoy some of the most powerful voices of tolerance and moderation. Their sermons, which were carried to our courtyard through loudspeakers, preached accommodation and talked more generally about humanity, good deeds, and the importance of faith in everyday life. These are spiritual values that we all share as People of the Book. Now we hear that the excellent imams have been replaced by government-appointed ones.

One can tell. The sermons now preach jihad and holy war and address themselves to the fate of sharia opponents. The sermons are increasingly becoming a tool of propaganda. From the loud microphones we are constantly reminded about ourselves as infidels. The imam one time took it upon himself to harass our youth during a drumming ceremony in the church. This behavior is unheard of. It is downright hostile and insufferable.

This shift is not a matter of one mosque only, but part of a concerted policy that is endorsed by the government.

The close connection between Islamization and Arabization came up during a discussion about Christian preaching in the North. A priest who was asked why the Catholic Church had not made adequate provisions for outreach to displaced persons in the vicinity of Khartoum replied:

There are a number of militating factors against baptism. Most of our preachers are displaced and therefore face tremendous instability and insecurity. The police raids and the destruction of the camps contribute to their isolation. Most of the people live very far. [There are too few priests to go around, so parishes are without] priests for long periods of time. The most important reason is the lack of confidence on the part of the priests or preachers in the usefulness of the Arabic language as the main medium of preaching.

Residence in the Arabic-speaking North has prompted the rapid adoption of Arabic by IDPs, but the church has failed to keep pace with its flock. Still, widespread resistance to state policies regarding religious minorities continues. In the face of pressures to assimilate, displaced southerners have sought to retain a sense of sovereignty and recover their sense of dignity and self-worth.

Framings

Urgent anthropology, like humanistic anthropology, makes peoples' own voices and viewpoints central to ethnographic inquiry. Responding to the urgency of the problems it explores, it goes beyond mere academic inquiry to allow its subjects' concerns to shape its major policy recommendations. This approach offers valuable frameworks for understanding and analyzing the complex existential conditions of present-day Sudan, especially the subjective formulations of the experiences of the internally displaced women who are the focus of this study. Throughout this book, I situate the innovative remapping of ideas about self and society that occurs as women adjust to displacement within the broader drama of war and political violence. By unraveling the intricately interconnected strands that make up the wide-ranging experiences of women who live in Izzbba, one of the largest shantytowns in Khartoum, I document the conditions under which they enact their lives as displaced persons, record their strategies for coping with their situation, and interpret the narratives in which they articulate and reflect on the ways they have changed in the process of adapting to displacement.

Although violence within Southern Sudanese communities played a role in dislodging these women from their homes, it is the war that affected them most profoundly. This protracted civil conflict has been the primary cause of widespread human rights abuses throughout Sudan. Not only did it imperil individual and collective security deemed fundamental by the United Nations Declaration on Human Rights more than fifty years ago, but it also constituted a serious infringement of the economic, political, and cultural rights of indigenous communities. War multiplies human distress and entails various forms of individual and collective trauma. Selfhood and personhood undergo dramatic shifts. Personhood depends on specific relationships and settings—a family, a village, a natural environment, with its geographic and spiritual dimensions—so the systematic destruction of a community's physical safety and cultural life strikes at its very foundations. The loss of communality means that identities must be considered afresh. The everyday experiences that accompany dislocation prompt a serious deliberation of the multiple, dialectical relationships between person and community, self and the world.

The effects of war on a displaced person's self-perception and sense of security are distilled in Maurice Eisenbruch's notion of "cultural bereavement" (1991). The loss goes beyond the death of loved ones and the loss of shelter to involve the loss of cultural moorings.[33] Eisenbruch's notion of bereavement helps us understand the testimony of T.P., a Kuku Christian from Equatoria who has lived in Khartoum since 1984. "Sometimes I say to myself, it is better to die rather than live in the conditions I am living in right now. I desperately want to reunite with my family members from whom I have been separated twenty years ago.[34] I cannot stop thinking about them. I hope to be able to go back to the South so that these feelings could get resolved." Forced migration, as this woman's painful situation attests, affects individual and collective self-perception, representations of self and others, and national and ethnic culture, as well as material and economic security (see Morawska 2000).

At the same time that forced migration entails profound loss, displacement also opens up possibilities for change. In rebuilding their lives, Southern Sudanese women have responded to the challenges of war, displacement, and resettlement in creative ways. The balance between embracing change and losing a sense of identity is a delicate one, though, when discontinuity is imposed and takes place all at once. Analyzing women's complex responses to their situation requires consideration of location, networks, and memory, factors that Peter Preston (1997) sees as crucial to the understanding of political and cultural identities (see also Faris 1989). These women's ideas about self, gender, and community are constantly being renegotiated. Not only have their previous conceptions of the social world been utterly disrupted, but they have relocated in a very different sort of place. Many internally displaced women have lived for an extended period of time in Khartoum, where they have come into contact with Arab Muslim populations and a mix of various ethnic, religious, and linguistic communities. The formation of new communities, networks of association and exchange, and mutual attachments has facilitated the reformulation of identities. In the words of L.K., who moved to Khartoum from Darfur in 1996, "I interact with my northern neighbors and have learned about *henna* (body paint), *dukhan* (smoke bath), and *dilka* (body scrub), among other customs. I'm prepared to embrace these customs."

I explore the narratives and testimony that I gathered from women in Izzbba and other shantytowns in Greater Khartoum from a feminist perspective. Forced migration has profound effects on women's gender identity, first and foremost because it disrupts the relationships that previously defined women's lives. Many lost their husbands, though some left abusive husbands behind. Women alone and with children or other dependents to care for mobilize their internal resources and turn to their neighbors to solve the myriad of problems they face. Women who head their own households can shed extended family members whom they do not regard as supportive and depart from the customary laws that favored their husband's relatives. Independence becomes an unavoidable fact of life, bringing both freedoms and burdens.

IDPs do not dwell on their bereavement, though the trauma they have undergone erupts into their lives in unexpected ways. Displaced women begin to create permanence in transience, or what Aihwa Ong (1995, 350), quoting James Clifford, describes as "dwelling in traveling." Prolonged residence in Khartoum amid Sudan's civil war has generated new symbolic meanings of space that, in turn, have created sustaining, affective relationships of interdependence among displaced people. Some shantytown residents go beyond the experience of displacement they share with other southerners and forge new bonds with their neighbors in the North, who are overwhelmingly from the poorer classes. Steven Feld affirms the salience of location in the crafting of the self: "The fusion of self, space, and time provides an opportunity for the experiential layerings from one's birthplace to other places lived and traveled in, to actively map place into identity, conjoining temporal and spatial projection, reinscribing past in present, creating biography as itinerary" (Feld, quoted in Battaglia 2000, 129). The narratives of IDPs shed light on the existential nature of identity, which is sensitive to changing circumstances and can be transformed through displacement. Responding creatively to the challenges of displacement becomes the stuff of personal narratives and the basis of a shared identity. Divisions among southerners in Khartoum have begun to give way to a greater recognition of southernness as a major marker of identity. At the same time, southerners have begun selectively to adopt culturally compatible customs from their northern hosts. Through these processes, displaced women renegotiate their sense of femininity and reconstruct their relationships with significant others.

TWO

Becoming Displaced

What happens to people when the landscapes of their lives—personal, social, and cultural—are landmined, when the maps of meaning that order people's lives are blown apart? What happens to people when what they believe makes them human—home, hearth, family and tradition—has been wrenched from their grasp?

—Carolyn Nordstrom, 1997

On a cold, windy day in December 2004 in Khartoum, while returning to Elemmarat, my hometown, after visiting the Libya Market in Omdurman, I had a conversation with my driver, a young man who had been displaced from Jebel Marra, Darfur. We talked about his new job as a driver in the capital city, the exploitation visited upon him by his avaricious employer, his family, and his determination to take a second wife when his financial situation improved. As he described the threatening circumstances under which he was forced to depart, he recited a poem by Idris Jammaa,[1] a gifted Sudanese poet:

> *In hathi kadaqiqin*
> *foq shokin nathru*
> *Wa qalou li hufattin*
> *yoma rihin ajmaaoh*

> *My fate is like a fistful of flour*
> *They scattered it all over thorny fields,*
> *And then they asked the barefooted to fetch it on a windy day.*

This recitation evoked the trauma of displacement, with its complex layering of meanings and emotions. When a person becomes displaced, connections with family and community are shattered beyond repair.

The United Nations Commission on Human Rights defines the internally displaced as "persons who have been forced to flee their homes suddenly or unexpectedly in large numbers, as a result of armed conflicts, internal strife, systematic violations of human rights or natural or man-made disasters, and who are within the territory of their own country" (UNHRC 1998a, 1998b). Remaining within the nation does not make displacement less traumatic or assuage the crushing emotions that accompany the journey. War that forces flight overwhelms the senses. "When you smell the smoke of gunfire and hear the ear-splitting bombing and see old and young people running in every direction, dust rising, you know that you are displaced and that your life has changed forever," remembers C.W., who has lived in a Khartoum shantytown since 1983. "We were not able to collect our belongings or think about where we are going, or what is going to happen to us or our animals. We just fled our village. There was no time. All of us just ran away, women, children, young people and old, we all ran and ran and ran away." Finding a direction came later; in the moment, flight was all that mattered.

Internally displaced persons (IDPs) flee in lorries and buses, by steamers, on army planes, and on foot. More often than not, the means of transportation—rather than a deliberate decision—determines the final destination. Some have become displaced within the Southern provinces; others have crossed the borders to neighboring African countries, while still others have settled in various localities in the North. War has been the primary force propelling the women of Izzbba to migrate to Khartoum (for demographic data, see appendix C). One-quarter of the women surveyed and interviewed said they came to join relatives, while others had come to look for work or to attend school. Chain migration and the presence of relatives or friends in the new settlement played a role in their ending up in Izzbba. Of the seventy-one respondents, 79 percent had relatives or friends in the area to which they moved. Despite this effort to cling to kin, family fragmentation was evident. Almost all said their family composition had changed as an outcome of displacement. This response is corroborated by other displaced women whom I interviewed in other camps and shantytowns. The overwhelming majority described the loss of property and family ties. In another setting, Kai Erickson poignantly described the consequent sense of exposure: they feel "alone and without very much in the way of emotional shelter. . . . the community no longer surrounds people with a layer of insulation to protect them from a world of danger" (1976, 240). War as an act of aggression and dominance obliterates people's basic means of survival: shelter, access to food, means of production, affective networks, and protection. The long journey from villages in Southern Sudan to towns in the North is protracted and arduous. The circumstances under which this journey is executed are almost unimaginably difficult. As I spoke with displaced women, I heard many disturbing stories about mothers forced to leave their children who died on the way, people assaulted, cattle and property stolen in broad daylight, and witnessing the butchery of loved ones. That so few women reported being sexually assaulted is evidence not of their safety but of their silence about this most traumatic of experiences.[2]

Philister Baya was brought up in exile in Uganda after her family was displaced from Mundri, Western Equatoria, by the civil war raging there. They were repatriated to their home after the 1972 peace agreement but displaced again in 1987, when the Sudanese government evacuated Maridi and her hometown was occupied by the SPLA. Fleeing civilians were caught in the crossfire in Rokon, and Philister's father, sister, and cousin were killed. After Philister made her way to Khartoum, she brought surviving family members to join her (Baya 1999, 61–62). According to Mary Hillary Wani, many southern women experienced great losses as they escaped war and famine in the South (1999; for additional personal stories, see U.S. Committee for Refugees and Immigrants 1999).

Even when journeys are undertaken under optimal conditions, migrants from rural areas face tremendous difficulties in finding a foothold in the city. Unemployment and underemployment are endemic (Gilbert and Gugler 1984). Adequate housing is hard to come by; minimal shelters are improvised from discarded materials. Information about how to manage daily tasks, such as fetching water and fuel, is exchanged among friends, and new arrivals lack social connections. In many poor countries, rural to urban migrants settle first in shantytowns on the outskirts of major cities. In Sudan, these areas are known as *sakan ashwai,* or squatter settlements. Similar settlements are known in Brazil as *favelas,* in Argentina as *villas miseria,* and on the U.S.-Mexico border as *colonias.* Shantytowns lack infrastructure and public services, but residents have some access to markets and casual employment opportunities. These new city dwellers live and work almost entirely in the informal sector (see Iliffe 1987; Tostensen, Tvedten, and Vaa 2001; for examples outside of Africa, see Schneider 1995; Lomnitz 1977; Goldstein 2003).

The problems migrants face are much more acute under circumstances of forced migration and sudden displacement, when people have no opportunity to ponder the risks and benefits of their move and to work out a plan in advance. IDPs from the South arrive in Khartoum having lost virtually everything: their homes, their possessions, and their access to resources. Husbands, brothers, and sons are off fighting or have crossed into other countries alone. A substantial number have been killed. Many women are in charge of their destiny for the first time. This dramatic switch from follower to leader is a mixed blessing. On the one hand, women discover a new sense of independence. Women in the camps and shantytowns of Khartoum want to make something of their lives. They do not want to depend entirely on humanitarian aid, even if they were provided with adequate sustenance; they want to support themselves and those who depend on them. On the other hand, it is almost impossibly difficult to become independent economically, especially in the isolated shantytowns, which are less regulated than the camps and farther from the city. Food is in short supply; children and adults ransack garbage cans and refuse piles for edible scraps. Electricity is nonexistent. Even water is scarce; the wells are few and far between in the desert, and no water is piped in. Although the government camps have tents, most IDPs construct their own shelters. Houses are built with adobe-like material known as *zibala,* composed mostly of animal dung, or straw known as *khaish,* as well as with plastic and other scavenged materials. The deterioration of IDPs' living standards afflicts every aspect of their lives in Khartoum. David Korn notes that "even if they were not poor before fleeing or being driven from their homes, the internally displaced quickly become the poorest of the poor, subject to abuse and exploitation and to rates of malnutrition, disease, and mortality well beyond those of the still settled population" (1999, 18).

Notwithstanding these devastating conditions, visitors to squatter settlements concur with Alan Gilbert's powerful observation: "the poor's response to poverty is rational, innovative, and nearly always more perceptive than often they are given credit for" (Gilbert and Gugler 1984, 84). Their creative responses to urban poverty are not always appreciated, however. IDPs are often held liable for squatting or settling illegally on unplanned land, which puts them at war with the government. In Sudan, the struggle over land is exceptionally sharp. Under government "replanning" or "zoning" and development schemes, land is sold at astronomical prices to realtors and foreign investors. The government then tries to evict the residents to make way for new construction, allowing a token few to purchase small plots but making no provision for the masses of the displaced. Each time, IDPs emerge as the perpetual victims of the sweeping drive toward capital accumulation and urban expansion.

Displacement epitomizes what Arthur Kleinman, Veena Das, and Margaret Lock (1997) call "social suffering," which (in Das's words) "brings into a single space an assemblage of human problems that have their origins and consequences in the devastating injuries that social force can inflict on human experience. Social suffering results from what political, economic, and institutional power does to people and, reciprocally, from how these forms of power themselves influence responses to social problems" (Das 1997, ix). The words of S.P.L, a shantytown resident, dramatize the cultural devastation that accompanies displacement:

> I fled to Khartoum running from guns. I worked in Juba as a cleaner for the Ministry of Education. Forced to leave my household and husband behind, I thought I was running to a safe haven, but when I arrived in 2000, I found myself in even worse conditions. I now live among relatives and friends, but I had given up my traditional culture. I spend my days in constant anxiety and suffering. I believe that continued residence in Khartoum will destroy my conscience of being. I want only peace and to go back to the South.

By the phrase translated as "conscience of being," S.P.L. meant her cultural self-understanding.

Arriving in the city brings no relief, except that it signals escaping the war zone. A Shilluk woman in Dar El Salam expressed appreciation for "fleeing the bullets." But being thankful for sanctuary does not keep IDPs from experiencing unspeakable suffering. In addition to formidable existential questions, IDPs have to grapple with physical and psychological stress from the horror of the war and its aftermath. These ailments seem to swallow up their lives. Little is done to help them cope with their experiences or construct new lives. A Dinka chief in Wad El-Bashir, a government-run camp, expressed his discontent with the situation: "Displaced people here are suffering tremendously. They are entitled to very little. A few humanitarian organizations are trying to help, but the numbers are way too high to cover. You are better off if you cross the border as a refugee. Your chances of getting help are better. Every day for a displaced person is a challenge."

Priscilla Joseph is currently an MP in the new government of National Unity, a member of the Peace and Justice Committee of the Sudan Council of Churches, and one of twelve executive committee members of the Southern Women's Group for Peace, which she cofounded. Joseph has organized numerous workshops for women on the Sudan peace process. Since 1986, she has served as a consultant and facilitator of training seminars for such organizations as Oxfam, GOAL SUDAN, and the Abieyi Peace Committee. She has done extensive course work at Eastern Mennonite University in Virginia on the fundamentals of peace building, philosophy, methods of conflict research, refugees, humanitarian assistance, ethnic identity, and conflict transformation, and authored several papers, including "Search for Sustainable Peace in Sudan," "Understanding the Civil War: Role of Media in Peace Building," and "South-North Conflict." Professionally, Joseph is a medical doctor on the teaching faculty at the University of Khartoum.

> Displaced women in general face a number of troubles, some visible and others unseen. These troubles are reflected in their practices and behavior. The most significant troubles that face displaced women are social, economic, and psychological. The displacement of families in war-affected areas has a major economic impact. Displacement leads to the loss of income-generating resources. Women in the South have a substantial economic role. Generally, the inhabitants of the South depend on agriculture, grazing, fishing, and hunting. War cuts off all these resources, as most of the people become internally displaced or refugees in the neighboring countries and depend on aid. Some of them work in marginal jobs. The woman in the South enjoyed a distinguished social status; even if she was poor, her dignity was respected. Now she serves at houses which subject her to humiliation and psychological as well as physical exploitation. In the capital, displaced women hardly find work except for marginal work that yields little income and exposes them to the risk of arrest by the authorities. Displaced women can sell tea or liquor, but selling alcoholic drinks leads her to prison, because it is illegal. War has a negative psychological impact on women. The woman who loses her husband, son, or brother either by death or departure undergoes psychological exhaustion. These women were once dignified and honored in their community; displacement exposes them to humiliating practices and leads to loss of self-respect and depression. (Joseph 2001)

The loss of women's status within family and community compounds the loss of economic resources.

Both governmental and international responses to IDPs' needs and concerns have been ineffective or entirely absent. David Korn sees the "selectivity" that characterizes humanitarian responses as "a major shortcoming" (1999, 56). In the absence of assistance from the central government, responsibility for the welfare of IDPs falls on the shoulders of local governments. In the North, however, the receiving communities lack sufficient resources; most locally born people live below the poverty line. The deficiency is compounded by the total lack of recognition that the protection and incorporation of IDPs within the social structure should be a matter of policy. Social neglect results in a continuing pattern of isolation and discrimination. The confluence of socioeconomic and political marginality exacerbates the suffering of the displaced. Sudanese and non-Sudanese NGOs, like their counterparts in many conflict areas, are making real efforts to aid IDPs. However, their resources are minuscule in relation to IDPs' needs.

In my conversations, I learned that many shantytowns were named by the displaced persons themselves. Out of frustration and despondency, residents of a shantytown in Omdurman called it *Kosom El Arab,* an exceedingly distasteful slur that can be translated as "Fuck the cunts of the Arabs' mothers." No one in town is troubled by the use of this derogatory term. In faraway bus stations, conductors call out loudly, "Come on, ride with us to Kosom El Arab, come on, there is room for two passengers to Kosom El Arab." IDPs from Kordofan and Darfur named their new abode *Zaglona,* meaning "They threw us away," when they arrived in steady waves in the wake of the famine and desertification that afflicted their homelands during the early 1980s. Some names are inspiring: Mandela commemorates the South African freedom fighter whose stirring story remains a powerful symbol of hope to those awaiting a miraculous discharge from hardship and desolation.

Thieves, Villains, and Lizards' Tails

IDPs are commonly depicted in a derogatory fashion and often encounter prejudice and discriminatory treatment from the host community. Frequently met with repugnance and disdain, they are seen as carriers of communicable diseases, thieves, pickpockets, and common criminals. An IDP camp in Omdurman became widely known as Ras El-Shaittan, the "devil's head," connoting the imagined malevolence and criminality of its denizens. My visit to Ras El-Shaittan coincided with that of social workers from Fellowship in African Relief, a charitable NGO aiding refugees and IDPs in Sudan. A grim resignation was written all over the faces of those who queued that day under a sweltering sun for oil and grits. These IDPs cannot comprehend how and why this off-putting appellation came to be imposed upon them.

Lately, a pronounced concern about the possibility that IDPs extort money from northerners and threaten to take revenge upon them has been voiced in Khartoum. A number of stories circulate as evidence of IDPs' malevolence. One person recounted to me an incident in which IDP "justice" was regarded as criminal aggression:

Paulino Mateep, that Nuer military officer, encouraged the establishment of special courts to try northerners who get in any trouble with southerners. . . . Paulino's courts are used for revenge, not justice. A young northerner who repairs mobile phones told us about his horrifying ordeal. A southerner walked in and asked him to repair his phone. The northerner looked at it and tried it many times, but he thought it [could] not be fixed. He gave it back to the southerner, who then accused the former of destroying his phone on purpose. He demanded a replacement. The northerner told him that the phone was already destroyed when he showed up. The southerner left the shop and showed up hours later with two men who forced the young man into an Amjad [a small transport van]. Three other men were armed with Kalashnikovs [machine guns]. They took him to a court that looked like a zoo. He was forced into a small hut to face the "judge." It was a mockery. They forced the young man to pay money or else he [would] regret it. These days you have to be very careful, because any IDP can invent a problem to get you in the stickiest situation of your life.

Mateep, who had reconciled with the central government after serving as a rebel commander, established informal tribunals in Khartoum, with the government's blessing, where chiefs and sultans would mediate conflicts.[3] To many who recounted stories of Paulino's courts, however, these tribunals are not places for seeking redress and restoration but sites in which group revenge is carried out with impunity. Approached with suspicion by many northerners, the setting up of these courts has led to circumspection and caution toward Khartoum's IDPs and deepened mistrust even further.

Disapproving attitudes toward IDPs flourish within their sending communities, as well as among their hosts. I was told by a Dinka priest that those who were compelled to leave have no standing with those who endured the war at home. He explained: "Just imagine for a minute that the sending community is a lizard. When lizards are in danger they dispose of their tails. But when they are out of danger, they are able to grow new tails. The discarded ones can never be reconnected to the lizards' bodies. This is the situation with the displaced. They are seen as lizard tails that have been cut off and can never be attached again." This image is not merely a metaphor for the irrevocable nature of dislodgment; it also bears centrally on the politics of repatriation, resettlement, and reintegration of refugees. How will IDPs be accepted by communities that dismiss them as lizards' tails, a pusillanimous lot who ran away during a time of crisis and have forfeited their place?

Given the growing divergence between those who left war-torn areas and those who stayed, some southern women residing in Khartoum are ambivalent about the prospect of returning to their former homes. The places they fled in the South have been destroyed; with their families shattered or scattered, there is nothing to go home to. Some IDPs have adapted to life in the North. They suggest that governmental and international agencies should provide material support for displaced women where they are, rather than focusing solely on return and resettlement. In numerous conversations, displaced women indicated their interest in what NGOs call capacity-building projects; they want to learn skills such as sewing, typing, and petty commodity production and to borrow seed money for small enterprises so they can earn money for themselves and their families. They also welcome "empowerment programs" that offer them access to information and resources they need to make decisions independently and act on their own initiative. Support for women in their present localities should be at the top of the agenda for the government of national unity. The fact that displacement is presumed to be temporary should not be used as an excuse to neglect the overwhelming needs of communities under siege.

"A Bleak Existence"

This chapter interlaces stories of displacement from people who inhabit shantytowns and camps for IDPs with analyses of their creative responses to their predicament. The majority of these narratives originate from the squatter settlement I call Izzbba; some come from another shantytown nearby, and a few come from residents of government-run camps.[4] The largest shantytown in Greater Khartoum, Izzbba is characterized by a significant degree of interethnic mixing, allowing for rich descriptions of diverse experiences and perspectives and enabling a complex ethnographic analysis (for demographic data about Izzbba residents, see appendix C). In these localities, I inquired about daily life, the obstacles that threaten residents, and their particular ways of surmounting them. Responses to these questions yield a vivid picture of the pervasive contraventions of elemental entitlements of IDPs. They also help to interrogate the institutionalized power of the state over vulnerable and dispossessed populations, primarily women whose lives have been marred by physical and psychological distress. Their lives in Khartoum's shantytowns entail a variety of encounters with the authorities that entangle them in a constant state of chaos. An Azande woman living in Mayo told me, "We wake up every morning to face yet another testing day." The narratives gathered in the course of this research demonstrate why we should frame displacement within larger discussions of women's rights as human rights and not just as a humanitarian problem that can be solved through charity and aid.

These women's narratives of the pain and suffering inflicted upon them are supplemented and extended by the comprehensive needs-assessment reports compiled by NGOs. Working for the most part in Lokichokio, a town on the Kenya-Sudan border where many refugees have congregated, and in Greater Khartoum, UNICEF's Operation Lifeline Sudan (OLS) was formed in 1989 to provide humanitarian assistance to approximately four million IDPs in the southern and northern sectors. Significantly, OLS negotiated with the Government of Sudan (GOS) and the Sudan Peoples Liberation Movement/Army (SPML/A) to deliver humanitarian assistance to all civilians in need, regardless of their location. Operating as a consortium of UN agencies (UNICEF and the World Food Programme) and thirty-five local and regional organizations, in 1997 it identified food security, health, nutrition, water and sanitation, and basic education as pressing needs. Disappointingly, those needs have not been met. Within IDP camps, people are suffering the worst effects of poverty. Malnutrition and infectious diseases form a malignant combination. Malaria is endemic; diarrhea is rampant, particularly among infants and children—to whom it is especially fatal. Lack of clean water makes sanitation impossible. A social worker in Soba Aradi told me, "The worst situation that is produced by lack of sanitation is the very horrible smell of human waste. It attracts flies and creates an intolerable stench that people are forced to inhale and live with. It is a glaring example of neglect and indifference. It reflects the seriousness of the problems that IDPs must contend with." The diseases propagated in such unsanitary conditions make the camps and shantytowns a site of excess deaths rather than a refuge from the fatalities of war.

When these Southern Sudanese women arrived in Khartoum, they joined an estimated 1.8 million IDPs living in the slums surrounding the capital city known as *sakan ashwai*, in squatter settlements such as Izzbba, Soba Aradi, and El-Baraka, and in the government-designated camps such as Dar El Salaam, Wad El-Bashir, Mayo, and Jebel Awlia. They came from the five main regions and counties of the South: Southern Kordofan,

Southern Blue Nile, Upper Nile, Bahr El-Ghazal, and Equatoria. IDPs descend from a variety of ethnic groups, but in Khartoum they linked up with the ethnically mixed community in their shantytown. Izzbba includes a wide array of ethnolinguistic groups: Nuba, 24 percent; Fur, 16 percent;[5] Arab, 15 percent; Dinka, 14 percent; Shilluk, 9.5 percent; Nuer, 5.5 percent; Bari, 4.5 percent; Fonj, 4 percent; Acholi, 3 percent; Moro, Zande, Latuka, and Firteet, 1 percent; and non-Sudanese, 0.5 percent. (See also Loveless 1999.) Ethnic mixing is not limited to that of Arab Muslim and non-Arab, non-Muslim peoples. Some Arabic-speaking Muslim IDPs, mostly from the western provinces of Darfur and Kordofan, arrived in the early 1980s, propelled by drought and desertification; they became the hosts of southerners. Now southerners are being joined by IDPs from Darfur. People and cultures from the far-flung regions of southern and western Sudan came together to give Izzbba its personality.

By all accounts, life in a shantytown is a chronic emergency. According to the OLS, "Sudan presents perhaps the most persevering situation of unmet needs by internally displaced persons worldwide" (UNICEF 1998, 17; see also UNICEF 1995, UNICEF 2001). When asked about the conditions in the camps and shantytowns, many women in Khartoum lamented that "death is better than this situation." Most had seen death firsthand, so the comparison was not metaphorical. Perhaps when they escaped the fighting, they had hoped to find a haven; instead, they were plunged into precarious circumstances where daily survival is a constant struggle and the fundamentals of existence remain insecure. These powerful voices resonate with those of IDPs around the world, whom Roberta Cohen and Francis Deng fittingly describe as "forsaken people" (1998a). As Ellen Johnson Sirleaf notes, "Disasters expose existing vulnerabilities in a most dramatic and unarguable manner" (1993, 303).[6] Natural disasters that result in the displacement of populations highlight the failures of despotic political regimes.[7] IDPs are incessantly confronted with managing quandaries they did not create under circumstances that offer them few resources. Listening to the personal testimonies and reasoned analyses of a wide variety of Sudanese women about life in squatter settlements yields insight into the experiences and perspectives of millions of citizens whose voices and viewpoints are seldom heard.

Continuing Violence against Women

Displacement is itself a denial of fundamental human rights, and displaced women suffer in ways that men do not. Their suffering flows directly from the gender-specific harms that afflict women and girls in times of conflict; civil war and political violence are all too frequently attended by rape, abduction, and forced servitude to irregular militias (Agger 1992; Eastmond 1993; Habib 1995; Hackett 1996; Indra 1998). Displacement compounds women's problems, as those who flee are especially vulnerable to sexual violation. In squatter settlements, shantytowns, and even government-run camps, violations of women's rights and assaults on their bodily integrity continue. The harrowing stories women told me reveal that in the context of ongoing Sudanese political conflicts, women and girls are fair game. Large-scale forced migration makes respect for human dignity all but impossible.

Although displacement is a traumatic experience for everyone involved, it is far worse for women and girls. In Sudan, relatively few women are exposed to the risk of dying in combat that affects male soldiers and fighters, but many women suffer from sexual violence in wartime, during their flight, and after their arrival in new communities. Most are left to deal with the significant physical and psychological effects alone (UNHCR 1995). Christina Dudu, a southern displaced woman living in Khartoum, outlined the gendered forms of exploitation, including sexual abuse, prostitution, and sexual harassment, that accompanied the mass flight of women and girls (1999). They had not experienced sexual violence at home in the South before the renewal of the civil war. Sexual acts become weaponized during conflict, and women and girls bear the brunt of brutal assaults inflicted on their bodies.

In enumerating gender-based acts of violence, rape heads the list of unspeakable crimes against humanity propagated in wartime. Rape has been one of the most serious problems that plague women in civil wars and other situations of political violence around the world. In the final analysis, rape is a specific form of punishment that women and girls face as sexed bodies. The far-reaching effects of rape have been illuminated by Tara Gingerich and Jennifer Leaning in their report on Darfur (2004). In addition to the immediate physical and psychological trauma of bodily violation, women must cope with a diminished sense of safety and feelings of vulnerability, attenuated connections with others and a loss of the sense of belonging, damage to their relational life, and disturbance of their expected life trajectory (2004; see especially appendix 2: 2–4, 6–8). The incidence of mass rape has severe consequences for the community, as marital and kin-based relationships are disrupted and communal trust is eroded. The trauma of rape is compounded in cultures where women's sexual purity is highly valued. Being raped constitutes a violation of self-respect, and reporting having been raped is an affront to the honor of the woman's family and community. Rape survivors may bear unwanted children, be deemed ineligible for marriage or remarriage, become vulnerable to pressures to engage in the sex trade, and be too shamed to reunite with their remnant families and return to their communities. Rape intensifies the fracturing of family ties and social networks that is a consequence of displacement, isolating women and increasing their burdens while undermining the ability of communities to provide mutual aid. Used as a weapon of war, rape is meant to demoralize everyone.

These wide-ranging and profoundly detrimental effects should force a reconceptualization of rape not merely as one of the spoils of war but as ranking alongside genocide as a crime against humanity. In considering why the gravity of rape has not been fully recognized by the international community, feminist legal theorist Catharine MacKinnon argues that a gendered logic is at work: "What is done to women is either too specific to women to be seen as human or too generic to human beings to be seen as specific to women. Atrocities committed against women are either too human to fit the notion of female or too female to fit the notion of human. 'Human' and 'female' are mutually exclusive by definition; you cannot be a woman and a human being at the same time" (1998, 44). Not only does rape affect women physically and psychologically, but it makes it impracticable for them to return to their communities afterward. It obliterates their sense of security and alienates them from their families and communities. The displaced women I interviewed had to varying degrees been both victims and witnesses of rape, yet few spoke of those experiences. The effects were evident in their silences, as well as in the fractures in personal relationships that followed. Rape violates a woman's sense of self, creates a rupture in her life history, and prevents her from dreaming of the restoration of past wholeness after the coming of peace. Having been a victim of sexual violence also renders women especially vulnerable to sexual exploitation after they are in camps and shantytowns.

Life Histories

These women's narratives are rarely presented in a vacuum; displaced women situate their autobiographical narratives in their cultural and social contexts. Their life stories emphasize the disruption of normal expectations and relationships. Some women adopt a longer-term historical perspective. IDPs often evoke historical injustices and suffering inflicted by northerners that goes back to the Ottoman Empire and Arab complicity in planning and executing large-scale slave raids. These remembrances are important avenues for mediations between present-day experiences and past events. The common lineage of memory and identity, which figures prominently in the personal narratives presented here, is illuminated through the work of James Fentress and Chris Wickham, who argue that the remembered events are those that identify the group, setting it in a context that differentiates it from others and validates its members' claim to belong (1992, 22). By telling stories of trauma that validate collective memories and shared understandings of identity, women victimized by rape and displacement attempt to reclaim their position as group members.

Women's experiences of destitution and distress during and after armed conflict in their communities of origin create a strong desire for involvement in conflict resolution. This investment was made with crystal clarity in many narratives and writings that I gathered from Southern Sudanese women who embraced the notion of feminism as praxis—not as a theory to guide their choices, but as a set of strategies they developed in reconstructing their lives independently under conditions of displacement. They spoke out about their suffering, not only as catharsis from the horror of war but also as a mode of recording it and, ultimately, healing its wounds by repairing intergroup relationships.

KARAK MAYLIK NYOK

This activist's story exemplifies the resilience of young women who determinedly pursue their dreams despite the disruption of family relationships and displacement of wartime.

> My name is Karak Maylik Nyok. I was born in 1973 in the Nuba Mountains, a place called West Liri, near Bantu in Al-Whada State, which lies in the far east of South Kordofan. Our tribe is Upper Nile Dinka. The majority of the Liri inhabitants are Nuba, with few Arab merchants and Muraheleen and some Dinka. The inhabitants held the Dinka responsible for the war.[8] This endangered the life of many innocents and made it miserable; Dinka were continually being chased by unknown people for unknown reasons. I was living with my family near a military camp. We were four girls and two boys. I didn't know then why we lived there, but I think it was because of the war, which I knew little about then. We had a big piece of land, which we used to plant with crops and vegetables. We had also a herd of thirty-eight goats and nineteen cows, which I used to take for grazing accompanied by my nephew Simon. I was happy and innocent.

But little by little the war started to creep into my life and shape my future. The first direct strike came when my uncle and my cousins were killed during the attack on Liri East in 1985. I deeply felt the loss of my uncle and cousins and ascertained that war would soon reach my home. It was spreading like fire, rapidly and indiscriminately. War came closer day by day, restricting our movements and threatening to engulf us. One day in August 1986, when I was eleven years old, I went into the forest as usual to graze the cattle. When I came back home, I found our house locked. I started to think fearfully about what might have happened to my family. "Did they kill all my family like my relatives?" I started to sob, lonely, with no one to console me, recalling my uncle's and cousins' deaths. I revived when our neighbor Al Zuara came and told me that my family was safe. But my father was taken hostage, and she asked me to go to Malak's house where my family was hiding. I forgot about the cattle that used to mean a lot for us and went with Al Zuara. There I met my mother, brothers, and sisters, and we all started to cry, missing our father. My mother mentioned something that meant he might be killed.

Without thinking, I found myself running blindly toward the police station, thinking that they would help me save my father. I fell and got up, tears blocking my eyes and sadness filling my heart. On my way I came across a group of Dinka. I saw my father with them and ran to him. My father was more scared when he saw me and in a whispering voice asked me to leave quickly, but I refused and preferred to stay and die with him. One of the men, a policeman, came and hit me. This made me cling even more firmly to my father's chest. We were no longer hearing their shouts or feeling their whips, but were listening to the rapid beating of our own hearts inside the truck into which we were now crowded. At 7 p.m. an officer from Nuer tribe came with the soldiers' salaries. He saw the truck full of Dinka people and inquired about them. The men told him that they were taking them to Kadogli, but the soldiers will slaughter them anyway. A spell of rage filled the officer and shouted at the soldiers, telling them that those people have nothing to do with the war and they are innocent. He forced the truck door open and let us out. My father took me by the hand and we ran home.

As these events became part of our daily life, my family started to think seriously of leaving the place. We were forced to leave our homes. So we left with some Arab merchants in a car heading to Kadogli. This was in 1986, after long years of suffering and lack of security in the mountains.

Our suffering in Kadogli was beyond imagination too. My mother worked as a food and spices seller. I wanted to go to school like my sister Auor, but my mother could not afford it. As I insisted on learning, a teacher who had a daughter my age named Habab offered to teach me with her daughter. She helped me to read and I joined the school at second grade with her daughter. At the end of the year I was at the top of the class and Habab came second. At the end of the second year I was promoted directly to fifth grade. So I persuaded my father to let me continue my studies. I was sent to live with my uncle Majak in El-Obeid. I was accepted at Alsafa intermediate school there. Though I used to walk two and a half kilometers to and from school, I was so happy to resume my studies. Unfortunately, my uncle who was taking care of me had to move to work in Juba.[9] After his departure, his wife, Mary, mistreated me. She has no children and she used to drink a lot. I usually spent the time after school with neighbors until she came late in the evening. When I complained to her, she used to shout at me that she had no children and did not want responsibility for any. Finally she stopped paying even my petty expenses. I wrote to my family, and they asked me to return to Kadogli. But the fighting broke out again there and I couldn't go. My father came and took me to Khartoum.

I lived there with one of my relatives in Dar El Salaam. This relative rejected the idea of my going to school and suggested I get married, which he thought would solve all of my problems. But I insisted on continuing my studies and he refused to let me stay with him. So I had to move to live with another relative in Haj Yousif.[10] I joined Al Umm High School. The school used to pay my bursary for the poor and displaced, so I depended on this to meet my expenses as well as my family's small needs.[11] In 1990 the camp was demolished and we were moved to Mayo camp.

Karak was finally reunited with her parents and siblings in Khartoum.

We faced many problems; my young brothers were unable to attend school anymore as we could not afford it, let alone my sister Auor, who had no chance to even think of going to school. I struggled and faced my problems alone. I never gave up until I sat for the Sudanese High Secondary School Certificate in 1993. I had to secure 4000 Sudanese dinars [US$15] to pay Juba University fees. At the same time, my father fell ill and had to stay in hospital for three months. I had no choice and I took the only possible decision and worked from house to house cleaning, washing clothes, and ironing. I lost my place at the university, but I was happy to assist my family.

Fortunately, I applied and was accepted for a secretary post in my state, stationed in the Ministry of Local Governance in Khartoum. But very soon in 1995 I was transferred to work in the South. My family refused and asked me to leave the job and look for another. At the same time, a teacher working in the South asked to marry me. My father talked a lot with me, reminding me of the hardships we encountered since leaving the mountains, in Kadogli, Obeid, and finally Khartoum, and how we suffered and separated. I married after a promise that I would be able to continue my studies. I married in 1995 in Mandela camp.

Karak married in order to remain near her parents and siblings, but her father's hopes that marriage would give her security and her own hopes of continuing her education were not fulfilled. Karak's life changed for the better when she was recruited by the International Rescue Committee[12] as a literacy teacher.

As I expected, marriage did not solve my problems. I thought of applying again to Juba University. My husband refused for no good reason.

In 1996 I volunteered in a primary school and I started to teach women in the evening. This convinced the public committee to pay me 1500 Sudanese dinars as an incentive every month. In 1998, the International Rescue Committee (IRC) launched a women's empowerment program in Mayo, Dar El Salam, and Mandela. I was lucky enough to be recruited by this program as a literacy teacher. I benefited a lot from this program, particularly from participating in the training workshops the program organized for women. Feeling slightly settled, I joined Juba University's evening program so I could work with IRC during the day. I continued to receive IRC training and support and was promoted to work in the empowerment program and then as a consultant in conflict resolution and peace-building programs. I directed my attention to serving the camp inhabitants.

In the camp we lack satisfactory security, health services, and education. The rate of unemployment is very high among men and women, as is illiteracy. The phenomena of child kidnapping and sexual abuse of girls and boys are prevalent, as well as family fights because of alcohol. Often men break into camp claiming to be policemen to take blood from children.[13] I realized that all these are attributable to the lack of awareness among displaced persons and lack of participation in public affairs.

Hence the idea of the community-based organization (CBO) emerged to participate collectively in addressing some of the camp's urgent problems. One of my achievements is the establishment of the Friendship Agency for Community Training (FACT), of which I am now the executive director. We have strong objectives for the CBO to address key problems of displaced persons and the homeless. We conduct training in literacy, small-scale industries, peace building and community conflict resolution, gender, health, family planning, human rights, etc. Current projects include the construction of a training center in Mayo and Mandela camps, a women's empowerment project in Liri, and peace clubs for children in displaced camps in Khartoum.

CBOs have been formed in many camps and shantytowns, assisting displaced women to cope with conditions of deprivation, nurturing their self-consciousness, and promoting their commitment to mutual aid and collective action.

"MAMA" KEZIA LAYINWA NICODEMUS

Kezia Layinwa Nicodemus, a former teacher in her sixties, has been the Sudanese People's Liberation Movement (SPLM) commissioner for women, gender, and child welfare for the past four years. The only female holding a senior leadership position in the SPLM, she focuses her efforts on mobilizing women and making their voices heard in the Sudan negotiating process. As a keynote speaker at the Sudanese Christian Conference for Peace and Unity in Houston, Texas, in 2002, Nicodemus discussed her efforts to help refugee mothers. She appealed to the international community to focus specifically on girls and women in development strategies in Sudan.

> I saw mass killings of my people with my own eyes. People were shot, their heads were cut off. In South Sudan no one came to our rescue. I hope the people of Darfur get their freedom so that together they can begin working for development. Northern Sudanese women also suffer. Their children are taken to war. They don't allow them to cry or mourn the death of their children.

> Every living thing in South Sudan recognizes the brutality of war. Even the dogs and chickens run for their lives when they hear the noise of the Russian Antinov[14] used for bombing. We see Kofi Annan as someone who is concerned with us. He wants us to talk about our destiny. In 1990–1995 we hid in the bush. My work on behalf of women and children continued. I was appointed by Garang and the SPLM to work

as a commissioner of Women, Gender, and Child Welfare. However, I work as a volunteer. No money, no bank. This shows you how bad the situation is. All people suffer. No markets, no shops. We live in grass-roofed huts. Small huts are usually built for children to sleep in. There is no infrastructure in my town. If you go to Maridi, Bantiu, there are no roads. We walk on foot and sleep on the way if we get tired. Work is difficult, but women need to empower themselves and to know about their rights.

I have a large family of nine children, one boy and eight girls. My husband is still alive, but he is sick. I am the only breadwinner. We brew beer. Getting food is a very difficult task. My older children live in America and Britain. Two of them are in Nairobi.[15] One is doing secretarial work just to be able to afford the house rent. But living in the country-side is so tiring, because there is no health care in Maridi. No doctors, no drugs. We have to walk for miles to find a health clinic, but still you cannot find medicine.

We have to put our heads together to end the suffering. Because—can you imagine?—the closest hospital is about 60 miles away and we have to travel. People actually die on the way. These hospitals are run by good people, and volunteers. Women die in labor. If they are lucky, they will find a traditional birth attendant. There is no support. Women are very poor. They are just grateful for whatever they get.

If we don't enlighten women and show them that they have rights, they will not know. Women are second-class citizens, both in the law and in the culture. There is no escape. That is why this job as a commissioner is important. A woman can influence policy makers. But as a woman I also face problems, although I am appointed by the SPLM. I am the only woman. I am glad that the SPLM promoted freedom and equality as main causes in the New Sudan, because as you see equality doesn't exist.

"Mama" Kezia's view that women's rights are intimately linked to peace and parity in Sudan is widely shared. Her clear conception of the indissoluble character of women's equality underlies her compassion for northern as well as southern women.

The contrast between the narratives of Karak and Kezia, who are engaged in collective action, and those of women who struggle with their circumstances alone is profound. Women who work with other displaced persons for change gain a sense of control over their situation, while those who remain isolated often fall into despair. IDPs' all-encompassing sense of victimization is epitomized in a statement by A.L.: "I moved to Khartoum from Kajo Kaji in 1997 and have since converted to Islam. I struggle to feed my family. My life is pure suffering. I don't think my life is going to improve. I have no hope. I don't believe I will be able to care for my children under these pressures. If we continue to live here, my children's education and well-being will suffer. Although this place is crowded, I feel that loneliness is consuming me. I have so many worries in my head. Loneliness and worries are consuming my life. I am just waiting for death." Similar sentiments were articulated by T.P.M., who moved from Equatoria twenty years ago: "Continued living as a displaced person has meant suffering, hunger, health problems, and poverty. Displacement makes one want death." The sentiment that displacement is worse than death is startling when voiced by women who are survivors, who did not sit down passively while war overtook them. After the emergency of flight had passed, they saw no viable future for themselves and their children.

These statements of suffering represent the sentiments expressed by many women I surveyed regarding what it means to be an internally displaced person in Greater Khartoum. Fully 95 percent of the seventy-one respondents described their experiences as negative and said they were "worse off" than before. Many see their limited access to basic needs—their lack of food, shelter, sanitation, and health care—as threatening to their survival and security as human beings. Women's responsibility for children and other dependents is an intense source of distress. Although having relatives with them alleviates loneliness, women whose sense of self–worth is invested in providing for others are deeply distraught by their inability to take proper care of their loved ones. Women who define themselves primarily as mothers and caregivers may be most demoralized by the fact that they cannot fulfill those responsibilities, even though it is not their fault.

Many displaced women's narratives are marked by a poignant contrast between their life before the war and their current circumstances. Looking back at what they have lost offers little comfort, because they know that the home they loved has been destroyed.

D.K.

I am a Christian and a Fujulu. I arrived from Juba to seek medical help for my father. After the war we were forced to depart. I struggle daily in my living situation, although I work as a midwife [traditional birth attendant]. I don't have money that covers my needs and living expenses. I suffer every day. First, there is no transportation where we live. You have to walk so far to be able to find transportation. Even the weather is unmerciful. It is causing a lot of suffering. The sandstorms and the heat make our life difficult. I always think of my childhood, when I would climb mango trees, help take care of the cows, fetch water, cut firewood, and sing and dance to *nugara* music. Life was good then. Now it is pure suffering.

K.J.

I came from Bahr El-Ghazal because of the war. I escaped with other people when the fighting erupted. I am twenty-five years old. Life in Khartoum is very difficult. I experience problems all the time. I try to sell tea in the market to make a living. Police harassment is unbearable. They try to pressure me. They even destroyed my equipment and my glasses once. They say I need a work permit, but it is very expensive to get one. I don't sell enough tea to have extra cash to get a permit. I always try to avoid the police by changing locations frequently. There is no comfort.

T.J.

This young woman, too, feels burdened by work in the city. Some of her sense of isolation may result from her being a follower of Noble Spiritual Beliefs, which cannot readily be transplanted to a new place.

I am twenty-nine years old. I am a Dinka. I arrived in Khartoum in an army plane in 1998. I miss the life that I used to live back home. I had favorite things that I used to like. Planting and fishing used to give me joy. I miss our cows and the beauty of nature in our village. Marriage celebrations, being with family and friends your age, religious occasions are no more. My life here as a displaced person is very sad because I struggle a lot.

C.J.

I am Koko from Kajo Kaji. I came here in 1986. Now I am fifty-five years old, I think. I am very uncomfortable in Khartoum. In my village in the South everything was available to us. We had our songs, dances, and traditions that we celebrated. We had food, too. We had meat, milk, and fruits. I attended church with my friends and prepared drinks. I feel that all of these things are lost forever. They will not come back. Since my journey, life has been nothing but suffering. Now, I have no money, no work, no food, no medical help, and no transportation. The police interfere in our life all the time. They add to our misery and fear.

The daunting material difficulties that displaced women face in Khartoum are compounded by their sense of cultural alienation from the Muslim, Arabic-speaking society around them. Indeed, the two problems are connected, as one customary means of earning money, brewing and selling alcoholic drinks, is illegal in the city.

Cultural Confrontations

The plight of women displaced from Southern Sudan is exacerbated because the civil war has forced them into locations where they are subjected to laws and regulations that pay no heed to their rights and dismiss the legitimacy and soundness of their cosmologies and modes of knowing. Familiar forms of sociability as well as income earning are disallowed. Philister Baya explains the extent to which displacement destabilizes the cultural life of IDPs and makes them subject to infringement by the police. "When we organize for social occasions such as marriages, funerals, and rites which are to continue late at night, we are required to get permission from the local authorities, namely El-Nizam El-Aam, to conduct such occasions. In most cases [they] go into houses to interrupt the occasions without good reasons. Christians are ordered to close their shops on Fridays, during *Jumma* prayers, by the same governmental body. On refusal, the Southern displaced women, who are struggling to maintain their living [by selling drinks], are dragged to the Public Order Court to be fined" (1999).

Almost two-thirds of the women I interviewed in Izzbba said they interact with northerners in some way or another (37 percent claimed they do not). Questions surrounding cultural continuity and change yielded a range of responses. While 16 percent indicated they are unable to keep their cultural practices, such as the consumption of alcohol, 73 percent said they would not embrace northern customs except for *tobe* (dress) and henna. The remainder indicated that their experiences have been mixed: they are able to keep some elements of their cultural practices while forgoing the rest.

My inquiries into the abrogation of cultural rights[16] produced mixed reactions, because displaced women encounter Islamic practices and Arabic speakers in particular contexts and respond to them in ways that depend on their relationships with their hosts. Displaced women disapprove of the government-sponsored Arabization and Islamization program and describe its damaging effects on them and, especially, their children. My interviews took place in a politically charged time during the proclamation of Khartoum as the "Capital of Arab Culture" in 2005 (*El-Khartoum Asimat el-thaghaffa El-Arabia*). Non-Arab, non-Muslim women emphasized the ways in which Arabism and Islamism are deployed to rewrite law and society in the Sudan.

A Catholic priest mapped out the specific ways in which war and displacement have violated the rights of southerners.

> War has negative impacts on our economic, social, and cultural rights. It contributed to the breakup of families and communities and led to coerced migration. Currently, people are resorting to beer brewing to support themselves and their families. Our culture has also suffered. Women get married in the style of customary marriage without their families' knowledge or approval.[17] Also important is the conversion of large numbers of Christian politicians and priests to Islam.[18] The problem is that people here are not aware of their human rights. They are not given equal rights to citizenship and face tremendous conditions of violence and social pressure. There is no freedom of expression, no religious rights. The most egregious forms of the violation of our congregation's human rights are the extreme poverty, unemployment, lack of health care, and the pressure that is imposed on them to abandon their education and join the military instead.

When asked how southerners are responding to the currents of Arabism and Islamism in Northern Sudanese society, the priest expressed considerable pessimism.

> People are working hard to resist Islamization. Some of them refuse to yield to the pressures imposed by the government and hold on to their Christian faith. Here in the churches we guide, preach, and encourage the observation of Christian beliefs. We have to fight the intruding cultures and hold on to our African and indigenous cultures. We also have to encourage the use of local languages. However, we still face significant influences in our daily lives. Some Christians converted to Islam. There are systematic violations of the rights of Christian people. Introducing Islamic cultures in school curricula is significant. The introduction and enforcement of Islamic cultures are pursued through various media. There are great restrictions on women's work in politics, and women's incarceration along with children is unmerciful. Here men are occasionally whipped and humiliated. Some are forced to enlist in the military to join the jihad, which is contrary to our religious beliefs. There is no freedom of expression. Instead, there is colonization and slavery.

This priest sees conversion as the result of coercion. His critique makes a historical conjunction between the Arabization and Islamization program and slavery and colonization by Europeans.[19] Like many Christians, Western as well as African, he also associates Islam with the oppression of women. While he condemns Muslim practices as demeaning to women, he does not reflect on women's gendered subordination in indigenous southern spiritual beliefs and rituals or in Christian theology and church hierarchy.

El-Mashru El-Hadari, "the Civilizational Project," indexes Islamist power. Even for secular Muslims in the Sudan, it marks a striking transition from tolerance to jihad. The program promulgates the view that Islamic civilization is superior to other cultures and seeks to reclaim what it posits as the "authentic" culture of the Sudan from the "corruptions" brought by colonization, westernization, and dependency on international capital. Although Islamist Hassan Turabi (1997) says this tendency represents a modernizing project within Islam, it imposes serious stresses on secular Muslims as well as on non-Muslims. Justifying the military conspiracy to overthrow the elected government, it seeks to attain unchallenged political authority and to enforce sharia. The "Civilizational Project" imposes the Arabic language and Islamic religion as a uniform national identity while suppressing the multiplicity of ethnolinguistic identities and religious affiliations in this complex society.

The "Civilizational Project" has had immeasurable consequences for the cultural traditions and worldviews of southerners in Khartoum. Joshua Diu, the principal of a remedial secondary school in Jabbrra, Khartoum, in August 2002 spoke eloquently on the contestation of identities as displaced people ponder the question, "Who are we becoming?"

> Young Christian and non-Muslim Sudanese are facing a cultural identity crisis as they lose their tribal settings at home and find themselves lost in a sea of Arabization and Islamization where they have to learn the Arabic language. We have to remember that Arabic is full of cultural influences. If the majority pick up Arabic, they will abandon their cultural background. Displaced people lost the support of their local environments. They find it difficult, especially in school settings, to integrate with southerners from other ethnic backgrounds. They don't fit neatly in Arab communities either. They get confused because they lost their identity. There are no opportunities for our young people to get an education. They lost their direction and don't know where to go any more. They carry the name of Sudanese. But what does it mean to

be Sudanese, especially after losing your values, your family, and your community? Today we have to think very seriously about the future. We need to restructure the South in ways that are conducive to rebuilding education and families and creating hospitable working conditions. At the moment, however, people have to contend with loss. They lack basic needs, and they also lack the ability to be creative or even to be |themselves.

Right now there are a large number of children who live on the streets of Khartoum. They turn to gangs and crime in order to sustain themselves. But that is to be expected, because they are not leading ordinary and stable lives in Khartoum. We have to remember that they are here against their wishes. Coming to the North is the only escape from the violence of war. Large numbers of our young people are dispersed in Egypt, Uganda, and Ethiopia, and all over the world. They are not playing a significant role as members of our society. In my school, children are bewildered about how they will survive in this tough place. Lack of stability, difficulty of integration, and second-class citizenship push these young people to hate their northern counterparts because they view them as oppressors. Islamization and Arabization add to the confusion about who we are. *El-Mashru El-Hadari* fails to recognize that when southerners convert, they do so as individuals, not as communities. There are a lot of cultural changes that we don't see as a positive step. Conversion, intermarriage, and the prevalence of Islamic education all combine to add to our struggles to preserve our sense of identity.

In Diu's eyes, all the steps displaced persons take to assimilate to their host society result from disorientation and domination. That some customs might be chosen as modes of adaptation to the host society is inconceivable to him.

The Law of Public Order, considered one of the most important features of the Arabization and Islamization campaign, is embodied in what came to be known as *El-Nizam El-Aam* for Khartoum State in 1996. This law, which was passed by the government to curb practices labeled "un-Islamic," is emblematic of the politicization of ethnoreligious identities and offers an authoritative commentary on the status of minority cultures under sharia.[20] Those who do not comply with its codes are brought to court. This law covers a wide range of issues. It limits the length and duration of wedding parties. It enforces the *hijab,* a form of Islamic dress with a headscarf and long-sleeved blouse. The law prohibits people from bathing nude or seminude in the Nile, a practice accepted under previous governments. It mandates gender segregation on public transportation, but that provision has been unenforceable. Both consuming and brewing alcohol have been prohibited for the first time. Many displaced women, who come from southern communities where alcohol was an accepted part of social life, rely on brewing and selling alcoholic drinks to make a living. Alcohol also has many uses in non-Muslim ceremonial practices celebrating birth, marriage, and death.

To guarantee the enforcement of this law, the government expanded the Criminal Procedures Act of 1991 and vested the Supreme Court, Courts of Appeals, General Criminal Courts, and People's Criminal Courts with full authority to imprison, fine, whip, confiscate property from, and enforce any punishment they see fit on those who violate the law. An ethnographic analysis of *El-Mashru El-Hadari* is ultimately an account of domination. I investigated the ways in which IDPs have adjusted to change with full cognizance of the structural constraints that mold the process of cultural production. The material bases of culture cannot be understood in isolation from the ways in which social life is organized. Inequality and hierarchy as structural impediments converge to force new ways of understanding the world.

Proverbs illustrate the attitudes that marginalize non-Arabs in Khartoum. *Adanu hammraa lai Adam,* "his ear is red to Adam," emphasizes an imagined "racial purity" that distances a person from his or her African roots. *Sajam el hilla El-dalila Abid,* "the village whose guide is a slave is doomed," denigrates southerners as militarily impotent and culturally backward. *Assa kalib lil nabih, wa assa farkha lil gabigh,* "get a dog to bark and get a female slave to do your dirty work," indelibly associates subordination with womanhood and Africanity. The denigration and peripheralization of non-Arab peoples and non-Muslim cultures is constructed within the context of specific power differentials within Sudanese society at large.

These declarations and laws are seen by southerners and by international observers as acts of infringement on the rights of minorities. According to a report put out by the Sudan Council of Churches Unit of Advocacy and Communication, "The Public Order Police are not bound by any geographical jurisdiction. Any of the units may make a campaign of searches (*kashaa*) in any place even if it falls within the jurisdiction of another unit. This makes it very difficult to know the jurisdiction to which the arrested persons are taken." The targets of the Public Order Police are primarily displaced persons, especially women held by the authorities

in Omdurman Women's Prison on charges ranging from prostitution to
alcohol brewing (1996).

The imposition of the *hijab* regardless of religious affiliation, as Susan
Sered contends, reflects the thinking of an "authoritarian institution with
a large stake in women's bodies" (2000, 17). E.K., a forty-five-year-old
Kuku Christian from Bahr El-Jebel, told me: "I came to Khartoum in
1995. Ever since then, I was not able to wear my traditional dress, and I
felt forced by law to cover my whole body. I am also afraid to brew. I face a
lot of difficulty as a displaced person, and I am not happy here. Continued
residence in Khartoum for me means greater despair. My children will be
lost to the culture of the Arab. There will be no housing to live in. Education for my children will be difficult, and I believe they will become slaves
of the northerners. My life itself is the most pressing condition. I think
peace is the only possible solution to my battle against Arab oppression."

Other women echo these sentiments. In delineating the detrimental
influence of displacement on cultural rights, I do not essentialize culture
or treat it as if it is frozen in time or carved in stone. In spite of contemporary academic critiques of the concept of culture, nonetheless "it proceeds." Clifford Geertz wrote: "No matter how much one trains one's
attention on the supposedly hard facts of social existence, who owns the
means of production, who has the guns, the dossiers, or the newspapers,
the supposedly soft facts of that existence, what do people imagine human
life to be all about, how do they think one ought to live, what grounds
belief, legitimizes punishment, sustains hope, or accounts for loss, crowd
in to disturb simple pictures of might, desire, calculation, and interest"
(1995, 43). Criticism of the ways in which Arabism and Islamism have
been mobilized by the Sudanese authorities was articulated in a plethora
of responses to my queries on the cultural rights of IDPs.

This opposition to official policy is encapsulated in a statement by
G.H.M., a thirty-year-old Dinka who has lived in Khartoum since 1983.

The biggest problem in the Sudan lies in the educational system and in
the various school curricula. This system is truly bad when compared
to other countries such as Egypt, Uganda, Kenya, and Ethiopia. These
countries promote a better understanding of their societies through education. Our system is entirely built on Arab culture and Islamic teach-
ings. Of course, it is widely held that this emphasis reflects the genuine
Arab identity of the country. Only eighteen days after the attainment
of independence, the Sudan decided to join the Arab League, whereas

Tunisia opted to wait for two years after their independence to join. The Sudanese social structure did not absorb basic facts about cultural and ethnic diversity. The effects of this stance were disastrous. The situation was aggravated since the Salvation Government took power. Once again, we see a greater leaning toward teaching the history of the Arab than that of the people of Merowe, Darfur, or the South. Here I don't mean to come across as hostile to the Arabs, but some balancing is necessary. We are by no means antagonistic to the Arabic language. Our children who were born here know it as the only medium of communication.

Another important component of the problem is the media. The media, especially the radio and TV, are government controlled and have no autonomy whatsoever. The media are used to further the state's agenda, including its attempts at spreading Arabization and Islamization. None of the programs move beyond Arab culture and the Islamic religion. Much effort has been expended to empower and promulgate these ideals. Islam is not linked to Arabism in other countries such as Kenya. A great majority of Muslims don't speak Arabic. I think Arab culture became dominant because it received coverage and support. If other Sudanese cultures were given the chance to be heard, they too would come to dominate. Print media are also to blame. There are no systematic writings about the peoples and cultures of the South. I think both the state and individual authors are responsible for this state of affairs.

If we consider how Arabization and Islamization have affected ritual practices, we encounter drastic changes. People used to dance in the nude. This practice did not stir sexual desire, as it was an accepted form of celebration. All these rituals—which were performed in a variety of ways, even in the South—were forced to undergo radical change because of urbanization and interethnic interaction. Ultimately, this will lead to the transformation of southern identities.

When we consider the question of Islamization, we find that responses vary. Among southern Sudanese people who converted to Islam, you find two kinds. The first group embraced Islam out of conviction. In the same family, you find religious diversity. My uncle is a Muslim. My Christian mother prepares his Ramadan break fast all the time. Another group is more dangerous. This group tried to take advantage since Nimeiri was in power. They are opportunists, and they continued to be encouraged by the Salvation Government, which gave more aid to Muslim converts than nonconverts. Finally, if we look at the civil service, we find a strong influence of Islamization, where the government expects people to break for prayer. Christians don't have the same break. Muslims take three days off to celebrate Eid, whereas Christians have only one day off.

Of course, we cannot really differentiate between "sincere" and opportunistic converts to Islam; under pressure of the so-called Civilizational Project, conversion is to some degree coerced or resisted. (In numerous conversations, displaced women made it clear that their cultural rights have been among the most serious causalities of war.) The loss of cultural integrity and community compounds the other losses IDPs have experienced and makes it more difficult for them to recover and cope with the circumstances in which they find themselves.

These questions of culture prompted me to ask displaced southern women about their interactions with northerners in the host community. The overwhelming majority of women I interviewed acknowledged that they interact with northerners in some way or another; only a small segment claimed they did not. Women's responses to questions regarding cultural continuity and change varied widely. While some indicated that they were unable to maintain their cultural practices, they still refused to embrace northern customs. Most vowed to retain their distinctive cultural identities but made some exceptions for local ways that were not directly associated with Islam or Arabic culture. The majority of women kept some elements of their cultural practices while forgoing others.

These experiences bring into focus the weight of cultural rights as collective rights and "the cultural health of minority groups" (Kukathas 1992a; see also Kukathas 1992b, 1998). Highlighting individual rights and personal freedoms should not be used to advocate a liberal tradition that has no roots in Sudanese society. Those who defend the liberal traditions of rights argue along these lines: "While we are right to be concerned about the cultural health of minority communities, this gives us insufficient reason to abandon, modify, or reinterpret liberalism. Far from being indifferent to claims of minorities, liberalism puts concern for minorities at the forefront" (Kukathus 1992a, 107). Sudanese who are outside of the Western liberal tradition espouse local and indigenous notions of rights that include culture as well as bodily integrity. In this ethnography, documenting the pervasive violation of the cultural rights of indigenous Sudanese problematizes and interrogates the institutionalized state power over minorities, especially such defenseless groups as displaced women.

Women's responses to questions about their cultural practices illuminate the centrality of time in effecting adjustment and accommodation. Length of residence plays a critical role in creating an environment within which cultural adaptation occurs. This process raises a fundamental question: What structural transformations accompany IDPs' adaptations in a predominantly Muslim and Arabic-speaking host community?

According to twenty-three-year-old V.R., a Dinka woman residing in Soba Aradi, structural changes come with resettlement in the North. She offered a perceptive analysis of the situation.

> When you ask about cultural rights, we have to remember that most of our traditions and rituals depended on our location in the South. Everything there was conducive to celebrating life and carrying on rituals that were tied to nature and to landscape. Our rituals were determined by the environment around us. We were forced to leave for a new environment that does not offer the same avenue for preserving traditions. Here women started to wear the *tobe*[21] and decorate their bodies with henna like northern women.[22] OK. These are beautiful things. Men, however, don't agree that southern women should do them. Women are more open in this way than men, who resist change. Marriage traditions also changed. My aunt decided to marry an Arab man. Everything goes. I can say that even religious conversion is not seen as a big deal these days. Converts are not automatically rejected, and their number is not high anyway. As for language, there are practical reasons. It is not really about any particular person prohibiting us from learning. I know that my local language is offered in a center in Klakala. But it is so far away from where I live. How can I learn it, then?

Displaced women agreed that they tend to be more flexible than men, who are likely to object to the changes that their wives and daughters adopt while living in Khartoum.

People conduct their lives as bearers of cultures that not only epitomize "aesthetic choices" but also mold their views on how to live and act in the world. The vibrancy and richness of the peoples and cultures of Southern Sudan have inspired anthropological knowledge. War and displacement are acts of violence that disrupt cultural continuity and destroy the collective reproduction of cultural life. Cultures are always on the move. What is at stake here is not only the ability of individuals to orient themselves in time and space but also the power of culture to transform daily life from an endless struggle to a communal celebration.

Economic Predicaments

Throughout my conversations with displaced women, I was impressed by their resourcefulness in eking out a subsistence for themselves and their children. Women who had been separated from their adult kin constructed networks of reciprocity and cooperation across ethnolinguistic lines. In Dar El Salaam, I was told by a group of women from Southern Sudan and Darfur that they managed to start a rotating credit association, or *sanduq*—a savings plan that is also popular among immigrants and refugees in the United States (Abusharaf 2002)—to pool incomes in order to improve their economic situation and, most important, to assist one another during hard times. "When a neighbor or someone else in her family gets sick, we also try to collect foodstuffs to bring to her. We collect oil, sugar, flour, and tea. It is true that we cannot afford large amounts of these things, but when you have a lot of people contributing, it makes a big difference." In Wad El-Bashir camp near Omudurman, a midwife from Upper Nile told me that through her work in a local cooperative, she had made a lot of Muslim friends. "Religion is something between you and God," she explained. Through these creative mechanisms, major gaps are bridged as interpersonal relations become increasingly defined by affection and mutual aid.

One of the grimmest daily tests facing displaced women is finding employment. According to a United Nations report, the major sources of income for IDPs are casual and seasonal agricultural labor and petty trade. Women supply the main income and carry out 70 percent of the work in their households (UN 2000, 54). Many displaced women in Khartoum will perform any tasks available to them, including domestic work for households of longer-term city residents. Urban poverty is the first problem that IDPs must contend with upon arrival in Khartoum, and it is still their most formidable challenge even after a decade or more of residence in the capital. Many years ago, Richard Sandbrook argued that "given the high rate of urban growth and the low growth of formal employment, the proportion of the economically active population in the informal sector is bound to expand" (1982, 59). These economic problems should be positioned within a systematic analysis of cities, urban poverty, and uneven development (Gilbert and Gugler 1984).

The majority of displaced women I interviewed pursue income-producing activities that fall under the umbrella of the "informal economy." Since few of these women had worked outside the home and/ or the rural economy, the nature of the jobs they secured in the capital city reflects this occupational background. M.A., a thirty-four-year-old from Yei, described her life before she was displaced in 1992 as "very good."

> Everything that my family needed could be gotten from the cultivation of the land that we owned. My relatives were all present, and my parents helped with food, which made things easy and simple. My life now is difficult, because I can't find work. My husband quit his job in the South and was supplied food by the Sudan Council of Churches. However, the Sudan Council of Churches stopped providing relief, and now I have to resort to brewing alcohol, which is another challenge. While moving, I sustained the loss of my household properties and my brother, and I was separated from my parents, sisters, and other relatives.

M.A. still does not know what happened to her missing brother. She finds it difficult to make a living in the city without productive resources and kinship networks.

C.D., who is thirty-three and a Kuku Christian, moved to Khartoum in 2000. Prior to her departure, she was a typist; she is now unemployed. "I moved to Khartoum because of the war, but my family is still back in Juba. Life in Khartoum is more difficult than my life before it: it is difficult to obtain work, transportation, and education for my children. I don't want to stay in Khartoum. The most pressing conditions I face are hunger and the lack of food, and the conditions in relation to my children. Returning to Juba is the only solution to my problems."

Economic rights are generally linked to established patterns of inequality. Gilbert and Gugler argue: "The patterns and processes of urban development are those of an unequal world. There is no way in which the process of urban development can be understood in isolation from the processes that generate that inequality" (1984, 8). Since displacement and forced migrations push most people into urban areas, the problems facing IDPs can be squarely positioned within broader frames of policy making in regard to development. Entering cities when employment in the formal sector is shrinking, rural migrants have few of the skills and connections required to obtain jobs and must utilize their previous knowledge and experiences to find work and generate income. Southern women brew alcoholic drinks because they have the necessary skills and find a ready market, even though it is illegal. S.M., a non-Muslim woman who arrived in Khartoum in 1996, lamented: "I am no longer able to make alcoholic drinks because of sharia. I am troubled by being viewed as an infidel under sharia."

Women with no other means of earning money resort to prostitution.
Yahya El-Hassan, a Pan African News Agency correspondent in Khartoum, described the result:

> Once in the North, [women] are forced to live in cramped camps around the big cities that lack all conditions of decent living. This situation forces women to compete for the very limited opportunities available, such as washers and maids. The rest opt for the brewing of local gin (*araqi*), or prostitution, two lucrative but dangerous businesses if the women are caught by the police. If convicted, the women are moved to an all-female prison. Recent UN research has found that over 80 percent of the inmates of Omdurman Women Prison in Khartoum are women from the South convicted of trafficking in *araqi* or prostitution (2000, 1).

Prostitution is seldom discussed openly, although its prevalence is generally understood. There is a continuum between prostitution and irregular relationships that desperate women may form in which they exchange sex for food and shelter. Displaced women who were raped by soldiers are especially vulnerable to sexual exploitation in Khartoum. Community health activists are aware of the need to inform women about how to protect themselves against HIV. The prevention of prostitution, however, requires the generation of employment opportunities.

Women voiced their anxieties about work under situations of increasingly intense economic pressure in a group interview I conducted in Dar El Salaam with displaced women from Darfur. Women contending with poverty become continually entangled with the authorities over what they can and cannot do. Some of these women moved with their husbands, who try to scrape a living by setting up stalls to sell fresh produce. They are constantly chased and harassed about permits they cannot afford (see also Loveless 1999).

Southern women tend to do domestic work rather than trading in the market. Some are paid weekly, but others work by the day. The economic position of their employers varies widely. Labor is so cheap that even women working in ordinary jobs can afford to hire a woman to do the laundry and heavy cleaning once a week. Although IDPs are confined to shantytowns, they form a pool of low-wage labor to families in the city.

Social Ties with Host Communities

Economic quandaries, the desire to surmount social isolation, and length of residence shape the social ties women fashion with others living in shantytowns and slums. Within the squatter settlements and camps, the hosts are IDPs who arrived earlier. While many came from other war-torn parts of the South, some are migrants from the West who moved to Khartoum decades earlier to escape environmental catastrophe. Beyond the shantytowns, in ethnically mixed slum neighborhoods, the host society is the North, Arabic-speaking and predominantly Muslim. IDPs have something in common by virtue of being displaced, even if they are very different culturally. And poor women have something in common, even if some are displaced and others marginalized.

Those hosts who are displaced persons themselves often assume the role of mediators between IDPs and the society at large. Women have developed robust ties and myriad associations in their present localities. During their years in Khartoum, southern women have connected with northerners as neighbors, employers, and even prospective spouses. In a group discussion, one IDP observed: "I have friendly ties with my Muslim neighbors. We help each other on many occasions. I have learned about henna painting and the northern Sudanese marriage traditions. I decided also to wear a *tobe*. If it were not for my money problems, everything would have been fine in Khartoum." Displacement has exposed IDPs to existential conditions similar to those of their northern counterparts, who are struggling every day against equally terrible odds to scrounge a subsistence.

In Khartoum's shantytowns, southerners and Darfurians have been exchanging the roles of guests and hosts. In the early 1980s, Darfurians were the receiving community to the large influx of southerners fleeing their homes after the declaration of sharia in September 1983 and the resumption of the war. Now, southerners are hosting great numbers of Darfurians escaping the carnage in their region. The newly displaced women from Darfur are met with mixed emotions ranging from total empathy and identification to marked resentment and lack of rapport. These responses are, above all, political. A social worker in Mandela recounted: "Some southern women in Mandela had a terrible fight with some Darfurians who appeared at a distribution center to receive relief items. The southerners asked these women: 'Didn't your people attack us in the South and kill our people because they were sure that they were participating in jihad? Why are you complaining now?' " Historical memory shapes this response: Muslim men from Darfur had served in the GoS armies that committed aggression against the South, and these southerners held the region's past collaboration with the GoS against those who had been displaced after they rebelled against the government and were victimized by its army and proxy militias. The acceleration of these disputes is, however, linked to the enduring dearth of relief supplies that tends to frame all Sudanese political disputes as quarrels over identity and resources (Mohamed 2000).

These frictions notwithstanding, the common denominator of these displaced communities is never lost. Forced migration has imperiled their livelihood and way of life. Displacement has entailed numerous encounters with the complexities of Sudanese politics, lack of educational opportunities, absence of health care, job scarcity, and cultural distancing. A Sudanese geographer, Mohamed El Hadi Abu Sin, suggests that "shared misery" prompts compassion and sociability (1995, 18). Communities that encompass the longer established and newly arrived, bridging the northern and western hosts and the southern and western guests, emerge over time in the shantytowns. Adaptability and flexibility enable displaced women to construct new social worlds. Women locate themselves within multiple contexts and situations. Initially, they have to establish themselves within communities that are religiously, ethnically, and linguistically different from their own. The language barriers are the first to be overcome, and today the overwhelming majority of southerners in the North are fluent in Arabic. Once they realize that they must settle in Khartoum for the foreseeable future, they take steps toward the consolidation of cooperative ties. Some women find others from their own ethnocultural and/ or religious group and construct new bonds with them, consolidating an identity as migrants of a specific sort after being lost among strangers. Other women construct social ties across ethnocultural and religious lines based on their common experience of migration or their geographic location within the shantytowns, or through their common occupations. Those with kin in Khartoum are more likely to be drawn into relationships with strangers by their relatives than to live within their extended family circle. Women find the city a fertile field for sociability.

Intermarriages are crucial vehicles for creating cultural exchange. In addition to establishing neighborly ties, women who arrive as widows may find opportunities for remarriage in surrounding northern Muslim communities. The majority of displaced women I interviewed knew of southern women who had married northerners and in the process adopted new practices. Intermarriage was most prevalent between younger women who had grown to maturity in Khartoum and local Arab, Muslim men. These realities call into question Francis Deng's argument that "the identity of Southern Sudan has been shaped primarily by the prolonged resistance to the imposition of Arab and Islamic culture from the

North" (1995). Resistance may have been predominant before large waves of forced migrants were set into motion, but now adaptation looms as large, as Deng himself lamented. Women's varied responses to forced migration undermine any monolithic or static concept of identity and show its ongoing redefinition and permanent restructuring. Self-definition and group identification are contingent processes that simultaneously inscribe and subvert the shifting boundaries of "Arab" and "African" identities in a country that prides itself on being a bridge between the Arab Middle East and the African world south of the Sahara. The pervasiveness of economic hardships has sent the vast majority of Sudanese begging regardless of whether they bear their tribal markings on their foreheads or on their cheeks.[23]

Living together in shantytowns has prompted IDPs to redefine their own identities and induced them and their hosts to rethink relations among different ethnocultural groups. These developments are regarded with some ambivalence by all those involved, for these changes are not entirely voluntary and new intergroup interactions are not always empathic or amicable. The repositioning of displaced persons in the North brought together Arab Muslim populations with non-Arab, non-Muslim peoples. It also brought into close association a wide variety of non-Arab, non-Muslims. Before the recent triumph of Islamism, Sudanese society was inclined toward secularism; religious affiliation did not assume any salience in daily interactions between Muslims and non-Muslims. Political decisions made these religious identities important. The process of cultural change among displaced people in general, and women in particular, must be understood in the context of war, violence, and forced migration. The adaptation of non-Arab, non-Muslim southerners to the dominant culture around them is rarely seen in positive terms. Indeed, some southerners regard it as another means of domination of the South by the North, a continuation of the war by other means.

Southern community leaders see the transformation of displaced persons as emblematic of larger losses. Many chiefs, teachers, and priests view this amalgamation as evidence of identities lost and homes ruined. In the context of war, violence, and forced migration, assimilation into the Arabic and Islamic practices of host communities in the North means annihilation of an "unambiguously" African world, even though the South was far from monolithic. M.M., who arrived in Khartoum in 1996, stated: "I am concerned that continued residence in Khartoum will lead my people to abandon or lose contact with their culture. Although we try to teach our children our culture, we often find it impossible to compete with Arab and Islamic culture taught to them in school. I feel that my problems are the problems of all displaced people; we are drinking from the same pot. The only acceptable solution to these complicated issues is peace." M.M.'s attitude toward the problem is complex. On the one hand, she worries about the loss of her particular culture under the hegemonic pressure of Arabic, Islamic forces. On the other hand, she feels that all displaced people, regardless of cultural origins, are in the same situation. Displaced women could, then, become a speaking force in support of the right to cultural integrity.

In *The Human Condition,* Hannah Arendt remarks that "all human activities are conditioned by the fact that men live together," but violence is the "only action that cannot even be imagined outside the society of men" (1958, 22). Displaced women's experiences and perspectives illustrate the power of the social, which underlies their work activities and their ideas about politics and culture. IDPs adopt patterns of conduct they encounter in host communities to varying degrees, ranging from minuscule changes to taking up core cultural customs. The process of change is gradual and selective; women move back and forth between cultures in a way that is not unidirectional. The adaptations displaced women make do not imply jettisoning their own idioms and convictions; rather, the process epitomizes a desire to craft new ways of being to fit new sets of interests and concerns.

These interactions, which are a critical force behind identity formation, must be situated within particular histories. IDPs' narratives illuminate the ways in which war, as an act of violence, has limited women's access to indigenous cultural activities by subverting the foundations of community life and affective networks at home. Displaced women's accounts reveal substantial variations in their responses to life in Khartoum. While some have exhibited tremendous adaptability, others have continued to cling to their identities, and still others resorted to accommodation and resistance at the same time. Southern Sudanese women's ideas about self, gender, and community are constantly being renegotiated. Contact with Arab Muslim populations and a mix of varied ethnic, religious, and linguistic communities have had an impact, but most important are the new communities, networks of associations, exchanges, and mutual attachments that displaced women have constructed in making Khartoum's shantytowns home.

Rising

Starting a new life in urban Sudan demands a whole series of adjustments and renegotiations that require tremendous emotional resourcefulness. Nowhere are the psychological scars of displacement more deeply etched than in the experience of suffering voiced by N.L.M. Sixty years old, she has been separated from her husband since she fled Kopoeta, Equatoria, in 1989 with her son. She works as a housekeeper but relies on her grown children for support. She describes her life before the war as much better, although she is relieved to be in Khartoum, away from the sound of guns. She lives far from other friends or relatives but has been able to maintain her culture through food and occasional dances. She has given up alcoholic drinks because of her new commitment to Christianity. She counts her separation from her husband as an improvement rather than a loss; as she put it, she is now "at peace with" her husband. She misses her children, who are working in the army, and makes do with the photos she has of them. When asked for an acceptable solution to the problems facing herself and others, she reflected that although peace would bring some joy, death might be the only solution to suffering.

To make sense of this sorrowful existence and of the new world that has sprung up around them, IDPs reflect on their lives, past and present. As they take up residence in the North, they analyze their own subjective experiences to fashion new frameworks to guide their interpretations of who they are and who they are becoming. Drawing on prewar realties is combined with a thirst for creating new futures. Within this context, we wonder: Are IDPs coerced into bending their ideas to fit into the new situation, or are they coalescing new and old life experiences to forge ahead in an environment brimming with trials and tribulations? This question cannot be isolated from the dominant state of affairs in which they find themselves.

Some women find hope despite the nightmarish experiences they have endured. Many women see shifting gender politics as a positive outcome of an otherwise dismal situation. Adopting new modes of cooperation and creating new forms of kinship with others in the community exemplify women's continuing efforts to find a footing. The fictive kinship networks they construct resemble those created by Africans who were kidnapped and enslaved in the past, demonstrating the resilience that makes culture such a valuable resource in new situations. Women's accounts demonstrate their flexibility and wits. In the midst of chaos, women are shedding skin, acquiring a say in their individual and collective lives, and improvising their own schemes for coalition building, empowerment, and self-sufficiency. Prevailing over deeply ingrained gender discriminatory practices embodies a specific type of moral victory over particular categories of dominance and transgression, for, as Pierre Bourdieu compellingly argues, gender discrimination is a paradigmatic form of symbolic violence (2004, 272). This aspect of the lives of displaced women shines brightly amid the mind-boggling problems that they face. With respect to shifting gender roles in conflict situations, it is important to probe the ways in which displaced women understand their position within the state, the family, and the society at large. Unquestionably, there are radical digressions from prewar norms and beliefs. Now, more than ever before, women come into view as providers in a new economy in which they are compelled to perform to the best of their abilities, regardless of their identities as female bodies. This sweeping shift from traditional gender expectations has led southern Sudanese women in Khartoum to profess that displacement has entailed gains as well as losses in the politics of everyday life. This trend is particularly important because previous gender relations were overloaded with systematic discrimination and domestic violence (see Wuol 2002).

The conditions that created antagonism in the South have not been replicated in the shantytowns and camps in Khartoum. Despite the competition for scarce resources, displaced women cooperate across ethnocultural and religious lines. Shantytowns are very peaceful places. The scenes of violent conflict at Soba Aradi and on Black Monday were exceptional and did not lead to the mobilization of political violence elsewhere in the vicinity of Khartoum. The communities that displaced women have created in the shantytowns resemble the New Sudan in microcosm, exemplifying the ideals of tolerance, pluralism, and peace for which the SPLM and the National Democratic Alliance stand in national politics.

THREE

Gendered Rituals

This chapter explores a specific example of how displaced women from the South who settle in predominantly Muslim, Arabized Khartoum thrive by crafting new meanings of self and community, time and place. As they negotiate peaceful accommodations with their new neighbors and selectively adopt or reject rituals they had not observed in their former homes, they perform their identity in specific social and political terms. Their experiences and perspectives are not homogeneous, but the changes that some make in the most intimate dimensions of the self are powerful illustrations of the negotiated, versatile, and situational nature of identity in the context of displacement and resettlement. Sudanese squatter settlements such as Izzbba are metamorphosing into spaces for resource mobilization and the reconfiguration of social relations. Among these intricately interwoven patterns, the most significant are forced migrants' engagement with urbanism and their adoption of gendered ritual practices of bodily modification. I use urgent anthropology as a lens for explicating the impressive strategies displaced women forge amid complex emergencies. It reveals the particular ways in which displacement shifts their frames of reference, as well as the confluence of culture and politics that they have innovatively remapped and effectively narrated. With respect to embracing traditions practiced by their new neighbors, closer examination of gendered ritual practices in the context of urban life reveals new ideas arising as focal points for reconfiguring a woman's place in the world and her relationship to the Sudanese polity.

Arabization and Islamization loom large as official government policy. Nonetheless, these forced migrants clearly distinguish between the rhetoric of the government and the practices of the neighbors with whom they interact and share a bond based on common economic marginalization and political disfranchisement (Ali 2005). To contend that displaced women have succeeded to a great extent in cultivating social networks

and institutionalizing ties to other segments of the urban poor does not mean portraying social life in squatter settlements as entirely amicable. Indeed, the crowding and competition for scarce resources cause discord, making the everyday cooperation that facilitates life in the shantytown a remarkable achievement.

The gendered rituals described in this chapter are among a myriad of bodily practices—such as adornment with henna, *tobe,* and gold jewelry— that represent how increased individualization that flows from women's relative independence of kin, their wage-earning opportunities, and their crucial contributions to their households help to redefine their position relative to premigration forms of authority. Among the more comfortable southern migrants, these practices are useful indicators of their adjustment to urban life and culture. These practices demonstrate how communities of forced migrants make headway in implementing everyday and informal avenues of peace and reconciliation.

These ideas were set out with abundant clarity in IDPs' accounts of social life as they struggled to improvise an existence under difficult conditions by using their wits and imagination. The decisions they make regarding the gendered rituals they encounter should not be articulated in oversimplified terms of sociocultural causes and personal effects, but instead understood as the result of conscious, careful processes of evaluation. Vivian, a twenty-three-year-old Izzbba resident, explains: "There is nothing wrong with the *tobe.* Most southerners now wear it, and there is no pressure on them, but they find it to be comfortable. As for henna, it is also acceptable, and personally I like it, and now it is becoming part of our marriage ceremonies. Women are usually more accepting of these traditions than men." Some attribute this flexibility to practicality. W.B., a Shiluk woman from Malkal, explains: "Some people learn about other people's customs. We have very important customs we cannot continue in Khartoum. It is very hard to find experts to do the branding and facial scars we used to have in the past." The pragmatism with which women approach difficult situations has played an important part in the process of selective adjustment.

Nurturing social networks supports and advances the lives of displaced women. This process was exemplified in a literacy class run by Amal Friends that I observed in El-Baraka in August 2001, before the government's closure and demolition of this IDP camp. A Darfurian woman I interviewed found that mutual concerns were far more significant than cultural differences among these women, who hailed from various parts of the South and the Nuba Mountains. She explained: "We do our best to live peacefully and solve the problems that occasionally arise. We learn about each others' lives prior to coming to Khartoum as well as presently." Urban life necessitates both individual resourcefulness and reciprocity.

The dynamics through which women form opinions regarding the adoption or rejection of practices of bodily modification that are new to them reveal substantial variations in the significance of these rituals and the meanings women attach to them. Forced migrants, though trying to decrease the social distance between themselves and their neighbors, articulate rationales for their embrace of these practices that often differ from how the same practices are understood among groups where these rituals are traditional (Abusharaf 2003). The specific contexts for understanding these processes of adaptation warrant elucidation. The first of these contexts is that of urbanization. These involuntary migrants left rural communities that were being destroyed and entered an urban world that is still emerging. Greater Khartoum exhibits what anthropologist Peter Gutkind defines as "some basic organizational and institutional characteristics of urban complexity" (1974, 123). Gutkind offers wide-ranging explanations of personal and group ties, work and mobility, family life, and the ideational world of urban societies. These elements are especially relevant to Khartoum's IDPs, who arrive from rural areas with their own quite diverse rules of operation. The dynamic institutional and spatial processes delineated by Gutkind and others who study refugees and voluntary migrants suggest that forced migrants' strategies cannot be understood as simply the effects of their new environment. Instead, migrants create new social formations in which complex ties to and among other urban slum dwellers are put together to different ends.

Taken together, religious conversions, intermarriages, economic cooperation, and bodily modifications constitute important indicators for ideational transformation. Displaced women express mixed feelings about these practices. Some resist and refuse; some resist and accommodate; while others see that, rather than entrapping themselves in perpetual self-pity and victimization, they must actively confront the pressures that render them vulnerable and powerless. This idea was captured in one displaced woman's recitation of an Arabic proverb: "Those whose hands are in the fire are different from those whose hands are in the water." In other words, the reasons why IDPs choose to accept or reject specific practices can only be elucidated by locating them within relationships constructed for different purposes and goals. This context is particularly significant when war-displaced populations move to areas that fall under the jurisdiction of the state whose policies have brought them misery and deprivation and uprooted them in the first place. To take the edge off this bleak reality, adaptability and openness come to constitute the master plan for charting peaceful paths.

Bodily Rituals

In Sudan, feminine and masculine identities are created and re-created through a multiplicity of gender ideologies and ritual practices. One of the most unexpected signs of identity transformation among a few Southern Sudanese women displaced to Greater Khartoum is their adoption of female circumcision, which was almost never practiced in the South but was nearly universal in the North.[1] Such a striking shift in regard to the body points to the contingency of identity and women's openness to change. This embrace exemplifies a horizontal transmission of tradition, not from one generation to another within an ethnocultural group but from one group to another in newly shared circumstances. Southern women encounter the practice in a variety of situations, and their responses to it vary markedly. All are culturally bereaved, forcibly separated from their kin groups and communities and unable to celebrate coming of age, marriage, and childbirth as they did in the past. While many southern women firmly reject the practice as alien and harmful, some adopt it as a way of cementing new ties in the North. In embracing female circumcision, they depart from their own cultural traditions and reshape their personhood as well as their bodies.

O.E.O., a Christian Acholi who moved to Khartoum from Torit-Tusa, Equatoria, in 1993, voiced her disapproval of the practice: "I learned about female circumcision in Khartoum. I believe that it should be abolished because of the complications it can cause during childbirth, menstruation, and sexual intercourse. I believe that God made women a certain way for a reason. I know a few southern women who have adopted it to fit into the community or because of intermarriage. I strongly disagree with it." Of the 150 women surveyed and interviewed in Izzbba,[2] more than half indicated an awareness of the adoption of female circumcision by women who either converted to Islam or married Muslim men. Respondents who did not adopt the practice express strong opposition to it. Those who adopted the practice because of their yearning to belong view female circumcision as a practical ritual that engenders a new sense of social personhood in Izzbba's cultural mosaic. Although the practice is deeply entrenched in the North, where 91 percent of the population still adheres to it, southern groups practice other culturally specific rites of passage that modify the body, such as facial scarification, branding, and the removal of teeth (SDHS 1995).

In the colonial past, British authorities were apprehensive that southern women might accept this ritual, which colonial officials regarded as not only alien to the South but also inherently repulsive (Abusharaf 2006a). For example, in 1938 D. Newbold, governor of Kordofan, wrote to the civil secretary about efforts to inhibit the introduction of this practice in "pagan" areas through "Arab" influence:

> The Nogok Dinka community of Southwestern Kordofan numbers 22,000 souls. The assistant medical officer of Muglad Dispensary, who is himself an Omdurman bred Dinka, states that female circumcision is not practiced by Dinka living in the Bahr-el-Arab area under tribal conditions, nor when they are living as wholly Dinka households in the Arab area of Muglad, but it is practiced by Dinka women living under detribalized conditions, i.e. in mixed Arab-Dinka households. I am instructing Chief Kwal Arob to use his court powers to prevent the spread of female circumcision as being against Dinka custom.[3]

By keeping northern influences at bay, colonial policies curbed the diffusion of this ritual to southerners. In the past, as in the present, interethnic mixing has entailed an energetic exchange of ideas and practices.

The adoption of female circumcision by some displaced women raises many questions. Is the decision to adopt female circumcision structurally integrated in the shantytown, or is it an individually based strategy? Who decides whether or not a woman or a girl will be circumcised? To what extent are these women being coerced? How has the loss of social, economic, and ethnic-group security influenced them? Has the loss of cultural life because of war and displacement led to the substitution of new rituals for old? If Southern women experienced sexual violation during flight, have they accepted a northern Sudanese rationale for circumcision as a vehicle for restoring virginity and sexual wholeness? How do women view this practice now, and have their views changed over time? Is circumcision the only northern Sudanese cultural practice that IDPs adopt? How does these women's situation in Khartoum threaten their own cultural survival, and how do newly adopted rituals related to the body restore their sense of well-being?

To place these questions within a wider context, I consider the significance of this ritual among northern Sudanese women and ask whether circumcision is a vicious act of mutilation and injury, or a virtuous act of purity and rectitude. In order to untangle the ideology that lies beneath the persistence of this ritual and compare it with the thinking of those who have just adopted this practice, I collected personal narratives from a group of northern Sudanese women who regard the practice as traditional. Although anthropologists have made important contributions to the study of initiation rituals, including genital cutting, little is known about the significance of these practices among people who newly adopt them. When we consider the adoption of female circumcision by some southern Sudanese displaced women in Khartoum, an entirely different set of rationales comes to the fore. Assessment of displaced women's accounts in Izzbba yields exceptional insights into the question of how cultures are made.

Female Circumcision in Northern Sudan

The practice of female circumcision is not universal in Sudanese society. Here, as in other African communities, its origin cannot be ascertained with any certainty. In part, this obscurity can be attributed to the marked sociocultural and religious diversity of Sudanese society. Most ethnographic studies of Sudan have judiciously distinguished Sudanese peoples according to discrete cosmologies and social categories based on ethnic, religious, and regional distinctions. Sudanese ethnic structure is, however, extraordinarily complex, with peoples of distinct origins living in close proximity over many centuries and interacting in a myriad of ways.

Among the groups that practice genital surgeries, both boys and girls undergo circumcision rites. While most observers ascribe the persistence of this practice to the negative attitudes held by women and men toward uncircumcised women, Sudanese linguist Abdallah Eltayeb points to similar reactions toward uncircumcised men: "Male circumcision was believed by the pre-Islamic Arabs to have something to do with the moon. They believed that the moon would partly circumcise an uncircumcised [boy by] causing the foreskin to contract, hence the abusive remark 'he is uncircumcised but for the portion taken by the moon'" (1955, 149). For females, the practice comprises a variety of ritualized surgeries, including clitoridectomy, excision, and infibulation, all of which have been performed for thousands of years. These operations are performed on girls ranging in age from a few days old to puberty. Trained or untrained midwives, traditional healers, barbers, and occasionally doctors perform these surgeries. Although the ritual is surrounded with joyous celebration and elaborate festivities for males, for females, with some exceptions, it is concealed and shrouded in secrecy. The reasons for female circumcision and the age at which it is performed differ across Sudan by region, ethnicity, and class. There is also variation in its prevalence, in the exact type of surgery practiced, and in the rituals associated with it (Abusharaf 2001, 2002–2003). As the narratives I gathered in the northern community of Douroshab[4] demonstrate, even women of similar regions and backgrounds understand the practice and its effects in quite different ways.

Despite the prevalence of the ritual, historically there has also been strong opposition that can be traced to the precolonial era, when indigenous efforts were made to extirpate the practice. The first resolute anticircumcision movement in precolonial Sudan was galvanized in the name of Islam. Before the annexation of the Sudan by Mohamed Ali and the Turco-Egyptian Empire in 1821, El Sheikh Hassan wad Hassona, then a powerful cleric, initiated a campaign to exonerate Islam and redefine its position, especially in the eyes of people who attributed circumcision to Islamic ideology. To this day, older women avow the miracles of this cleric, who convinced many that people can be circumcised without genital cutting, when they utter the following words:

> *Ya Barakat elsheikh Hassan* [The infinite blessings of Sheikh Hassan]
> *Wad Hassona,* [the son of Hassona]
> *Tabab el majnnona,* [the curer of the deranged]
> *El sabbah el bit mahssona.* [Whose female client woke up one morning beautified by Sunna circumcision even without cutting.]

Other equally influential religious clerics, such as Sheik Hamad wad Umm Marioam and Farah wad Takttook, voiced their vehement opposition to female circumcision. These holy men influenced local discourses on culture, tradition, religion, and sexuality as early as 1861.

Ironically, colonial intervention against the practice helped to engender opposing forces supporting it. In 1945, after nearly a half-century of British colonial rule, the government imposed a law prohibiting infibulation, the most extreme type of genital operation (Abusharaf 2006a). Subsequently, a midwife in the town of Ruffaa, on the eastern bank of the Nile, was sentenced to six months in prison for circumcising a girl. Ustaz Mahmoud Mohamed Taha, the leader of the Republican Brothers political group, led a protest against the British action that soon developed into a popular uprising (El-Bashir 1994). Taha's protests had little to do with male supremacy or, indeed, with gender or sexuality; instead, they

followed from his view of British intervention in the cultural life of Sudanese people as a vile, disparaging attack on their sovereignty and identity.
His action was situated within the nationalist, anticolonial struggles being fought at the time.

Despite Sudanese resistance to colonial intervention, the British stead-
fastly pursued their anticircumcision campaign. The British sought the
support of prestigious political and religious figures with sizable follow-
ings to support the law in 1946. Imam Abdel Rahman Almahdi of the
Ansar sect and Ali El Merghani of the Khatmiya, who wielded considerable power in Sudanese society because of their social positions, wealth,
and piety, were asked to approach their followers and others who invoked
religious arguments in support of circumcision. The imams contested the
authenticity of the most famous sayings of Prophet Mohamed that appeared to condone, if not recommend, female circumcision.

In the end, the British laws were ineffective. As political theorist Mona
Abul Fadl pointed out, colonial rule had brought to Sudanese society
the notion that things could be different, that nothing was given, and
that whatever existed was subject to challenge and transformation (1998).
While opening indigenous society to change, colonial domination also
suggested that nothing was sacred and, indeed, that local traditions were
inferior or "backward" compared to metropolitan enlightenment. Many
people harbored a deep suspicion of British proscriptions and refused to
heed them. Despite the ban and the threat of incarceration, the majority
of Sudanese women continued to practice infibulation (*elkhifad elpharoni*).
Fifteen people were reported to have been prosecuted for infibulating
their daughters in 1948, which testifies to the fact that the law did not end
the practice. The ritual was simply practiced clandestinely.

From the time of Sudan's independence in 1956 until the end of the
1970s, new plans were formulated to stop female circumcision. Attention
focused on the social and cultural aspects of the ritual that accounted for
its persistence. More recently, several organizations, including the Sudan
National Committee [Against] Traditional Practices Affecting the Health
of Women and Children (SCNTP), the Red Crescent, and the Mutawinat
Group, have sponsored research on effective strategies and experimented
with a variety of approaches to female circumcision, including community
outreach through the use of mass media, audiovisual aids, and publications. Another approach incorporates efforts to end female circumcision
into existing programs concerned with public health, family planning,
maternal and child care, midwifery training, and nutrition. Despite the

strong anticircumcision campaign in Sudan, however, the practice has persisted. To comprehend the ideas of women who adhere to this ritual, we must examine the gendered ways in which these women view themselves, their society, their universe, and their place in it.

Listening to Women's Narratives about Female Circumcision

My use of personal narratives regarding this sensitive subject is prompted by methodological considerations. By quoting speech directly, although anonymously, I highlight the ideological complexity within which decisions to engage in this practice are undertaken. After two periods of fieldwork, it became clear to me that the status of women in Douroshab is not low, as Western critiques might lead us to expect. Women determine when, how, and where a girl will be excised. Women alone perform female circumcisions. The considerable influence women wield in their community is evident from the wide range of their responsibilities and from the pivotal roles they play in family and community life. The ritual does affirm one generation's authority over another, but this authority should not be dismissed as an expression of "false consciousness" in which women perpetuate their own subjugation. Nor can the motives behind genital surgeries be traced to patriarchal power or values, for no singular, oppressive patriarchal system leads women to perpetuate their own injury. Within the complex symbolic and social context of circumcision practices, women see their participation as voluntary. Collectively, they exercise power over bodily rituals signifying femininity.

Relying on first-person narratives replies to the tendency to speak for the excised woman that mars much of the scholarly and popular literature on female circumcision that originates and circulates in the West. Third-person reporting, as a rhetorical strategy, not only reflects the shortcomings of certain feminist discourses but demonstrates their inability to comprehend the complexity of life experiences in modern African societies. Finally, the meanings of female circumcision to its adherents are best illustrated through narratives. British anthropologist Marilyn Strathern suggests that "in people's lives . . . ideas cannot possibly have a life of their own" (1988, 310); ideas come to life in the context of the elaborate and nuanced personal stories that describe their meanings. These narratives provide an understanding of the ritual as presented in women's own words, which voice their own truths and the meanings they find in lived experience.[5]

ACHIEVING FEMININITY AND PRESERVING PURITY

As an older woman I interviewed in Douroshab put it, "circumcision is
what makes one a woman." A prevalent justification for circumcision is
the belief that female genitalia are ugly and misbegotten, and the clitoris "revolting." If left unexcised, these women say, the clitoris can continue to grow and ultimately "dangle" between a woman's legs. Here the
ritual enters the realm of the cosmetic: it is a repudiation of the otherwise loathsome appearance of female genitalia. This perception is widely
shared by northern Sudanese women. I was told by an older woman that
the midwife who performs the surgery is often reminded by the kins-
women of the soon-to-be circumcised girl to *sawihoo amalas wa samih
zai dahar elhamama*, "make it smooth and beautiful like the back of a
pigeon." The ritual not only is a fastidious technique in pursuit of an
aesthetic, but performs a gendered reconstruction of the body. From this
point of view, circumcision liberates the female body from its masculine
properties. This idea is related to the belief found in ancient Egyptian
mythology that the gods are hermaphrodites.

One of the women I interviewed, S., aged sixty-two, defined circumcision as a vehicle to achieve femininity. "I was given pharaonic circumcision when I was eight years old. . . . I still remember the operation being
painful, but to this day I believe it is necessary." She explained this rationale for removing the external genitalia matter-of-factly, in anatomi-
cal detail, as a way of averting a masculinization of the girl's developing
body: "These parts, especially the clitoris, can get very big. I heard from
some people that women who are not circumcised have clitorises that are
as big as a little boy's penis. I haven't seen it myself, but people who told
me swore that this is the case. . . . I believe it because just as the rest of a
girl's body parts grow when she grows up, her clitoris also grows. . . . Circumcision is what makes one a woman, because by removing the clitoris,
there is no way that her genitals will look like a man's. The woman with
a big clitoris is just like a man. How can a woman carry such a long organ between her legs and pretend that things are normal? That is why we
say that pharaonic circumcision is good, because after it is done the girl's
genital area becomes very beautiful and smooth (*malsa*)." Although S.
was aware that the less extreme form of genital excision called sunna was
favored by younger women, she insisted that all her daughters be given
pharaonic circumcision, as she had been.

In a culture with a strong belief that the clitoris is homologous to the
penis, the possibility that the clitoris will grow as a girl matures excites

discomfort, anxiety, and fear. Not only is excision an effective way of removing an excessive organ, but the surgery comes to represent the ultimate seal of femininity. The flat patch of skin created through clitoral excision and infibulation becomes a "symbolic wound" that attests to the specificity of cultural constructions of gender and womanhood. This narrative is a powerful reminder of how female bodies are re-created and socialized in different cultural contexts.

From the perspective of women in Douroshab, the virtue of purity is achieved through circumcision. These women refer to the genital operations as *tahara,* which in the etymological sense denotes cleanliness and purification. Anthropologists such as Mary Douglas (1966), Ann Sutherland (1976), and Soheir Morsey (1993) have painted elegant portraits of how notions of purity and impurity operate as elaborate moral codes and as cherished ideals in the cultures they examined. To paraphrase Morsey, the importance of social personhood in women's lives is manifested on a daily basis and informs their concept of the human body's need for purification and cleanliness (79). Sudanese justifications of circumcision as a purificatory operation are no different. External genitalia are seen as potential sources of pollution and defilement, *najasa,* which is a much-deplored state to be avoided at all costs. The concept of *najasa* denotes the antithesis of *tahara;* circumcision is a tool for avoiding *najasa* and transforming it into *tahara.* The concept of *najasa* encompasses both physical and moral impurity in diverse situations. For instance, women are implored to perform ritual purification known as *ghusl,* or bathing, after menstruation, intercourse, parturition, and other activities deemed polluting or *najis.*[6] Becoming pure and clean not only helps these women reestablish their social personhood but also differentiates them from other women who do not practice circumcision and are therefore impure.

A. believes that a woman who can practice sexual restraint enhances her status as well as ensuring her purity. She is proud to belong to the Jaleen, an ethnic group that, because of its history as merchants, is found throughout Sudan. A. recalls her own painful circumcision by a midwife at the age of eight. Married at nineteen, she is the mother of three daughters, the oldest five and the youngest only one.

I got married and from the first day, I suffered. After giving birth, like all the other women, I demanded reinfibulation. I have to tell the truth: circumcision does not allow women to want sex. Now, I only have relations on Thursdays, because my husband's job in Khartoum is demanding. Being in transit and in crowds every day from Douroshab to Khartoum is a big problem for him. When he comes home, he just wants to rest. I have no problem with this, because I believe that having sex all the time is bad. It lowers a woman, reducing her status in her husband's eyes. Once a week, once every two weeks is okay.

A. is convinced that an uncircumcised woman craves sexual intercourse, so she will become more subservient to her husband and at risk from other men's advances.

Z. advocates a moderate form of circumcision for the sake of cleanliness, a more secular form of purity. She positions sunna as a compromise between the pharaonic tradition and modern notions of bodily integrity: "Most of the people in Khartoum do not practice pharaonic circumcision because they believe that it is not necessary. . . . The people who support sunna (I am one of them) believe strongly that it keeps the genital area clean. By removing the clitoris, which is the source of bad smells and secretions, a woman's body becomes very good smelling and clean. . . . A woman should not be left uncircumcised, but at the same time her body should not be injured badly. . . . She can have a good marriage, and does not have to suffer from pain. I think that if women believe in the benefits of sunna, men will not have any problem." The shift in preferences that Z. articulates is a common trend across the country. In some families, the older daughter is infibulated while the younger ones are given clitoridectomies, continuing the practice but modifying its severity.

The practice of female circumcision inscribes prevalent ideologies, politics, and values regarding femininity and sexuality. To these three women, circumcision is important because it enacts gender and collective ethnic identity, serving to distinguish between themselves as pure *taharat* and others as polluted *nijsat* women. The politics of conformity go beyond keeping clean; they have to do with one's character, sociality, and personal and collective identity. As Simone de Beauvoir put it, "Marriage is the destiny traditionally offered to women by society" (1952, 425). The virtues requisite for marriageability, especially virginity, modesty, and an unblemished sexual reputation, are an integral aspect of gender ideology among women in Douroshab and other circumcision-practicing societies.

SELF-RESTRAINT AS A MEANS FOR NEGOTIATING POWER

To S., a Muslim high school graduate of Jali origin who works as a typist in a government office, female circumcision is not a symptom of women's oppression but a potential source of their power. She articulates this rationale to explain why she supports the practice, even though she knows it has been called into question. Her explanation is straightforward in its assessment of the balance between pain and pleasure:

> Many people in the Sudan are starting to change their views about the circumcision of girls. They tell us that it is painful and violent. My own view is that there's no difference between boys' circumcision and girls' circumcision. Both are painful, so how come they're not saying boys' circumcision is also violent? . . . I don't support ending this custom, because I don't believe in the new message. I am 100 percent behind pharaonic circumcision. My reasons are simple: sex with an infibulated woman is more enjoyable than with uncircumcised or sunna circumcised woman. When the vaginal opening is narrow and tight, the woman enjoys the friction, and the man enjoys a long intercourse rather than *akhtif wa aajri* [hit and run]. This is my experience from two marriages. . . . Infibulation is smoother and much nicer looking than having big labia. The other reason is that sex is better with pharaonic. . . . As a grandmother now, my infibulation did not eliminate my desire to have sex even at this age. People say that if you cut the clitoris you don't enjoy sex, but we can say to the same people: do you think if your tongue is removed you will stop feeling hungry? The same with sex. These people need to know that if a woman has a good husband, sex can be good even if she is circumcised, and can be very bad if she is uncircumcised and has a selfish husband. The issue is a good marriage. Now I have sex almost five times a week. It is very enjoyable and I know too about orgasm, *tharwa.* I have *tharwa jinsia,* that indescribable sense of pleasure that gives one the feeling of touching the sky. It makes one shiver.

This narrative powerfully problematizes the notion of sexual pleasure itself. Michel Foucault is correct to argue that there is no "pathology of pleasure," no "abnormal pleasure" (quoted in Halperin 1995, 93–94). The widely held assumption that circumcision reduces desire is not supported by this narrative. Heidi Skramstad (1990) has also reported Gambian women who believed that genital cutting did not reduce their enjoyment of sexual intercourse. Foucault's conceptualization of power as neither an institution nor a structure but a "complex strategical situation," a "multiplicity of force relations" simultaneously "intentional yet 'nonsubjective'" (Foucault, quoted in Smart 1988, 77), reminds us to inquire: How is power exercised? By what means?

To N., a young married Dongulawi woman, "circumcision is a source of empowerment and strength." She believes circumcision endows women with a remarkable ability to exert self-control, to take charge of their "natural" desires, and to display sexual restraint. Self-mastery, a disposition seen as a virtue that is promoted through genital surgery, is the reason for her undeviating support of pharaonic circumcision. Infibulated women, she maintains, are able to drive hard bargains and have a say in household politics and decision making. Their controlled sexuality allows them to achieve these goals in the face of scarce resources, hardship, and constrained socioeconomic circumstances. Women exercise power not only over their own sexuality but also over their spouses.

N., now twenty-six, has been married for five years and has a son who is almost two. Her husband works as an accountant in Saudi Arabia. She explains, "I was not able to accompany him for financial reasons. We wanted . . . to save money, so that we can build a house. He visits me once a year." Her personal situation, while difficult, also has its compensations. Indeed, the theme of gains through losses informs her perspective on sexuality and marriage, and she situates circumcision firmly within that context. Although her female relatives advocated infibulation, "for men the story is different": "When I got married and went on my honeymoon to a hotel in Khartoum," she says, "my husband was very angry. He told me that among men there is teasing about one's sexuality and ability to have an encounter without being rejected by the wife. [But] I did not allow my husband to come near me because of my fears. It took several months for me to have normal relations with my husband. But in spite of this, after I gave birth, I wanted to be reinfibulated. I did it for myself, for I wanted to restore my body. . . . Because after the midwife delivers the baby, the genital area becomes ugly looking." Her affirmation of the value of infibulation is based on a clearheaded assessment of power relations in marriage.

Pharaonic circumcision is good for women. It protects the dignity of women. The woman will have control over her body, and she will not run around with men. I think that a woman who is not *mukhafada* [reduced] has endless problems. I want to say to everyone who does not prefer circumcision that it gives women a lot of power in the household. For example, if she has a fight or if she wants her husband to do something for her, her circumcision will allow her to take control and be able to refrain from sex for a long time until she brings him to see the problem exactly from her viewpoint. I don't think that uncircumcised women can do that; those women, when they fight with men, maybe two days later after a fight, if the man touches them, they become aroused and immediately forget the problems just to have sex. That is why in Sudanese families, women are very, very strong. I swear that in some houses the woman is so strong that her husband can't breathe without her consent. I think this is true because of her power over her sexual desire. Men are weak, weak, and weak. They will do everything to appease a woman for sex. And the circumcised woman understands how to take advantage of the problem and turn it around for her own ends. A woman can make her husband wait for a long time, till he is no longer able to stand it. I think that because of these things, pharaonic circumcision is a good thing for women, because it helps your relations with the husband. . . . Relationships between men and women become very equal and strong. Circumcision gives a woman that power.

N.'s statement pertains to the exercise of power in a specific sociocultural context and familial situation. Given the prolonged marital separation necessitated by male labor migration, infibulation and reinfibulation may make husbands more confident in the chastity of their wives and protect married women's reputations.[7] N. sees circumcision not only as an effective tool for controlling her "natural" desires but also as a way for women to exercise power in their daily affairs. This narrative contradicts the feminist assertion about circumcision as the signifier of women's victimization by male dominance and proposes an alternative view regarding women's agency within the household.

The narratives of N. and S. make opposing claims about the effects of circumcision on women's capacity for sexual pleasure, revealing the differences behind the performance of the ritual in the same community. Rituals are open fields for reinterpretation. While most northern Sudanese women regard female circumcision as a means of attaining femininity and purity, they differ profoundly as to its effects on female sexuality. There is no consensus about the central values promoted by the practice beyond the core set of gender ideologies. This fluidity renders rituals of bodily alteration subject to adaptation by other groups for quite different purposes.

F., like N., proposes that female sexuality can be manipulated to gain respect and attain status within the family and community. This fifty-five-year-old mother of five girls told me, "Circumcision protects the girls from getting in trouble and protects them from engaging in sex. I think that it is very important for the virginity of women to be protected if they want to get husbands who respect them." The most impassioned, ardent advocates of the ritual are women themselves, who hold that by perpetuating circumcision they are protecting their daughters' virginity

and hence their reputations. Here, ritual becomes a mirror for larger conceptions of what constitutes morality, good behavior, and sexuality. "I
agree that pharaonic circumcision is painful. But still I am for it. . . . The
woman who is circumcised behaves in a way that forces people around
her to respect her. But a woman who is not circumcised cannot enjoy the
same status. Men respect women who have self-respect and who do not *Modesty*
get involved in sexual relations." F. adduces the strong position of women
in Sudanese society as evidence of the value of this custom.

> It is a good practice that we inherited from our grandmothers, people
> who knew how to handle men. None of the Sudanese women who are
> infibulated are weak or powerless. . . . If you look around, you can see
> that Sudanese women work hard and many hold high positions in soci-
> ety. Look at women in places where women are uncircumcised. Some of
> them can't leave the house without their husbands. We don't have these
> problems in Sudanese society. Pharaonic circumcision ensures the wom-
> an's strong place in the family. She is very trustworthy because she does
> not allow men to take advantage of her. She is her own person, even
> for the man she is married to. This is a source of respect, and I think
> it is more important than how painful it is. The wound heals, but the
> relationships remain strong. By preserving her reputation, a woman will
> become powerful and respected by members of the community. Look
> at other countries. Premarital sex is common in places where women
> are uncircumcised, which not only undermines the reputation of the
> woman but taints the entire lineage by her uncontrolled sexuality and
> lack of self-restraint.

In these conversations, sexuality is represented as a double-edged
sword: it can be a source of tremendous strength if controlled and safe-
guarded, but it can also be a source of weakness and deviance. Northern
Sudanese women who support circumcision evaluate it in relation to the
position of women in societies in which circumcision is not practiced,
rather than perpetuating it blindly as a tradition handed down since time
immemorial.

CIRCUMCISION AS A RELATIONAL ACT

Marx's theory of relationality is helpful in shifting our emphasis from
questions of individual choice to overdetermined social formations. In
analyzing individuality and community in Marx's theory of social reality,
Carol Gould points out that for Marx, there is an "ontologically independent entity that one could characterize neither as an individual nor

as society, but only as a system of relations." In that sense, "we would have an ontology of pure relations, with 'entities' having no independent ontological status whatever except as modes of relations or moments of relationship" (1981, 31). This critical approach has the advantage of enabling the particular form of social organization of Douroshab women to emerge more fully. Contrary to the widely held views found in most Euro-American literature on the subject, the relational rather than the individual context is the most significant aspect of circumcision rituals.

A., a forty-eight-year-old Douroshab resident who completed middle school and works as a typist in the Ministry of Education, declares: "Customs are unbreakable. That is why I believe in circumcision." Her description of the meaning of "tradition" highlights the philosophy of the individual-in-relation. Like many of the women I interviewed, A. emphasizes personhood, bonding, and the creation of femininity. Her narrative situates this practice as an act that affirms kinship among women across the generations. She acknowledges that circumcision is "a painful experience": "You have to understand why our mothers were keen to do it. They did it out of concern because they did not want to break with their tradition." As an adult, she says, "In spite of my suffering during delivery, which was also a problem, I was determined to have the *adal* [reinfibulation]. Because when they cut you open [to deliver the child], the genital area becomes ugly looking . . . in my view, this was necessary because the women I know do it to look good." Now the mother of a son and two daughters, she carefully considered the matter of her older daughter's circumcision.

> I wanted to be like everybody else in my family and my neighborhood. My daughter is now experiencing trouble; when she gets her period she can't move. I think that the problems I would face with my family would be greater and harder to deal with had I decided to abandon this custom altogether. The pressure did not come from my husband. My husband did not have any say when our young daughter was circumcised. I did not consult him or let him know, because this is a sensitive issue and it was my decision. My husband does not usually interfere in my business. But my relatives, especially my mother and my aunts, were the ones who wanted pharaonic. Now they want pharaonic for my younger one, too. They will be unhappy if I choose other types, because the opening is not as small as in the pharaonic. I am convinced that circumcision is painful, but . . . our relatives do not do it because they want to hurt us. They are just following their community and their families. I feel that in the name

of custom my relatives did that to me, and in the name of custom, I did it to my daughters. All of these things are in my mind. I understand them, but I have no way of changing them just because other, more educated women come to tell us how bad circumcision is. If I leave my daughters uncircumcised, my relatives will talk and gossip about me. I will not be able to bear it. In the future, if my daughters want to change I might give them advice, but I will not try to change their ways because the new generations have different ideas.

A. has an unusually clear view of the role of kin-based and local norms in defining acceptable practice. She accedes to the prevalent custom but acknowledges that other considerations may prevail in her daughters' future.

Intimately linked to the idea of community solidarity is the indigenous conceptualization of rights. Since the individual lives within a larger collectivity, these rights are not seen as individual possessions, as commonly held in Western thought. People take greater freedoms within this community to instruct and advise one another about every facet of their lives. Long-established practices of mutual cooperation and interdependence underline a fundamental point: that the concept of rights "as inalienable, interconnected, and indivisible" cannot be grasped in isolation from the dynamic social relations of the collectivity. I heard over and over again that many women continue the practice in order to secure social belonging, kinship identification, and loyalty.

WHAT VALUES, WHOSE VALUES?

Although northern Sudanese women acknowledge the ascendancy of custom as the underlying force behind the maintenance of female circumcision, their southern counterparts do not. We must consider the espousal of a new custom within the broader contexts of social action (James 1972). We must also concede the difficulty of grasping the intricacies of changing values and ideologies. Understanding shifting values is an exasperatingly complex problem. Morton Klass raises critical questions in *Singing with Sai Baba*. "[How] are values expressed? Can we ever be sure the same value is present even when two people make the same choice in different situations? Is it possible that one and the same value may be expressed by different choices in varying circumstances?" (1991, 10)

The question of why some southern Sudanese women started to take on the practice of female circumcision following their arrival in Khartoum in 1989 is especially difficult. Northern women justify their support of the practice by arguing that it preserves virginity, enhances femininity, and increases the purity and cleanliness of the body. The practice is intimately linked to sexual politics and attitudes toward sexuality and reproduction, which lie at the heart of significant cultural and religious beliefs among the Sudanese. Intermarriage has sometimes entailed taking on the practice. It does not, however, require belief in the values espoused by northern Sudanese women among whom the practice is a long-standing tradition. Not to be underestimated is the societal pressure that southern women encounter in their new communities.

In 1997, an all-day workshop called "The Differences Which Unite Us" was organized by Women Action Group to facilitate dialogue between southern and northern Sudanese women. This encounter yielded significant insights into how each group perceives the other. Southerners expressed deep resentment of how they felt northerners regarded them:

> Northerners discriminate against us racially and religiously, for example, in having to wear a tobe and behave as they do, which is "not our way." Northern women support jihad in the South by giving their sons for the war; they even prepare special foods for those going to the war in front of southerners whose relatives in the South will be the ones to die. Thus many have no concern for the feelings of others. The northerners treat us in a superior manner; they are hypocrites and actually despise southerners. Northerners laugh at us for not being circumcised.

Although many northerners deny that they support jihad, since their sons are conscripted into the military without their consent, their stereotypical attitudes toward groups that do not adhere to female circumcision are important to consider, especially as the two groups start to interact and intermarry.

Documenting the Adoption of Circumcision by Displaced Women

Recent years have witnessed a growing body of anthropological perspectives on female circumcision. The reason for examining this contested practice in depth is not to demonstrate that southern women who come from groups where it is not performed have adopted it in the North, a fact that has been confirmed by concerned activists and health workers in the region, or that those women who have adopted the practice express their own justifications for espousing the ritual, although those differ from

why younger girls are circumcised. The key point is that displaced wom-
en's adoption of female circumcision cannot be isolated from relations of
power, agency, the making of self and community, and the subjective formulations of experience of people undergoing massive transformation.
Current efforts to understand this practice among women displaced
from southern to northern Sudan are prompted by a desire to prevent its
widespread adoption. Advocates know from their experiences in other
settings that strategies to curtail the practice must be based on an adequate understanding of women's own situations. According to Sudanese
university professor and anticircumcision activist Ahmed Abdel Mageid,
"Many Southern displaced people in Khartoum started to adopt female
circumcision. I call this negative acculturation" (2001, 24). NGOs and
community activists have documented its rising incidence among IDPs.
During my visit to Sudan in 1996, concern over the spread of this ritual
was mounting. According to one social worker from a local NGO, "While
we are trying very hard to curb the practice among people who practiced
it for thousands of years, now we [have] started to receive news about its
spread among southerners who did not know about it before."

The United Nations report on humanitarian operations in Sudan states
that "traditional" northern practices have become common among displaced people, and female genital mutilation[8] is practiced in its most drastic form—infibulation or pharaonic circumcision (2000, 59). Incidence of
the practice was discussed in a proposal prepared by the Sudanese National Committee on Traditional Harmful Practices Affecting the Health
of Women and Children (SNCTP). Amna Abdel Rahman, who heads
this committee, proposed bringing a training and sensitization campaign
to the displaced. She explained the urgency of this project:

> Due to the high rate of illiteracy in the camps, displaced people are igno-
> rant about the eradication of harmful practices, female genital mutila-
> tion in particular. According to reports collected from established clin-
> ics in the camps and other teams, FGM is now being practiced in the
> camps. Some families bring their young girls to the clinic to be circum-
> cised, although this is usually refused. Circumcision for both boys and
> girls has been reported in some camps, e.g., Carton Kassala and Dar El
> Salaam, mainly among the displaced from the Western Sudan. Since
> different groups are accommodated together in one camp, Southerners
> have already started to adopt female genital mutilation as an urban fash-
> ion and as assumed religious requirement. (1995, 2)

SNCTP has tried to promote alternative employment for midwives who derive substantial incomes from performing circumcisions.[9] I was told by the president of the organization that southern midwives who learned how to perform the operations from their northern counterparts could also work as agents for change if they were informed about its deleterious effects on childbirth. The strategy of finding alternative sources of income for midwives and traditional birth attendants has been one of the most effective tools in the fight against female circumcision in Sudan. In 2002, I accompanied SNCTP social workers to Wad El-Bashir, one of the largest camps in Omdurman. The workers planned the visit to inquire about the progress of a store where midwives were employed as vendors. Ten southern midwives were present at the time. They expressed frustration with the work in the store, but ended the meeting by reiterating their commitment to its success. The inclusion of southern midwives in the Inter Africa Program, which allows them supplementary sources of income, remains a powerful symbol of the momentous role they can play in either the proliferation or the obliteration of this tradition.

Coverage of the spread of the practice was also the focus of a recent Reuters news article, "Sudan Peace May Help End Female Circumcision." Reporter Andrew Hammond writes that war has encouraged the spread of female circumcision in Sudan, but peace could give a much-needed boost to efforts to combat the practice.[10] Hammond quotes Samira Amin, a founding member of the Sudanese Network for Eradicating Female Circumcision: "A 2001 survey of street children who live in the capital's displaced communities showed 67 percent of them had undergone what medical textbooks call genital infibulation. These are people from the Dinka tribes in the South, the Nuba Mountains, and the Felata in the west, who did not do this before. It is a transmitted trend." Dr. Constantine Jervase, a surgeon from Bahr El-Ghazal, observed:

> The practice had extended to tribal groups in the South before the war brought northerners and southerners together in the shantytowns of Khartoum. They are just copying it from the Arabs. If they show their neighbors they are now using the same culture and system they might be able to get some assistance. The internally displaced are concerned with how to survive, and that can mean acquiring certain things to please their masters. If the south becomes a different country something has to be done because it won't disappear just like that. Something has to be done to fight it, just like the northerners are doing, by campaigning and enlighten[ing] people.

Anthropologist Hamid El-Bashir authored another important document evaluating the SNCTP's efforts to end female circumcision. El-Bashir tells the story of a thirty-seven-year-old non-Muslim Shilluk midwife serving her displaced community in Goz Al Luban, a camp near Kosti city in central Sudan.

> In 1978 I was selected to join the midwifery school in Malakal. The midwives who came to train us from Khartoum told me that I had to get circumcised since I myself would be a midwife in the future. I was about to accept but, due to the unexpected sickness of my mother, I quit the training program to sit next to my ailing mother. Now, seventeen years later, I joined the midwifery school in Kosti in order to graduate after one year [of] training and be a certified midwife to serve the community of the displaced Southerners in Goz Al Salam displaced camp. I was really surprised when they taught us this time in the midwifery school that female circumcision is bad and we shouldn't practice it. I told them, but it is Islamic; they said no, that is not true. That is only a wrong popular belief.
>
> In my family we are very much mixed: My sister Nabita is a Muslim (through marriage); I'm a Christian (by birth); and my daughter Suaa'd is also a Muslim. Nabita became Muslim when she got married to a Muslim soldier in Malakal in late 1960s. He became part of our family and he told my sister that they should circumcise me. My sister liked the idea and called the midwife, but I ran away and hid with my aunt for few days. When I came home they were laughing at me and accused me of being a coward and not daring to have a small operation like circumcision. So I never got circumcised until I grew up and got married to a Shilluk man and had my daughter Suaa'd. Suaa'd became a Muslim through her uncle (my brother-in-law) Mubarak, who was [a] primary school teacher. She was living with him when she was young. He circumcised her with his daughters in 1980, and from that time she automatically became Muslim. Three years ago, Suaa'd got married to a Christian man from the Shilluk tribe, but she is still Muslim. Now Suaa'd is living with us in Goz Al Salam displaced camp.

El-Bashir's observations have been corroborated by Susan Kenyon, whose ethnography *Five Women of Sennar* (2004) reported the taking up of female circumcision by numerous groups of southerners and West African immigrants. A 2002 AFP news article, "Female Circumcision in Sudan Resists Abolition Efforts," states, "The Christians [who] escaped from the South have adopted circumcision. They think this practice will

ease their integration into northern communities." This is the governing question in the context of displacement and forced migration: Does the adoption of circumcision reflect an attempt by displaced women to reduce the social distance between themselves and their hosts?

B.L., who is Fujulu, speaks matter-of-factly about her circumcision as an aspect of her becoming a Muslim:

> I joined my mother in Khartoum and adopted female circumcision as part of my conversion to Islam. All the women I heard about who converted to Islam decided to get circumcised. Men too get circumcised when they convert to Islam. It is part of the religion. I can describe my life in Khartoum as "good" because I live with my relatives. Financial hardships, however, have taken their toll on me. . . . I regularly interact with northerners. I live with them and learned about their food, crafts, marriage, witchcraft, and sorcery. I am prepared to embrace some of these practices. It is also true that I resent the fact that northerners despise southerners and call them "slaves" and "servants." When I got married to a Muslim in the North, I got circumcised. The most important reason behind my decision is my conversion to Islam.

The prejudice that northerners display against southerners particularly rankles B.L., and she states clearly that conversion to Islam is part of becoming socially acceptable in the North.

Several southern women were circumcised in the context of marriage to Muslim men. L.N., a Bari Christian, came to Khartoum after she married:

> I moved from Juba in 1999 with my husband, a northern Sudanese man whom I have since divorced. My parents moved to Khartoum after me. During my first year in Khartoum, I lived with my husband's family. After the first year, I faced discrimination from my husband's family as a southerner. I became ill and I believe that my mother-in-law bewitched me. After divorcing my husband, I lived with my parents, but my child died as a result of these troubles. I believe that my marriage to a northern Sudanese man was a waste. I maintained aspects of my culture even when living with my in-laws. I respected them and cooked southern food for them. My child was named in the Bari birth tradition. While living with my in-laws, however, I found myself in a different society where I learned about northern foods, *dilka, khumra, karbaret,* henna, *dukhan,* dressing with *tobe,* and other traditions. I was circumcised by my ex-husband's family during the delivery of my second

child and I find it normal. I believe that sunna circumcision, in which only a small portion of the clitoris is removed, is acceptable, but I do not support pharaonic circumcision, which removes much more. I know many women who adopted it and either married Muslims or who grew up in Muslim communities and do not want to be degraded as *nijis* or impure.

L.N. positions her postpartum circumcision within a context of pressure from her in-laws. Although she does not make it the center of her grievances against her husband and his family, her circumcision was the last straw in a marriage in which she felt marginalized despite her efforts to adapt to northern culture.

F.M., a Christian from Juba, underwent circumcision in preparation for her marriage in the mistaken belief that her husband would expect it.

I met my husband when I was still in the South. He is a northerner and Muslim. When he asked to marry me, I decided to get circumcised. I did not ask him whether he wanted me to be circumcised or not. The only thing I was sure about was that most northern women are circumcised at an early age. So I had the operation. I thought this would be good since northern men are always with circumcised women. The operation itself was not easy, especially for somebody who is an adult. I stayed in bed for a few days until I recovered completely. When we got married, I told my husband and he was very disappointed and cross with me. He said that when he asked to marry me, he knew very well that southern women do not undergo the surgeries like northern Sudanese women. He also mentioned that this surgery is not necessary. But from my standpoint at that time, I felt the opposite. I thought this is the normal way to be for northerners. My idea about circumcision has not changed. I am not worried about it and I know so many southern women who had circumcisions since they [married] Muslim men. You never know. Some men are supportive of it, others are not. I am happily married now.

Although there is no established link between religion and genital cutting for females and some clerics deny the custom is Islamic, in many communities circumcision is believed to have religious significance.

M.J., a Christian nurse from Juba, told me her story during a visit to the camp where she has been employed at the health center for two years. She has firsthand knowledge of female circumcision: her southern Christian husband, who lived in the Arabic-speaking Muslim town of Kosti, coerced her into undergoing the procedure. Her story illuminates the ways in which her husband's exposure to northern practices affected his beliefs about sexuality.

> My experience is very strange. I am a Christian woman who heard about female circumcision, but it did not occur to me to form a strong opinion about it since it did not concern me. I married a Christian man from Bahr El-Ghazal. It is his original home, but he looked for employment in Kosti and moved there a long time ago when Nimeiri was still in power. He had interactions with people in Kosti who are Arabs. He has good relations with them, and I think that is why he liked this practice. Men talked to each other about it. This is how he found out and insisted that I get the operation—and went far enough to tell the midwife who delivered my child to cut and sew. Of course I was very tired of being in labor and felt little pain because I almost passed out after the child was born. This situation made me question him. Although we stayed [together] for a while after this incident took place, eventually I got a divorce.

In this case, too, being involuntarily circumcised after giving birth accelerated the end of the marriage. The husband had absorbed the belief that circumcised women afford greater sexual pleasure to men, so he insisted his wife undergo the procedure when she was in no position to resist.

see p. 202

In the context of migration, husbands' and wives' acceptance of female circumcision as essential to femininity was an attempt to fit into the host community. In his book *Human Societies,* Abram de Swann explains the need for belonging and affection: "People need the regard of their fellow human beings. They see themselves 'through the eyes of others'—as they think they are seen. In this way they form a self-image, which is determined by what they think other people think of them. They do not worry about everyone's opinion, but single out people from their past and present surroundings who are important to them. Thus people are also dependent on others for something as personal as their self-image or identity" (2001, 8–9). These interviews with southern Sudanese women demonstrate their effort as forced migrants to secure a foothold in the host society.

Female circumcision is a ritual contributing to the cultural construction of gender, womanhood, and "appropriate" sexuality, and is seen by practitioners as a part of the process of achieving full personhood within their culture. However, displaced women adopt this practice as adults; it is rarely performed on young girls. When I asked S.S., a resident of the shantytown, about the practice, she responded:

Personally I am not supportive of circumcision, but my older sister is. We both arrived in Khartoum in 1994 from the Nuba Mountains. Some Muslim Nuba practice female circumcision if the child has *duda* [vaginal itching, caused by worms]. The majority of women don't. My sister and I are Christians. When we arrived here, we found that some Nuba and southern women started to adopt female circumcision. My sister made up her mind to undergo the procedure. She went to a midwife who performed a lot of surgeries on women her age. She had the surgery, and she was lying on her *angaraib* [bed] in pain. I was trying to stop her, but she did not listen to me. I resisted this practice because I am afraid of the pain of the cutting. I asked my sister, why did you do this now? All your life, you were not circumcised. What are you doing this for? She was in pain and she kept telling me *sakit sakit* [for no reason]. But no one gets circumcised for no reason, especially if you are a grown woman. I know one thing: my sister wanted to be like other women she met in Khartoum. She thinks that Khartoum people's ways are better than ours. But all these women who were circumcised were not young women. They all learned about circumcision because some neighbors do it and tell them about it. Now they think it is a good idea. I will not do it as long as I live.

Since in the North the procedure is performed on girls of six to nine years of age, the adoption of the practice by adult women is a major departure. Many would argue that the embracing of this practice by adult women underscores the voluntary character of their decision.

According to Carol Ember and Melvin Ember, however, "A subordinate society may acculturate to a dominant society even in the absence of direct or indirect force. The dominated people may elect to adopt cultural elements from the dominant society in order to survive in their changed world. Or, perceiving that members of the dominant society enjoy more secure living conditions, the dominated people may . . . identify with the dominant culture in the hope that by doing so they will be able to share its benefits" (1973, 496). What is especially remarkable in the acceptance of female circumcision by displaced southerners is that people who are "just as powerless" actively broker the practice. Although female circumcision is perpetuated by the dominant northern Sudanese society, the practice was introduced by members of the displaced groups who arrived in Khartoum from western Sudan in the wake of the drought and desertification that swept their region in the early 1980s. Now they lead other displaced women down this path to cultural adaptation.

Several women stated that they underwent the procedure after marrying Muslim men. This situation differs from the northern context, where women perform this custom to please themselves. Indeed, a great number of women who did not adopt female circumcision knew of others who did so because of men's influence. In their view, whether the woman adopts the practice or not is left to the husband's discretion. For example, a twenty-eight-year-old Dinka woman, R.A., who moved from Bor in 1990, stated: "I believe that female circumcision is harmful to women. . . . I knew of southerners who adopted it as they were forced to do so by their Muslim husbands, who deceived them into believing that it was part of overall cleanliness, and who did not care about their wives' well-being. I believe that female circumcision was a misled attempt to correct God's way of making women."

There are some exceptions to this rule, however. While the majority of displaced southern women who adopted female circumcision were married to Muslim men, some of them were not. H.L., a Christian Bari from Juba, arrived in Khartoum with her northern Muslim husband in 1990. Although marriage and migration brought her into close contact with northerners, she did not convert to Islam or adopt circumcision. In fact, she maintains that her husband agreed that if they have a daughter, she would not be circumcised. The women who resist the procedure suggest that women who adopt it are either deceived or coerced. Their objections are fundamental: for example, that God did not create women's bodies with defects that require surgical modification.

Notwithstanding the importance of intermarriage, in a forced migratory context it is reasonable to suggest that the adoption of the practice is a strategic move by IDPs to find a place in the host society and reduce the distance between themselves and their hosts. Although women in Izzbba spoke openly about their attitudes toward female circumcision, their profound reticence regarding rape made it impossible to ascertain whether some women had adopted the practice as a paradoxical way of restoring bodily integrity following sexual violence during war and flight. There is no doubt that displacement has reshaped the ways in which southern Sudanese women view themselves, their communities, and gender relations and has profoundly transformed their notions of home. Several grassroots workers told me that the majority of displaced women see the practice as an urban innovation.

The acceptance of female circumcision is not structurally integrated in the shantytown. Rather, it is an individual strategy that women have undertaken to adjust to new realities. Ethnic mixing introduced women to this practice. When I asked about the extent to which these women may have experienced coercion, responses were mixed. Some of the women indicated that they came to the decision totally on their own. Others highlighted the momentous role that their in-laws played by demanding that they undergo circumcision. The majority of women who did not adopt the practice believe that southern women accepted it because they were deceived by husbands and others who extol the values of female circumcision. For those who acquiesced to the practice, the decision was produced by unique circumstances encountered in the new location.

However, embracing rituals does not always reflect identical values and moralities. In his work on the Ndembu of Zambia, Max Gluckman notes that while it is important to establish common explanations for ritual phenomena, "it is essential to grasp that there are fundamental differences between them and also between modes of interpreting them" (1997, 40). Acquiescence to new norms and belief systems can be seen as one of a series of adjustments women make to overcome their sense of cultural loss and marginalization. The situation in Khartoum has undoubtedly undercut women's ability to uphold some of their cherished traditions. They seek alternative practices in an effort to make an otherwise intolerable situation more endurable.

Dukhan as Metaphor of Reconciliation

Southern Sudanese women's participation in a ritual bodily practice known as *dukhan* with their northern, Arabic-speaking counterparts reveals complex ways of remaking self and home and serves as a metaphor for intercultural reconciliation. In considering the unfolding subjectivity of southern Sudanese women in Izzbba, we must acknowledge the contingency and situationality of identity formation. As Peter Preston put it, "the sphere of practical activity constitutive of self-identity" comprises "locale, network, and memory" (1997, 39). The making of self is facilitated through both the performance of old traditions and the adoption of new rituals.

Dukhan, or smoke bath, is a beautification ritual practiced by women in northern Sudanese provinces.[11] After large numbers of southern displaced women settled in northern-dominated communities, they became acquainted with *dukhan,* as well as with henna and other forms of body adornment. This ritual is open only to those who are married or about to get married. Associated with sensuality and eroticism, it is believed to boost sexual gratification. A series of steps must be followed carefully before bathing in smoke. To start, a blend of scented *shaff, talih,* and sandalwood is placed inside a hole. Enough charcoal is lit to produce scented smoke. A *birish* rug, woven from palm tree branches, is then placed over the hole. To bathe, a woman strips naked. Her body is thoroughly rubbed with *karkar,* scented oil made from animal fat, orange peel, and clove essences. The woman sits over the hole, allowing the rising smoke to fumigate her body. Women rarely perform *dukhan* alone. Usually, they rely on the help of female kin, neighbors, and friends to add wood as needed or to provide water to compensate for the massive amount of sweat released during the bath, which can last for an hour or more. A body scrub known as *dilka* is then used to clean the body and to reveal a glistening skin. A warm shower concludes the process. Although women insist on the benefits of *dukhan* for health reasons such as curing bodily aches and pains, its links to sexuality cannot be ignored. *Dukhan* is frequently regarded as a symbolic invitation for sex in a society where women's expression of sexual desire is condemned. To participate in the *dukhan* ritual is to engage in a cult of femininity in which clear rules about the construction of ideal womanhood are followed with passionate precision.

Displaced women who adopt the practice of *dukhan* have incurred the harsh censure of southern men. T.M., a forty-seven-year-old male social worker, expressed his antipathy toward the ritual by saying, "I don't know why these women are doing *dukhan*. As men, we hear that *dukhan* is performed when a woman is too wide and that *dukhan* helps tighten her. The southern women here are mostly single or widowed. What do they need it for?" His comment implies that *dukhan*, understood as an invitation for sex, is incompatible with the chastity expected of unpartnered women without husbands. But the women themselves offer more nuanced reasons for adopting *dukhan*. One Dinka woman explained she learned this custom by watching her neighbors and imitating their actions. By practicing this ritual, displaced women gain a new understanding of self while forging a new community. Connections with their neighbors compensate for lost social networks and idioms that gave meaning to social existence before their displacement.

Although not all southern displaced women have adopted *dukhan*, the custom shows how women respond to new social contexts. Rites and rituals such as *dukhan* cannot be isolated from the larger setting of social action. As Wendy James shows in her analysis of the politics of rain control among the Uduk, "To perform a . . . ritual is not simply to carry out a naïve 'symbolic' act which is supposed to have instrumental efficacy. It is to make a calculated move in a very real game of social and political maneuver" (1972, 33). The adoption of *dukhan* plays a useful role in building bridges across ethnic communities. Creating neighborly sociality, *dukhan* celebrates belonging rather than distance from others. Women find ways to make a place for themselves in a new multicultural scene.

In exploring the effects of forced migration on cultural transformation, I focused on gendered rituals that enable women to reshape "strategies of selfhood" in their new surroundings as they struggled to create a sense of centeredness and direction. In such situations, the self becomes entangled "with other subjects' histories, experiences and self-representations" (Battaglia 2000, 116). Women's inability to carry on southern cultural traditions in their new settlements affects their evaluations of new customs. Displaced women list a whole litany of lost cultural rights: the right to brew alcohol; wear traditional dress; perform ethnic dances; and perform marriage, birth, and death rituals in the same way they were celebrated at home. Access to cultural life is intimately linked to questions of peace and the ability of individuals and communities to live securely and freely in their environment. Describing the experiences of Togolese, Russians, and Polish Jews in the introduction to their book *Ethnography in Unstable Places,* Carol Greenhouse, Elizabeth Mertz, and Kay Warren note that people strive "to manage their everyday lives against a palpable transformation of the world they thought they knew but now feel pressed to reassess through the lens of their everyday circumstances (2002, 3). The residents of Izzbba with whom I had extensive conversations would readily recognize this observation, both experientially and intuitively, as reflective of their own lives. Women had to assume new roles as they struggled to create a space for themselves in the host community's established order.

Negotiating identities is not synonymous with abandoning other forms of subjectivities and understandings. Ideas about self in times of difficulty are necessarily a product of rich imaginings. These IDPs provide ample illustration that identities are ever-shifting, contingent, and "multiply referenced" (Peteet 2005, 4). Any static notion of "identity" is entirely inappropriate to the Sudanese context.

Whether adopting female circumcision, decorating the body with henna, or engaging in *dukhan,* these ritual acts form part of a public presentation of self that nurtures a sense of neighborly sociality. Displaced women have to elbow their way into a multicultural mosaic that prompts them to compose new concepts of self and community. Their narratives challenge essentialist concepts of identity, as the discursively constructed aspects of personhood are contingent upon the existential realities surrounding displaced women. The actions recounted in this chapter not only exemplify IDPs' inner strength and adeptness but also serve as "the groping footsteps" (Bateson 1989, 34) toward harmony and peacemaking in this war-torn nation. In these everyday ways, both the displaced and their hosts are reflecting upon their inherited cultural meaning systems and continuously renewing, elaborating, and altering them as they encounter one another and create common lives in the fluid setting of the shantytown.

1. Rogaia Mustafa Abusharaf (wearing tarha) and midwife (wearing tobe), Wad El-Bashir camp, ca. 2003. Photo by author.

2. Achol Rehan with her three daughters, Gogrial, Bahr El-Ghazal, ca. 2004. Photo by author.

3. Sondra Opeca, at Women Waging Peace conference, Washington, D.C., 2004. Photo by author.

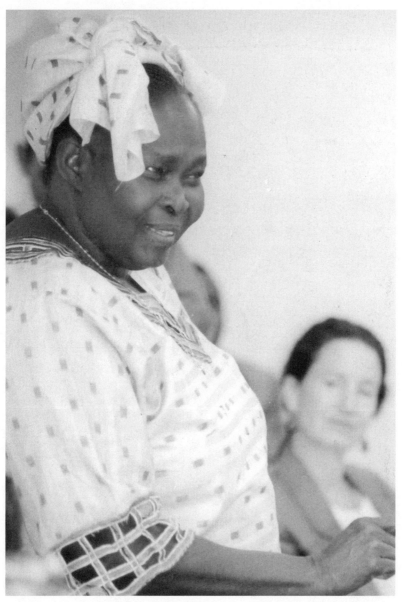

4. "Mama" Kezia Layinwa Nicodemus, Women Waging Peace conference, Washington, D.C., 2004. Photo by author.

5. Karak Maylik Nyok in canoe, Malkal, Upper Nile, 1990s. Photo by author.

6. Priscilla Joseph, Women Waging Peace conference in Washington, D.C., 2004. Photo by author.

7. Angelina Bortolo Odengala with her five children, Wau, in the early 1980s, before displacement. Photo by author.

8. Women in front of cathedral, Ammarrat, 2005, after cleaning the church for Christmas. Angelina Artolo Odengala is standing in center rear. Photo by author.

9. Women cleaning cathedral; St. Mark killing the dragon in rear. Photo by author.

10. Women cleaning front steps of cathedral. Photo by author.

11. Men in white jalabia addressing southern and Darfurian women gathered under tree in Kordofan, photographed by Karak Maylik Nyok.

12. Karak Maylik Nyok's grandmother (wearing lau), Upper Nile, during the 1990s. Photograph by Karak Maylik Nyok.

13. Four women from Darfur, Mandela camp 2003. Photograph by Karak Maylik Nyok.

14. Women Waging Peace conference delegates from Sudan, with two WWP staff members, Washington, D.C., 2004. Photo by author.

FOUR

Negotiating Peace

One branch in bloom said to his neighboring branch, "This is a dull and empty day." And the other branch answered, "It is indeed empty and dull."

At that moment a sparrow alighted on one of the branches, and then another sparrow, nearby. And one of the sparrows chirped and said, "My mate has left me."

And another sparrow cried, "My mate has also gone, and she will not return. And what care I?"

Then the two began to twitter and scold, and soon they were fighting and making harsh noise upon the air.

All of a sudden two other sparrows came sailing from the sky, and they sat quietly beside the restless two. And there was calm, and there was peace. Then the four flew away together in pairs.

And the first branch said to his neighboring branch, "That was a mighty zig-zag of sound." And the other branch answered, "Call it what you will, it is now both peaceful and spacious. And if the upper air makes peace it seems to me that those who dwell in the lower might make peace also. Will you not wave in the wind a little nearer to me?" And the first branch said, "Oh, perchance, for peace' sake, ere the Spring is over." And then he waved himself with the strong wind to embrace her.

—Khalil Gibran, "Peace Contagious" (1932)

Women's narratives give voice not only to their suffering in societies riven by war but also to their active efforts to make peace. Displaced women are deeply invested in conflict resolution. In the shantytowns, camps, and slums of Khartoum, they practice reconciliation on a daily basis as they mix and mingle with displaced women from other ethnolinguistic groups and interact with Arab, Muslim women in the surrounding community. Necessity forces them to shed the deference to men that was expected in their communities of origin; they exhibit independence and resourcefulness as they struggle to support themselves and their children. Many women become more assertive politically as well, seeking to play a role in the formal peacemaking process in their country. This chap-

performativity

ter moves from the informal bridge building women undertake in the shantytowns to the organized efforts of women's groups to participate in building a New Sudan.

As active agents in reconstructing their own lives and that of their nation, displaced women undertake feminist transformation. Both in and out of war zones, Sudanese women embrace feminism as a powerful language for challenging authority in all its layered complexities. Awut Deng Acuil, the founder of Sudanese Women's Voice for Peace, observed: "In the South, women interested in finding ways to put an end to conflict had no official place to hold their meetings. We used to congregate under a tree and talk all day about ways of addressing war and peace. Of course, passersby always looked at us as just women chatting." Demonstrating women's determination to have a voice in the peace process, Acuil was a member of the Sudanese People's Liberation Movement (SPLM) negotiating delegation at the Intergovernmental Authority on Development (IGAD) peace talks. Cofounder of the Sudanese Catholic Bishops Regional Conference (SCBRC), the Sudanese Women's Association in Nairobi, and the Sudanese Women's Voice for Peace, Acuil worked with the New Sudan Council of Churches to establish conflict resolution initiatives and peace agreements among clashing Sudanese groups. She also established the Pankar Peace and Good Governance Grassroots Initiative. Acuil was the secretary of information for the West Bank Peace Council in the Bahr El-Ghazal region and was awarded the Inter-Action Humanitarian Peace Award for her efforts in building peace and women's rights in Sudan. Since 1999, she has been a member of Inclusive Security: Woman Waging Peace. Activists like Acuil are "masterful mappers" and "demythologizers." These terms are offered by Cornel West in his brilliant essay "Theory, Pragmatisms, and Politics," in which he defines "demythologizing" as "a mapping activity that reconstructs and redescribes forms of signification for the purpose of situating them in the dynamic flow of social practices" (1993, 89). In Sudan, the simple act of meeting to discuss common problems is subversive. In addressing issues of war and peace collectively, women undertake a simultaneous interrogation and transformation of gender relations and ideologies.

The portrait of feminine submissiveness that pervades anthropological analyses of Southern Sudanese societies, from Edward Evans-Pritchard's *The Nuer* (1940) and *Man and Woman among the Azande* (1974) and Francis Deng's *The Dinka of Sudan* (1978) to Sharon Hutchinson's *Nuer Dilemmas* (1996), is modified by locally grounded studies conducted by Sudanese women themselves. While inequitable gender ideologies and the assumption of male dominance are widespread, women do not passively accept their subordination. As they resist the constraints others seek to impose upon them, women question the norms that prevail in their communities and come into conflict with the reigning powers within kin-groups and localities. In the context of a protracted civil war, the violence against women that is implicit in male dominance in ordinary times comes to the surface. For the same reasons, women's struggles to attain personal independence and dignity take on a political character. Women making peace are asserting themselves as active citizens.

Suzanne Samson Jambo is the NGO coordinator for the New Sudanese Indigenous Network (NSIN), which comprises 42 nongovernmental organizations. The NSIN is a forum for Southern Sudanese civil society groups to address such issues as human rights, participatory governance, development, postconflict strategies, and advocacy for a just and lasting peace in Sudan. Jambo helps indigenous Sudanese women's NGOs integrate gender-sensitive international, regional, and local human rights provisions into their programs. She has worked with international organizations such as Amnesty International, the UN Children's Fund, and the UN World Food Programme. Jambo holds professional degrees in law and applied social sciences. Her efforts exemplify the fusion of scholarship with activism.

In *Overcoming Gender Conflict and Bias: The Case of New Sudan Women and Girls,* Jambo observes that "traditional practices such as arranged marriages, bride price and dowry payment are the norm, and girls are usually married off to the highest bidder." She notes that these practices are compounded by a culture of violence emanating from decades of militarization and armed conflict (2001, 5). Because war is a gendered act, it has profound and enduring social and political effects, refashioning structures of gender relations as well as definitions of nationhood. Focusing on Sudanese women living in Bahr El-Ghazal, Equatoria, Upper Nile, South Kordofan, and South Blue Nile and those living abroad in Egypt, Uganda, and Egypt, Jambo documented the dual victimization of women by male dominance and warfare. Casting the same wide net in her research as in her organizing, she probed the issues with grassroots women and men, elders, chiefs and paramount chiefs, governors, commissioners, civil and traditional judges, and political leaders. Jambo concludes that the discrimination manifest in abusive marriage practices must be redressed through careful implementation of public policies to empower women economically, protect their legal and political rights, and raise their standing in society. As women constitute 60 percent of the population, improving their position is in the best interests of Sudan.

The systematic efforts of southern women to challenge their subordinate status and make peace in their country demythologize conventional gender norms that plague women throughout their lives and exclude them from political decision making. Women view facing up to militarization and the propagation of political violence by successive governments in Sudan as a critical frame of reference in their advocacy efforts. Sexual violence against women, including rape, sexual slavery, and torture, goes beyond being merely spoils of war; the bodies of women and girls are converted into targets to be violated as a means of attacking other men. As Alexandra Richards, president of Australian Women Lawyers, affirmed: "Women have every reason to reject militarism and war because they destroy the life they have given and nurtured, but also because militarism and war feed male aggression of which women become particular victims" (2000).

Women in Sudan and the Sudanese diaspora have established networks and organizations to raise awareness about the human costs of the conflict and to call for the comprehensive implementation of the peace agreement. As breadwinners and decision makers, women are starting income-generation projects, some in fields as nontraditional as carpentry. Women from the North and South have organized to meet the needs of orphans, street children, and others in dire economic straits.

Sudanese women are urging the international community and their country's male leaders to advance the inclusion of women in peace building and reconciliation. When the Government of Sudan prevented women from boarding a plane to take them to the Naivasha talks in Kenya, women from the South joined northern women to protest their exclusion from the peace process. At Naivasha, women's organizations were forced to present their recommendations to the parties by pushing their manifestos under the closed doors of the conference room. Sudanese women have played no role in the African Union-sponsored Darfur peace talks in the Nigerian capital, Abuja. Indeed, women have consistently been sidelined by the North-South and Darfur peace processes (Abusharaf 2005b). Although many women's organizations were registered observers with the Intergovernmental Authority on Development (IGAD) and presented technical papers to negotiators in the Machakos talks, they were not formally involved.

Addressing the root causes of conflict in Sudan must include promotion of women's economic empowerment. In some war-affected areas,

three-quarters of the surviving inhabitants are women; women constitute the overwhelming majority of adult IDPs and refugees. Women head
households, yet they do not have legal access to land or resources because
of discrimination in statutory and customary law. Sudan is not among the
180 nations that have signed the UN Convention on the Elimination of
All Forms of Discrimination Against Women (CEDAW). Formidable difficulties were identified by the Working Group on Women's Participation
in Peace-Building Processes in Sudan in 1997. According to Amna Abdel
Rahman (1995), this working group enumerated the problems militating
against gender equality in the peace process. Familiar peacemaking mechanisms and systems of kinship are eroded and replaced by civic organizations that lack female representation and a relation to the homeland, especially when these organizations are based outside of the affected areas.

The commanding words of Kezia Layinwa Nicodemus ("Mama"
Kezia), head of the SPLM's Women and Gender Commission, attest to
women's steadfast determination to end these inequities: "We are speaking in one voice today. We are women from all over Sudan and we are a
voice for peace. We speak in one language regardless of our divisions. We
have been given 25 percent of the seats in Southern Sudan's constitution.
But we have to push to make this a reality. Sudan is a country of men and
we have to work hard with the support of the international community to
train our women to be leaders" (Abusharaf 2005b, 44–45).

At the present time, as an outcome of the work of women like Mama
Kezia, understanding of the dynamic interactions of gender, violence,
war, and peacemaking has increased. This concern is also expressed in
other countries emerging from war, as well as by transnational bodies (see
Ignatieff 1984). The United Nations Security Council cemented its interest in women's role in peace building when it passed its landmark Resolution 1325 (UNSC 1325) in October 2000, which affirmed that maintaining
and promoting security cannot be accomplished without women's vigor-
ous input in negotiating and implementing peace. This acknowledgment
illuminates the significance of gender as an organizing principle in societal structures that mold the politics of war and peace.

Sudanese women who recognize the centrality of gender to war and
peace through their own bitter experiences seek to play an active role in
peace talks. Agnes Nyoka, the coordinator for Sudanese Women's Empowerment for Peace (SUWEP), a Kenya-based organization that en-
gages refugee women in dialogue regarding the Sudanese peace process,
has participated in numerous conferences relating to peace in Sudan, including the Ethiopia-Sudan Development Marketplace and Knowledge

gender =
central to
war
+
peace

Forum in February 2003. As a guest speaker representing SUWEP at the conference, she shared her expertise on the importance of the link between government and civil engagement of the local community. Nyoka is also affiliated with the Sudanese Women's Christian Mission for Peace and participated in the Racism and Gender Conference in September 2001. As she put it: "Dialogue is very important to resolve and prevent conflict in Sudan. As women, decisions are being made for us. The GoS and SPLM are using arms, and we carry UNSC 1325 in our arms to promote inclusion."

Women's yearning for the security that peace brings is evident in the conflict in Darfur as well. When I interviewed Rose Lisok Paulino in Khartoum in August 2005, she was in the process of leaving for the West. The substantial attention she paid to the security of displaced women in Darfur's displaced camps results from more than empathy and identification; it reflects Paulino's passionate beliefs about citizenship, nationalism, and collective experiences. She offered me a poem that encapsulates her views on the worth of surmounting violence and implementing democratization through mutual acceptance and tolerance:

All of you Sudanese women with tears in your eyes turned to the sky in a large and painful begging, from all parts of Sudan, from peace talks to roundtable conference, from Addis Ababa to Abuja, from Abuja to Nairobi, from Nairobi to Asmara, from Asmara to Cairo, from Cairo to IGAD, mobilizing only men and capitals—Why not mobilize women, children, and old people, who are always yearning for peace?

But you will never see peace

If you don't understand yourselves, if you always fight, if you always hate each other;

If you act like people not from one country;

If you don't work for your country Sudan's own happiness.

Yes, I'm this secular five-letter word. I am not new for you Sudanese people.

Yes, I'm peace, peace, peace. It's me, the softness of your temporary quiet times.

It's me, the soft perfume for thirteen years of your life.

It's me: Love, Respect, Recognition, and Tolerance.

It's me: Freedom, Equality, and Justice. I will raise you Sudanese in front of all nations in the world; I will develop your country, Sudan, and your women and children.

I will quench their thirst, heal their limps, satisfy their hunger, and give them access to power.

I would make Sudanese happy for your whole life if you see me.
I am peace, peace, your intimate friend, Sudanese people.

Rose's poem is part of a tradition of resistance literature, in which Sudanese women poets reflect on the politics of war and peace. In a senior
thesis on women and peace building in Sudan, Joice Michael Khamis
documents the historical role of *Hakamat,* folk singers whose poems and
songs focus on their communities' longing for durable peace (Khamis
2002). When it comes to peacemaking, Sudanese women let their imagi-
nations run wild. Through prose, poetry, storytelling, and singing, these
women are promoting respect for human rights in the country.

The unfolding political subjectivity of Sudanese women in general and
southerners in particular is evident in their various avenues of peacemaking. Women are the main stakeholders in inculcating a culture of peace,
which was defined by the United Nations General Assembly in its 53rd
session as "a set of values, attitudes, traditions, and modes of behavior."
The breadth of this definition suggests that peacemaking begins and cul-
minates in the daily interactions among people in diverse communities
cooperating to achieve common goals.

Abstinence as Resistance

Throughout my conversations with women whose lives have been disrupted by war and now reside in shantytowns, I was awed by their
resourcefulness and imagination in finding ways to generate and enhance
reciprocity among those from different places and faith traditions. I was
especially struck by women's participation in ritualized bodily practices
as a means of effecting reconciliation. Decorating the body with henna,
wearing the *tobe* or *hijab,* and taking a smoke bath, *dukhan,* nurture intimate connections among women in the shantytowns and with their
Arab, Muslim neighbors in the slums. "Victims have much to gain from
being able to let go of hatred, even when the perpetrator is unrepentant,"
writes Martha Minow in *Between Vengeance and Forgiveness: Facing History after Mass Violence* (1998, 19).

The fierce rivalry between the two largest ethnic groups, the Dinka
and the Nuer, is one of the most insistent discords in the southern region. A Human Rights Watch report cited a Nuer chief as saying: "They
used to tell us that the reason why the Nuer and Dinka fight each other
was because we are ignorant. We don't know anything because we are
not educated. But now look at all that killing! This war between Nuer

and Dinka is much worse than anything we experienced in the past. And it is the war of the educated elite—it is not our war at all." This enmity, which escalated considerably in recent years, was a topic of extensive deliberation during the 1999 Wunlit Nuer-Dinka reconciliation conference. Held in Bahr El-Ghazal under the auspices of the New Sudan Council for Churches (NSCC), the People-to-People Peace and Reconciliation Conference provided a space for participants to vent grievances and to formulate long-term strategies to end the raiding of cattle, the capture of women and children, and the destruction of livelihoods. A conference observer started his comments on the peace talks by describing a beautiful scene: "The conference opened out of doors in multi-faith style with Dinka and Nuer spiritual leaders, masters of the fishing spear (Dinka) and earth masters (Nuer), forming a big circle around a tethered white ox Mabior, chanting their desire for him to take away all the bad blood between Nuer and Dinka" (HRW 2003).

Women at the grassroots level have undertaken to reconcile their peoples as well. Achol Cyer Rehan, the director of Women's Association of Gogrial County in southern Sudan, organizes women in their efforts to increase opportunities for economic development, education, and peace building. In 2002, under Rehan's leadership, the Women's Association of Gogrial County partnered with the Boston-based humanitarian group My Sister's Keeper to develop two grinding mill projects in the villages of Panliet and Akan. She has served as a liaison between southern Sudanese villages and soldiers' camps, sending small delegations of women to the camps to advocate an end to the violence. She facilitated dialogues between northern and southern Sudanese women regarding rights to dry season grazing lands. By coming to an agreement in advance, the women avoided a renewal of conflict. In November 2003, she was elected chairwoman of the Women's Association of Bahr El-Ghazal, where she has been able to extend her ingenuity, resourcefulness, and energy to women's associations throughout southern Sudan.

At the conference held by Inclusive Security: Women Waging Peace in 2004, Rehan described the powerful process of peacemaking among Nuer and Dinka women in her home community in Bahr El-Ghazal:

> Women from Dinka and Nuer groups were sick and tired of the fighting between the men in their communities. The Nuer and the Dinka did not see eye to eye. They fought like mad people all the time. They made life difficult for everyone, especially the women. The conflict continued unabated until one day, the women from the quarreling groups sat

together and started to talk. They talked and talked and talked. Finally, they reached a brilliant idea: to stop preparing food and to abstain from having sex with the husbands unless they stop[ped] the ruthless violence. The Dinka men went home in the evening and asked the wives: we want to eat. The women answered by saying they were afraid to go out and especially to go near the river to bring fish. At the same time, the Nuer men noticed that their wives were following the same procedure. This strategy continued for a long time. Finally, the men began to figure out that they were in the same boat when they began to describe the women's fears, and worse, their abstinence, which they couldn't bear. Nuer men too exchanged information and stories about their hunger. In the end, some wise people from the fighting groups decided to send mediators to effect reconciliation. They realized that fighting was not serving their purpose in life. When the women knew and ascertained that the men were indeed making peace, they resumed their duties to collect food, prepare meals, and sleep with their mates when night fell.

Abstaining from sex is a political act that shows that there are other ways of solving conflicts than carrying arms. Within the patriarchal order of things, the Nuer and Dinka women who participated in the boycott have drawn attention to their plight, which otherwise could have been ignored. Their genius in bringing about reconciliation was a tremendous step in resolving conflicts by conversation. This tradition, which is widely practiced in numerous African societies, could not have been revived at a better time. Peace was restored in the village, and everyday business was conducted as it used to be before the unfolding of the intense confrontations. The notion of using sexuality to protest the wide-ranging atrocities in the community is not only a powerful commentary on the women's inner strength but also an embodiment of what Marguerite Waller and Jennifer Rycenga call "frontline feminisms" (2001).

Recuperating the desire of Sudanese women to stimulate reconciliation within their discordant communities make public exemplary ways to negotiate and sustain peace on the ground. Narratives of suffering and victimization under circumstances of violence are central to our understanding of the unfolding of political subjectivity. So are testimonies of women's peacemaking. As Sudanese women living in and out of shantytowns and camps for the internally displaced indicate, peace can be brought about by means of everyday practices, negotiations, and reflections. These efforts attest to the demise of the private sphere, within which women were formerly relegated. The private and public domains are inextricably linked, and the connections become especially visible when circumstances of war and peace challenge the most fundamental assumptions about state and society.   .

Making Connections between Feminism and Peace

The close connections among feminism, peacemaking, and the revolutionary transformation of Sudanese society were central to the thought and action of Fatima Ahmed Ibrahim, the first president of the Sudanese Women's Union (Abusharaf 2004b), and continue to shape feminist praxis today (Abusharaf 2004c). Priscilla Joseph, the Khartoum physician who cofounded the Southern Women's Group for Peace, is active in conflict resolution programs across Sudan. She offers an extended analysis of the centrality of women's advancement to social recovery from the consequences of war and displacement. In her view, the independence that women have been forced to develop should be enhanced by access to resources and extended by their inclusion in political decision making.

> To understand the challenges facing us today, we have to know where we are. We are emerging from war. We have been dispersed. Some of us have been influenced by various cultures different from our own. Those of us who stayed have had to shoulder new responsibilities. Husbands have been away, and roles have shifted. Women found strength and discovered that they can do things. We ask: what is our dream when we move? All women think that life will improve. They think of access to resources, housing, literacy programs, schools for their children, and health care. Women think that they will have space with men on political issues. They want to have a say in the family. They hope that reconciliation will take place even among the various tribal groups within the South. . . .
>
> Women have been grouped into single mothers and widows. The challenge is to create targeted programs for capacity building. Women should be empowered to look after themselves as they have been doing throughout the conflict phase. Rural women have significant problems, including how to succeed in bringing the town to the village. Running water, shelter, electricity will be necessary in order for them to redirect their energies from fetching water to literacy classes, for example. We think that there will be opportunities for business and agriculture. The Government of Sudan should assist returnees by improving communications, transportation, etc. That is how we look at the situation when we discuss return.

I think that women will continue to endure hardships. Social pressures are so great in our society, including arranged marriages, social obligations, and the taxing demands of large extended families. Women are supposed to bow to these pressures. Sometimes the simplest tasks turn into a nightmare. . . . Women are expected to cook for tens of people at a time. They still face the challenge of being accepted by men who are brought up to think that women should serve them unconditionally twenty-four hours a day. Although housewives have their share of troubles, women politicians are facing serious issues as well. Because most of them have been elevated by men, they don't defend other women's agenda for change.

To get somewhere, we have to stress the importance of incorporating affirmative action programs in the current constitution with emphasis on creating laws to prevent discrimination against women and traditional harmful practices such as early marriage and the mistreatment of widows. It is the responsibility of women politicians to purse these changes in our communities. Postconflict capacity-building programs including economic development and literacy must be made available. Education should be made compulsory, and parents who refuse to send girls to school should be brought to court.

I am convinced that the key to women's liberation in our communities is economic empowerment. Special micro-credit programs will be helpful to get women into the market. Women have talents in areas such as farming and food production. These are all central issues to women's advancement in our current situation. The situation of Sudanese women from the rural areas in the North and the South is very similar. That is why continued peace and feminist activism is critical for all Sudanese women.

If we move to the IDPs, the question becomes: What are they going to do now? Can they continue to live and work in Khartoum? Can they find work upon returning to the South? Can they manage to use existing relationships so that they can secure work regardless of their place of residence?

These issues are intimately tied to the implementation of peace and reconciliation. Today, there are active paramilitary groups in the South. We decided to engage most of them in conversations about halting the bloodshed. Civil society organizations also initiated a South-South dialogue to address the conflicting views and restore peace. These measures were undertaken prior to the signing of the formal peace agreement. Again women played a paramount role in conflict resolution, especially in the reconciliation that took place between the Nuer and the Dinka. Now there is a new program in Rumbek . . . [that] offers insights into what it means to be a feminist in a traditional society.

The programs that Kuch and other feminist peacemakers organize seek to empower women to address the problems they now face and to exemplify the equality, mutual respect, and nonviolent processes of negotiation and conflict resolution that they envision as fundamental to the New Sudan.

Listening across Differences

The Women Action Group (WAG), founded in March 1996, facilitates dialogue between women of the Christian South and the Muslim North (WAG 1997, information packet). WAG's activities exemplify what anthropologist Douglas Fry (2005) terms "the human potential for peace." Comprising roughly 50 women from each region, the group designated Lillian Harris to facilitate workshops and discussions pertaining to conflict resolution. WAG demonstrates how conversation can be effectively employed as a means of enhancing understanding. Communication, mutual respect, dialogue, and camaraderie are seen as building blocks of a just society. In a just society, writes John Rawls, "the liberties of equal citizenship are taken as settled; the rights secured by justice are not subject to political bargaining or the calculus of social interests" (1971, 4). The desire to achieve fairness through discussion and acknowledgement of similarities and differences figured prominently in WAG's inaugural workshop. "How we would do this was not clear, but we anticipated that if genuine dialogue—as opposed to debate—became possible within the group, the way forward would likewise become clear," remarked one of WAG's organizers. According to WAG's mission statement, "Efforts to achieve WAG's objectives have employed the methods of personal healing and group reconciliation; venting our own pain, learning to listen sensitively, affirmation of the viewpoints and identity of others and identification of common hopes and concerns. Although enormous patience is sometimes required, we have found that by looking together at our individual and collective pain, we have been able to understand that often our differences actually unite us" (WAG 1997, conference proceedings, 1). Listening and acknowledging the legitimacy of differences occupy center stage in WAG's agenda.

A WAG workshop titled "The Differences Which Unite Us" was organized to inaugurate the art of conversation and listening as useful justice-enhancing mechanisms. Commenting on this event, Harris stressed the value of "listening therapy" in enabling women to voice grievances and search for answers to their predicaments. Finding expression for unresolved emotions and feelings has been identified as top priority. As Harris put it, dialogue seeks "to build bridges between northern and southern women and to promote mutual venting of negative emotions and feelings of anger, pain, confusion, aloneness, and helplessness which arise from the maelstrom of war, displacement, social prejudices, and cultural transition. It was felt that if each side could listen attentively to, accept, and begin to understand the agony of disempowerment of the other, then true mutual healing and group reconciliation would begin" (WAG 1997, conference proceedings, 2–3). This active and empathic listening generated a vision of a democratic path to peace.

The existence of prejudice within ordinary discourse was carefully examined when southern and northern women identified derogatory terms used with reference to each other. Disparaging language and its wider sociopolitical implications furnished the subject matter of "words which divide us," an innovative exercise that offers important insights into the process of peacemaking.

"Words which divide us" were listed as follows: human rights, peace, *jihad, mandu-kuru, kafir,* slavery, Arab, *jallabah, bang-bang* or *gwang-gwang.* The participants divided into two groups of Northerners and two groups of Southerners to define these words and report back. From this group discussion, which lasted about twenty minutes, it emerged that the most divisive words are *kafir* (non-believer), *abd* (slavery), and *jihad* (holy war).

The first group of Northern women regretted the reappearance of such words as *abd* and *kafir,* which they thought were remnants of a dark past. Slavery is a situation of exploitation and racial inequality. There is at present a deliberate effort to deny our African identity by portraying a positive image of what it means to be Arab, while anywhere we go in the Arab world outside Sudan we are called *abd.* The word *jihad* particularly provokes us, because how can we call for peace and call for *jihad?* Statements by the second group of Northern women pointed out that there are different views of these words. For them, peace means no war, no discrimination; *jihad* is fanatic, the elimination of opposition. The first Southern group of women considered that all these words taken in isolation—*jallabah,* Arab, *kafir,* slave—have divided us, but today they have brought us together: we are in harmony here, which means we share commonalities. *Jihad* is used politically today and people say that it signifies struggle. The second group of Southern women considered peace as signifying stability, unity, justice, and living in harmony. *Jihad* is a religious war for conversion to Islam. Slavery is looting for the spread of Islam. *Mandu-kuru* and *bang-bang* are the people moving upstream (Arab or Arabized, of mixed African and Arab ethnicity). Finally, *kafir* is someone who has no religion and will go to hell as long as he is not a Muslim (WAG 1997, conference proceedings, 14–16).

As the conversation drew to a close, both northern and southern women expressed interest in their commonalities as women living under a male-dominated military regime rather than in their ethnolinguistic, religious, cultural, and historical differences. The absence of democracy, sexual inequality, discriminatory laws against women such as the Public Order Act, lack of freedom of expression, shared victimization by war, and the second-class citizenship of all women regardless of their ethnic, religious, or cultural affiliation must be disputed to construct the circumstances of justice that are fundamental to mutual tolerance and the enjoyment of human rights.

Challenging Tradition

The Sudan has been at war with itself since the onset of independence in 1955. The North-South conflict, while the most prominent, is not the only source of turmoil. Recently, the conflict in Darfur has claimed many lives and displaced many people. The Comprehensive Peace Agreement between Khartoum and the SPLM does not speak to the full complexity of the ongoing conflict in Sudan, and the various peace agreements among warring parties in the West have failed to yield positive results. The long history of human rights abuses and the deep ethnic and religious rifts within the country make reconciliation and the transition to peace especially difficult.

Opening up channels of communication and dialogue have been equally significant in more formal discussions about peace. Harvest for Sudan: A Women's Peace Initiative (2000) received considerable support from President Jimmy Carter and former First Lady Rosalind Carter. Sudanese women leaders from the North and South, the Nuba Mountains, the East, and the Ingessana Hills outlined the objectives of Harvest for Sudan: to "give visibility to the impact of the conflict on women and their children; highlight the crucial role of women in promoting conflict resolution, healing and peace building; strengthen the emerging coalition of women for peace in Sudan; formulate strategies for the implementation of the IGAD; launch a women's peace platform for Sudan" (Riak 1995, 2).

During this workshop, participants emphasized that a peaceful life free from violence and access to food, health, and education are basic human rights; and that women have a unique experience in resolving conflicts in the home and at the community level (Riak 1995, 5). The main recommendations for producing a long-lasting and sustainable peace revolve around political, educational, coalition building, and networking strategies. Participants saw political strategies as primary means for mobilizing and empowering women: eliminating political factionalism, formulating clear human rights policies, continuing conversation and dialogue among various women's groups, and appealing to international and transnational bodies to mediate various peace initiatives and processes. Peace education topped the agenda; modes for promoting a culture of peace included the use of drama, music, poems, and songs. Raising awareness of differences among the wider population was also designated as a peace-fostering mechanism. The Harvest for Sudan trained women in negotiating skills as a central component of coalition building, since it allows the exchange of ideas between different women's groups in war zones and among women living in Sudan and abroad.

Women's efforts at reconciliation and problem solving are vital components of peace and reconstruction. Sudan urgently requires a broad, nationwide awareness-raising campaign about women's rights that speaks to men and women as well as young people. Women's land tenure, title, and ownership rights must be clarified and an enforceable legal framework set in place that reconciles competing claims to land and enables women and female-headed households to hold and defend their ownership. It is essential to educate the population about the diversity of customary laws with an eye toward revisiting customs that discriminate against or disadvantage women, such as female genital mutilation.

Women's Visions of Peace

Mary Hillary Wani, a peace activist who works with women to form cooperative savings and credit funds for self-managed enterprises, suggests that Sudanese women's participation in peacemaking is built upon their customary roles in resolving conflicts within their families and communities. "Traditionally, women play a crucial role in resolving conflicts, both within a family and inter-tribally to safeguard the welfare and continuity of the community. The involvement of women in the quest for peace is not coincidental, but is the fulfillment of a role that is deeply rooted in many societies." Rather than defining peace in the abstract, Wani adopts "the definition as projected by the majority of displaced women": "In simple terms, they define peace to mean: security and the right to move without restriction; love, unity, and solidarity; justice, freedom, and the absence of all forms of discrimination; having a house, a job, and land to cultivate; having enough food; being free of disease; the right to education for our children; freedom of worship; the right to our historical heritage; and participation in decisions and plans that affect our lives" (Wani 2001). This practical description of peace delineates the priorities that women believe must be addressed.

In 1997, women from all sides of the fighting and representing a range of nongovernmental organizations and political groups gathered in Nairobi, Kenya, to hammer out a platform for peace negotiations. Mary Hillary Wani summarized the consensus that developed there, which provided a foundation for later peace conferences. "In Nairobi, Sudanese women from the southern and northern sectors met and came up with a minimum agenda for peace, which was developed and firmly elaborated in the Maastricht declaration. There still remains a dire need to develop a common vision and a joint action plan for all women to work towards." The main points included in the declaration are "development of a broad culture of peace at all levels; empowerment of women to contribute to a just and peaceful resolution of the conflict; development of a plan for the implementation of the minimum agenda for peace; education of women in mediation and negotiation to enable effective participation in nonviolent conflict resolution; establishment of links and networks with relevant international organizations and the media, to support and advocate for a just and sustainable peace; establishment of regular meetings with IGAD leaders and the Secretariat for the Sudan peace process to ensure women's perspectives on human security, conflict resolution, and development in Sudan; and representation of women in the negotiations" (Wani 2001).

At the same time that women sought to further the process of peacemaking, they aimed to alleviate the suffering produced by war and displacement. Preserving lives through providing food and medical care to those in combat zones and displaced camps and "bringing this war to an end" were recognized as indissolubly connected. Women sought to draw all sectors of society—men, elders, and children, as well as other women— into the peacemaking process and to train others in conflict resolution. The meeting in Nairobi expressed special concern about young people moving to Western countries to escape the conflict who are unaware of "what awaits them there"; since youth represent the future, it is essential to Sudan that they remain at home and commit themselves to rebuilding the nation.

Wani concluded: "The Sudan is a multi-cultural, multi-ethnic and religiously pluralistic country. To ensure the sustainability of peace, women should strive to create awareness of . . . [and] respect for the various cultures, religions, and ethnic groups; freedom of worship," and tolerance regarding "the question of identity."

> Educational programs for creating awareness and working on [these] points . . . should be introduced and maintained until such a time that the population has rid itself of all prejudices that have been perpetrated deliberately by undermining some sections of the community or, in some instances, as a result of ignorance. The present educational curriculum, from the basic level, is biased towards one culture and religion; the history of the South is at most neglected or misrepresented. To consolidate peace, the curriculum has to be revised. Peace education has to be incorporated at all levels to replace the current war culture that is advocated in the mass media everywhere. Women could start by educating members of their own families, friends, neighbors, and the community at large. (Wani 2001)

A long list of educational venues, media, and strategies followed.

In the end, the advancement of women and the process of peace building are seen as profoundly interconnected goals: "These [programs and activities] will prepare and guarantee the full participation of women and other sections of the community in postwar development; [they] will also build a capacity to deal more constructively with conflicts before they become full-blown" (Wani 2001).

Women's Voice in Formal Peace Forums

One of the most notable formal peace forums took place in Maastricht in the Netherlands, where people from the South, North, East, and West gathered to draw up a declaration supporting peace and buttress their allegiance to dialogue and fruitful exchange. This initiative, which was held on April 13, 2000, consisted of civil society working committees, the National Democratic Alliance, nonpartisan working groups, Nuba women's committees, and SPLM working groups. Created in late 1997 in Khartoum and Nairobi when these various groups were formed by different parties and interest groups, the initiative had a long gestation. The Maastricht forum was an exemplary occasion for forging coalition politics, and participants relied heavily on IGAD, global women leaders, and representatives of international donor bodies, the EU, OAU, the Arab League, and the UN. Central to the building of bridges across ethnic, religious, and political affiliations, the women in this forum stressed the shared predicaments that face women as women. Women are overburdened by the devastating effects of war, yet their ability to draw from a wealth of unconventional methods of conflict resolution is also vital to the visualization of a long-term and all-encompassing plan of action. While the entire draft declaration is a powerful instrument of peacemaking, item four is of special relevance to women.

> We, the Sudanese women, decide to immediately undertake the following actions: develop a broad culture of peace at all levels; empower women to contribute to a just and sustainable peaceful resolution; further develop the Sudanese women's minimum agenda for peace in relation to the declaration of principles; develop a plan for its implementation and communicate its contents to all parties; educate women in mediation [and] negotiation to enable effective participation of women in nonviolent conflict resolution; establish links and networks with relevant international organizations and the media to support and advocate for a just and sustainable peace.

These women see the "culture of peace" not only as a source of benefits for women but as their own creation.

Peace forums have been held in the United States as well as Europe. For example, the organization Inclusive Security: Women Waging Peace hosted sixteen Sudanese women peace builders for meetings, presentations, and events October 8–15, 2004, in Washington, D.C., and New York City (see Abusharaf 2005b). The gathering was intended to raise the voices of Sudanese women advocating that the U.S. government, the United Nations, international governmental and nongovernmental organizations, and think tanks promote the inclusion of women in efforts to bring peace to Sudan. "Peace in Sudan: Women Making the Difference" was an opportunity for Sudanese leaders and other experts to develop concrete recommendations for policy makers. In light of the ongoing challenges in the country, which prevented some parties from meeting directly at home, this forum was a rare opportunity for women to share their views on how to bring peace and stability to Sudan. The participants identified and discussed four major themes that highlight the many obstacles and challenges women face in Sudan's peace process. They suggested ways that major actors, including the Government of Sudan, the Sudan People's Liberation Movement/Army (SPLM/A), regional organizations, the international community, the U.S. government, and civil society and humanitarian organizations, could remedy the situation. They focused on four areas: addressing the root causes of the conflict and promoting the economic empowerment of women; mobilization for negotiations; enabling the resettlement of internally displaced persons and refugees; and addressing the crisis in Darfur. I attended this conference as a concerned Sudanese and also served as rapporteur to aid in the writing of the final recommendations that the delegation produced.

Sudanese women's organizations put forward comprehensive demands to establish structural, procedural, and substantive equality within the peacemaking and national development process, including ensuring that foreign and Sudanese women are represented in all missions, negotiating sessions, and needs-assessment teams sent by foreign governments and international organizations to assist Sudanese peace building; establishing an internationally sponsored commission of inquiry and commission for truth and reconciliation; designing a protocol for accountability and transitional justice mechanisms, especially with regard to gender-based violence; removing impediments to civil society organizations and repealing restrictive laws that inhibit freedom of movement, so that women's NGOs throughout Sudan can work together; establishing mechanisms to clarify and strengthen the roles and relationships among NGOs, civil society, and government entities dedicated to assisting women; convening periodic national women's consultations at which female representatives of the grassroots, government, and nongovernmental organizations throughout Sudan, representing all ethnic and faith-based groups, can discuss shared priorities and concerns; establishing a ministry and presidential adviser for women's affairs to ensure gender mainstreaming; supporting gender training for political parties using national and international experts and national women's organizations; ratification and observance of the Convention on the Eradication of All Forms of Discrimination Against Women (CEDAW) and the UN Convention on the Rights of the Child; raising the minimum age for marriage to eighteen; ensuring that disarmament, demobilization, and reintegration efforts include female ex-soldiers; including women in UN and African Union peacekeeping units; training and involving women in the security sector as police, military, and security officers; monitoring to ensure women are at least half of the beneficiaries of all assistance efforts in all sectors; and ensuring women's access to reproductive health care.

During the Sudanese women's visit to Capitol Hill, Congresswoman Eddie Bernice Johnson (D-TX), a member of the Black Caucus, commented on women's peace-building efforts: "You are making a difference in your communities. Your inspirational stories of reconciliation between former enemies promote a broader understanding of the issues involved around the conflict and the people, particularly women, needed for the resolution. You shine rays of hope for women in other conflict areas and let them know that violence is not the model, but organizing for peace bring[s] women, their families and their communities an indelible peace that everyone need[s] and deserve[s]."[1] One of the participants, Sondra Sudi Opeka, grew up in Khartoum and became actively involved in feminist politics. In response to my inquiries about her work on women's rights in Nairobi and South Sudan, Opeka explained:

I got involved in feminism in 1997, after I visited Southern Sudan with a group of church leaders, who went to different areas in Eastern Equatoria for a needs-assessment mission. I saw the situation of my sisters. I was really touched by it. Immediately, I joined other women's groups upon my return to Nairobi. These groups were focusing on women's rights in Southern Sudan. My strategies for empowering women include awareness raising and education. By letting women know that they have rights and entitlements, they begin to find ways of addressing their own problems and in so doing they will begin to heal. My involvement in the women's rights movement has taught me that women are just as able as men to hold office and make policies as their male counterparts. As peacemakers and as future voters, they are the majority of the population. Women's vote can change the political picture dramatically. Right now, Southern Sudanese women are the most marginalized of the marginalized. Socially, economically, and politically they are severely disadvantaged. War and violence are creating enormous problems. Even as we are entering a period of peace, women in the South have only one commission out of twenty-one commissions, the commission concerning gender and child welfare. You can imagine the extent of the continuing marginalization. Women are certainly capable of holding other offices and assuming other affairs that do not necessarily involve women's issues. This is why addressing the status of women should be situated within political, economic, and social programs. My main occupation right now is to help promote education about justice, democracy, and development through Sudanese Women's Empowerment for Peace. Affirming citizenship and respect for Southern Sudanese women's rights is an utmost priority.

Women in this peace network stressed that increasing to 50 percent the target for women's participation at all levels in all governing and deliberative bodies in Sudan, including land commissions, oil commissions, party lists, and elected and appointed bodies in national, local, and regional governments, both transitional and permanent, should be the uppermost concern to the Government of National Unity.

Sparrows Flying in Pairs and Branches Bending Together

Throughout my conversations with women in Khartoum's shantytowns and camps for internally displaced persons, and with other activists, the call for peace has been positioned at the forefront of their priorities. Above all, women aspire to fashion an environment free of physical, psychological, and symbolic forms of violence. In Soba Aradi, J.Y., a Fujulu Christian who was displaced from her hometown in Yei in 1993, avows: "I pray that peace [will] come so that my family [can] return to their land in the South and live as they did before the war." S.D., a Bari from Western Equatoria, views peace as the only answer to her prayers for stability and opportunity for her children: "The demands of life in Khartoum are difficult. It is becoming worse every day. I am worried that my children will grow up uneducated and lacking any sense of cultural or familial identity. I hope that peace, resettlement in the South, and reunification of families will help me solve these pressing problems." Women in Sudan have demonstrated a commitment to act as agents of change in the continuing peace efforts. Although they have for the most part been excluded from the formal negotiations, Sudanese women in the country and those displaced in neighboring countries have established organizations and networks to spread understanding about the human costs of the war and to demand a comprehensive plan for the implementation of the peace agreement. They are strengthening the constituency for peace throughout the country. It is essential to draw on the assets, experiences, and dedication of these women in order to set into motion a peace-building process that resolves the underlying political problems, addresses ethnic cleansing in Darfur, and builds permanent reconciliation.

Sudanese women's peace activism has been anchored in manifold formal and informal gatherings through which they chart peaceful paths. Recent discussions of transnational feminist thinking and praxis are beginning to take such activism into account. As Michaela di Leonardo put it in her introduction to *Gender at the Crossroads of Knowledge,* women "occupy specific locations in nexuses of multiple stratifications" (1991, 31). Women's investment in peace does not pertain to any "natural" attributes or "maternal" roles but bespeaks their interest in rebuilding community, generating reciprocal exchange, gaining equal citizenship, strengthening governance, and promoting democratization. Women whose lives have been shattered by war and displacement do not seek to replicate the conditions of oppression from which they suffered in the past or the divisions that gave rise to prolonged armed conflict. Their stories, testimonies, and plans for action seek to remedy the conditions within which victimization is produced. Through equitable participatory processes, they seek to remedy both violence and oppression and, in the process, to make peace and promote equality in their nation. Weaving experiences of the past and visions of the future has been important to the feminist project in Sudan. Through systematic interrogation of the material and ideological institutionalization of male dominance, they are positioned to perform a vital role in postconflict society. As gender-based violence, war, and displacement have combined to generate a legion of struggles, women have created new spaces within which political subjectivity and agency are entering the everyday language of struggle for change. As Amartya Sen argues: "The active agency of women cannot, in any serious way, ignore the urgency of rectifying many inequities that blight the well-being of women and subject them to unequal treatment. Thus the agency role must be much concerned with women's well-being also. Similarly, coming from the other end, any practical attempt at enhancing the well-being of women cannot but draw on the agency of women themselves in bringing about such change" (1999, 90).

As catalysts of change, displaced Sudanese women are making considerable contributions to the field of transnational feminisms. Feminism here is seen as a vehicle for solving pragmatic concerns ranging from the institutionalization of women's rights to the creation of accountability mechanisms to end traditions of impunity. Women articulate the varied meanings, uses, and ways of nurturing a culture of peace, and in so doing they are providing new and powerful ways of understanding what an anthropology of war and peacemaking might look like. Whether under a tree in Bahr El-Ghazal or in a luxurious conference hall in Washington,

D.C., whether bathing in smoke or abstaining from sex, these acts have afforded women the opening they need to articulate their collective concerns as both victims and actors, while creating the infrastructure conducive to peace that has been undermined by competing masculinities and extreme circumstances of political violence. In drawing a link between feminism and peace, these women herald momentous transformations in Sudanese society. Through everyday practices and the strategic deployment of the concept of women's rights as human rights, peace feminism is altering the meaning of peace from the mere absence of war to a more inclusive embrace of tolerance and accommodation of difference.

EPILOGUE

"This Is My Country"

On November 1, 2007, on Al Jazeera TV's *This Evening,* correspondent Adil Faris reported from Juba, the capital of Southern Sudan, on a most alluring beauty pageant. For the first time since the Comprehensive Peace Agreement (CPA) was signed, young women representing the ten states of Southern Sudan gathered in Juba.[1] Contestants attired in formal and informal dress and in "traditional" costumes were judged on their beauty, intelligence, and commitment to solving the problems facing youth in Southern Sudan. Each young woman's "folklore, social presence, and past migratory biography" featured prominently, and each was evaluated by the extent to which she embodied her own ethnically specific culture. There was more to this occasion than meets the eye, for it offered an opportunity for commentary on youth culture, social heritage, and politics. Uncertainty about whether stability would prevail in the region was mixed with youthful hopefulness. In Southern Sudan, even the most straightforward of events has been fraught with uncertainty about these communities' very survival, much less their ability to sponsor beauty pageants and other cultural events. Organizers were careful to include contestants from as many ethnic groups as possible. Although the most hotly debated question was whether a Dinka or a Nuer would win,[2] judges and participants were determined that this contest not become yet another arena for competition between these two large ethnocultural groups. The pageant sent a strong message that factional differences should not be allowed to pose obstacles to local diplomacy and intergroup mediation, so it did not mirror the contentious panorama of southern ethnic politics. Rather, the worries it expressed are intertwined with several arrangements sculpting national policies, local governance, and social equity that exemplify the process of transition in a society trying to emerge from the shadows of war.

As I write this epilogue, Sudan remains prominent in the international news media not primarily because of the incomplete implementation of the CPA but because of the continuing conflict in Darfur. On July 14, 2008, President Bashir was named by the International Criminal Court in The Hague as responsible for war crimes and crimes against humanity—specifically, that he "masterminded and implemented a plan to destroy in substantial part" three "tribal groups" in the western region because of their ethnicity.[3] Accusations of genocide hang over Sudan's president and his government. Yet, for many Sudanese, the questions of stability and re-settlement in the South, the role of Southern representatives in the central government, and the planned referendum regarding the future autonomy of Southern Sudan are burning issues. As a southern man observed, "The war in the South was not a primary concern for international activists, unlike the one in Darfur that dominates the media. We are not angry that atrocities in Darfur are very well covered, but we are disappointed that the war in the South was totally ignored." The relationship between Southern Sudan and the northern-dominated government is at the cen-ter of recent political developments. The first vice president of Sudan's Government of National Unity, Sudanese People's Liberation Movement leader Salva Kiir Mayardit, decided to freeze his party's participation in the central government because of the slow implementation of the provi-sions of the Machakos Protocol that formed the basis for the CPA. Re-becca Garang, government minister and widow of John Garang, voiced similar dissatisfaction and called for continued international pressure on the government in Khartoum to honor its commitment to the consolida-tion of the CPA.[4] The protocol and CPA crafted specific principles and procedures to ensure self-governance, the right to self-determination, equitable political participation, women's rights,[5] security, democratiza-tion, and "equalization and allocation of nationally collected revenues." The CPA also delineated measures with respect to transitional processes in Southern Sudan, such as disarmament, demobilization, reconciliation, land ownership, the sharing of oil development and revenues, and rein-tegration of refugees and displaced persons. These provisions taken as a whole are essential to ensure voluntary return to the South. If fully imple-mented, they will support sustainable constitutional options and facilitate ethnic reconciliation.[6]

IDPs express considerable, and understandable, reluctance to return to the South under the prevailing conditions of instability. Stemming the region's continuing loss of population demands major reforms and respect for human rights, as well as a regional and global environment through which positive energy can be channeled for the improvement of the lives of those who have borne the brunt of war. Conditions of possibility for return are hampered by the wars in Darfur[7] and the East and the exclusion of many political players from the peace agreement between the Government of Sudan (GoS) and the Sudanese People's Liberation Movement (SPLM). The high expectations of return that followed the signing of the CPA in January 2005 have diminished markedly (Morris 2007). Only 1.2 million IDPs are reported to have returned to the South; unlike refugees who were staying in camps in neighboring countries, the internally displaced lack support from national and international agencies. These obstacles were corroborated by the deputy governor of Rumbek in response to my question about his government's plans for returnees. He enumerated substantial impediments related to the limited absorptive capacity of Rumbek, its desperate need for services and funding, difficult intercommunity conflicts, and serious problems of land-mine clearing, the deadly legacy of the fact that during the prolonged civil war Rumbek was a garrison town.

These difficulties deter IDPs from acting on their long-held desires to return to the South. The impossibility of the situation there was reflected in an interview I conducted with a social worker in Mayo, Khartoum, in 2005 about residents' responses to the CPA. She explained: "People are extremely relieved about it. They are very willing to go back. The problem is that buses leave Mayo for Southern Sudan packed with people; but the same buses come back packed with people fleeing the South." The chronic inattentiveness to IDPs' interests intensifies their quandary about returning. IDPs are not greeted with open arms. Their social personhood is subject to hostile scrutiny by those who never left, who see the IDP as the quintessential persona non grata and as "lizard tails" that can never be reattached to the body from which they had been severed. Graham Wood and Jake Phelan's investigation of Western Equatoria, the focal point for refugees repatriating from Uganda, the Central African Republic, and the Democratic Republic of Congo, reveals deep divisions regarding the potential "effects of returns on physical resources, how 'stayees' perceive returnees and the potential fault lines between those who stayed, those who fought and those who left" (2006, 49).

In speculations about southerners' desire to return, the concept of home held by Sudan's refugees and IDPs goes unheeded, and experiences of loss and healing are reduced to their bare bones. The intricacies of the decision to stay put or go back were articulated in a conversation I had with a refugee in a Rumbek marketplace. David, who had arrived in the town from Kakuma camp in Kenya to "see for himself" what repatriation might entail, told me that he left his family behind in Kakuma because the situation in the South is uncertain and far from conducive to return. He was planning to go to Juba to inspect the possibilities of resettling there instead, since that town is undergoing rebuilding. Relationships between place and identity in the context of prolonged residence elsewhere are constantly measured by IDPs and refugees like David, who are all too aware that the road to return is difficult.

In May 2006, when I was fortunate to visit Rumbek, a town in the Lakes State in Southern Sudan, I glimpsed the realities of life in a community from which IDPs and refugees have come (see Brookings Institution 2002). A useful description of the place was provided in a Rift Valley Institute course bulletin: "The town of Rumbek traced its evolution to the days when it used to be a *zeriba,* a fortified camp, established by ivory and slave traders in 1850s. It was later controlled by the Turco-Egyptian State during the 1860s and 1887. The town enjoyed a rich history and its name was taken from a local chief. The most recent history of Rumbek shows that it was briefly captured by SPLA in 1986 and recaptured in 1997. It assumed a role of an administrative centre and indeed the political centre of South Sudan under SPLA control" (2006, 8–9). To a visitor's eye, not only has the town been permanently marked by political violence, but the busy trade for which the town was known is at a complete standstill. Only a place that was not so entirely destroyed could seem more deserted. The roads are quiet, save for a few UN and other humanitarian aid vehicles. Local men ride beautifully decorated bikes or motorcycles, while women and children walk long distances. All are trying to outwit the myriad visible difficulties and invisible dangers that confront them.

Along with other members of my group, I paid a visit to a nearby Dinka shrine to learn about venerated ritual practices, such as sacrifices to deities to protect the community and bless it with abundance. These rituals are customarily performed by the highly revered Spear-master. The Spear-master of this shrine happened to be in Khartoum, but a welcoming ceremony proceeded. During this visit, I observed creolization from Arabic mixing with local languages. Anthropologist John Ryle has argued compellingly that Arabic can be counted as one of the numerous Southern Sudanese local languages (2005). In addition to the *tobe,* which is worn along with other forms of dress, the Muslim call to prayer is heard at dawn from a local mosque. I was told the mosque was founded by a Muslim Dinka, but the congregation consists of northern and southern Sudanese Muslims, Somalis, and Indians.

In Rumbek, I was reunited with my friend Karak Nayok, founder of DIAR, an organization that takes its name from the Dinka word for women. Karak repatriated with her family to Rumbek in 2005 after the signing of the CPA and is enraptured at being back in the South. Since her return, she joined a major NGO and resumed her own work in DIAR, through which she arranged an extraordinary celebration of International Women's Day. The women of Rumbek paraded through the streets holding banners hailing the New Sudan and demanding programs to end domestic violence, sexual abuse, poverty, and HIV/AIDS. Alas, Karak's family is not as euphoric. Karak spoke eloquently about her family members' various and complex responses to repatriation. "My mother is not excited about our return. She feels alienated from the Agar Dinka who constitute large numbers in our neighborhood. We are Attar [Dinka] from Upper Nile. She says she felt more at home in Khartoum. My teenage sister is also upset. She misses life in the city. As for my children, they too are not happy, although they have started to accept their new life. My son asked me one day why we returned. I told him this is our land, it is your land. He responded, 'What do you do with it?'"

What can be done with land that has been looted and left uncultivated? The question of material resources is a high priority, since it represents not only a point of friction but also a building block for overcoming the hostility among diverse communities that is exacerbated by competition. The settlement of disputes over access to scarce resources requires revamping current policies regarding postconflict reconstruction through observing the rule of law and establishing good governance and accountability mechanisms. It takes time for local diplomacy and reconciliation processes to emerge in these unstable settings.

This ethnography documents displaced women's refusal to concede defeat in the face of their extraordinary troubles. Their forced removal from kin networks has increased their autonomy, sharpened their subjectivity, and required them to redefine home. Life in the shantytown is a relentless struggle for self-definition as women forge new ties and seek new avenues for inclusion. The fact that IDPs have lost relatives and friends to war makes the decision to return far more emotionally taxing. To those who have survived the massacre of their family members, return is tantamount to "reunification with graves." Their narratives and silences about their experiences of displacement reveal a deep sense of loss.

The emotional, interpersonal, and cultural as well as material resources of southern communities have been irreparably torn by war. D. J. Parkins has pointed out that forced migration is quite different from voluntary migration, not only because the displaced lack material resources but also because "the very foundation of their societies" has been disrupted; they are required "either to re-establish or re-define personal and collective origins" (1999, 303). Sudanese IDPs had no opportunity to bring anything, whether useful or symbolic, when they fled their shattered homes. Traditions incurred a massive blow. People were bereaved of many social and cultural practices, including age classes, clan classifications, childbirth rituals, kinship rules, language,[8] betrothal and marriage rituals, laws regulating inheritance and property ownership, rules of compensation for injury, distribution of resources, totems, magic, oath taking, rainmaking and sacrifice, supreme beings and guardian spirits, initiation, burial, and meals shared around the evening fire.[9]

Because displaced women have been affected by war differently than men, they remain the main stakeholders in community reconstitution and nation building. They search for effective strategies for reintegration and resettlement that are consistent with their own visions for the future. The late Sergio de Mello articulated the guiding principles: "Internally displaced persons [and refugees] shall enjoy in full equality, the same rights and freedoms under international and domestic law as do other persons in their country. They shall not be discriminated against in the enjoyment of any rights and freedoms on the ground that they are internally displaced" (UNHRC 1998b). Espousing these principles, Sudanese women peace activists drafted policy recommendations to ensure the successful return, resettlement, and reintegration of refugees and IDPs in their home communities.

Restoring the balance that John Garang intended in his vision of the New Sudan is vital to the welfare of all Sudanese. It not only acknowledges the equality of all Sudanese but posits a new relationship between the center, *el-markaz,* and the periphery, known in political discourse as *el-hamish,* the margin. This process as inscribed in the CPA takes into account the diversity of cultures, modes of knowing, and religions in Sudan and creates the conditions of possibility for a society that transcends the narrowness of "the Civilizational Project" that has imposed Arabization and Islamization on indigenous peoples with a myriad of distinct cultures, religions, and languages.

From Khartoum to Kakuma, IDPs and refugees constantly recalibrate relationships between place and identity in the context of prolonged displacement. In many cases, the southern villages from which they were forcibly removed are no longer home, both because these communities were destroyed by war and because displaced persons have adapted to their new places of residence. Mark, a young Dinka, told me in 2004, before the CPA was declared: "When people go back, they are happy to be reunited with family and friends. When I left, I did so alone. My parents died, our neighbors ran away too. My childhood friends fled also. If I go [back], who is going to welcome me?" What IDPs have made of their existence outside Southern Sudan is the most significant aspect of their experiences, notwithstanding the formidable difficulties they still face. As waves of forced migrants continue to arrive in Khartoum because of the Darfur crisis, the lack of infrastructure in the South, and the political disputes in the East, IDPs develop a shared consciousness vis-à-vis the overpowering politics of the state. With the formation of the Government of National Unity, these concerns became even more significant, as IDPs see little progress in their shared struggle for dignity and restoration.

A.D., an ethnic Balanda woman living in Khartoum, articulates the attitude of many southern IDPs in the North toward the question of repatriation.

> Last week I was running errands in Khartoum marketplace. I was stopped as I was entering the shop by a young northern lady carrying papers in her hands. She told me, "Sister, I am a college student and I am studying the return migration to the South. Are you going back now peace has been achieved?" I was not happy about this question. I just told her, "This is my country. Khartoum is the capital of Sudan and I am Sudanese. I can live wherever I choose to live, just like you. You may ask a foreigner, an Ethiopian or a Palestinian, whether they will go back home, but you can't ask someone from the same country." I said those words and left.

A.D. seeks acknowledgment of her right as a citizen to continued residence in the capital city; her consciousness also reflects the local connections she has developed over time.

The sense of belonging articulated by IDPs demonstrates that the desire for repatriation is not unanimous among southerners living in the capital. Comparison with Iranian refugees who settled in Sweden is instructive, despite the marked differences in the two groups' situations. Refugees' concepts of home and return shifted as they recognized that their exile was not temporary; many become involved in Swedish society and politics. Other examples of transformation in concepts of home, recalibration of citizenship, and reintegration abound (see Graham and Khosravi 1997). Whether a shantytown or a community of exiles, these locations are converted into worlds in motion through the agency of the displaced. Composing a life amid change and uncertainty, they carry out systematic critiques of society in ways that transcend essentialist notions of identity and show that selves are fundamentally "experiential concepts" (Erchak 1992).

How, then, did the women whose voices and viewpoints are recorded and analyzed in this ethnography summon the resources needed to navigate through a complex scene of political violence, and in what ways have they responded to these dilemmas? What does life in Izzbba tell us about African civil wars, the social world of squatters and shantytown dwellers, and sustained individual and collective efforts to alter the organizing principles of society? An urgent anthropological lens focused on practical strategies and visions of moving forward illuminates IDPs' stubborn refusal to concede defeat in the face of daunting difficulties and highlights what they have accomplished through the creation of urban networks. Despite their pervasive sense of loss, processes of individualization and the construction of group solidarities occur in a complementary manner. Against all odds, the subjects of this ethnography defy stereotypical representations of women as passive victims of war and oppression; they refuse to inhabit and explicitly repudiate this subject position. Instead of dwelling on injuries that beleaguer their lives, they have posed questions, confronted unjust treatment, and reclaimed their enormous power as breadwinners and guardians.

This point was compellingly rendered in a story told by an Azande woman who estimated her age as about fifty:

> Since I arrived many years ago, I have been working hard in Khartoum as a domestic. I still live in Mandela and spend a long time getting to work and returning after sunset. My husband stays home, drunk. He got used to beating me up, especially when he is drunk, and that means all the time. I asked myself: Mary, aren't you the one who is supporting this bastard? Isn't he eating and getting drunk with your money? I got out and fetched the largest stick I could find. I started to beat him up so severely until he started to crawl on his stomach. I wish I did this earlier, but I think that when he bit me on the face I started to take my revenge. Now he is silent.

Mary's story skillfully triangulates forced migration, change in gender relations, and the active reassessment of the self in northern Sudan, as it turns on challenging the male authority that derived from the husband's identity as provider. In a situation where she struggles daily in a casual labor market characteristic of the slums, she rejects what had been regarded as an accepted Azande practice of the husband disciplining the wife.

Displacement alters life experiences and redefines cultural dynamics, among other crucial dimensions of the body politic. These concrete forms of empowerment have propelled these women to analyze culturally sanctioned discriminatory practices and critique the unfair mind-sets that governed time-honored and customary rules of conduct. Without romanticizing the gains resulting from displacement, which came at the cost of great pain and irreparable losses, I emphasize that the experiences displaced women recounted worked in fascinating ways to increase their relative autonomy and sharpen their ideas on previously held interpretive and intersubjective frames of reference. Constructing mutual aid networks, revisiting traditions, and making consistent local efforts at reconciliation are all interwoven in practice. Through economic and social ties among one another and with their new neighbors, women in Izzbba have attained knowledge of city life and work and adopted innovations ranging from bodily rituals to informed feminist praxis. IDPs' narratives are chronicles of convalescence and change that defy simplistic notions of refugees and IDPs as victims in locations of organized violence. Building bridges across environment and culture is a sign of hope when the state has failed to attain this goal.

Equally important, this ethnography raises the question as to how to explain the intermingling of culture and politics in the urban milieu of squatter settlements. IDPs' adoption and rejection of gendered ritual practices and their explanations for their decisions attest to the dialectic between ruptures and continuities in this dynamic setting. The espousal of new modes of dress and adornment and of practices of permanent bodily alteration entails a certain level of recovery of gendered aesthetics regarding the embodied self while shedding light on very specific and selective forms of adaptability and transformation. These processes were uncovered through multiple narratives and interpretive commentaries about these practices in quite different cultural settings, showing their importance for understanding the complexity and heterogeneity of Sudanese society as a whole. In focusing on traditions of ritual bodily modification, this ethnography moves beyond stereotypical representations of cultural traditions as "frozen in time," fixed in form and continuing by inertia. As Eric Hobsbawm and Terence Ranger (1992) have pointed out and numerous anthropological investigations illustrate, tradition is constantly invented and reinvented in light of changing circumstances. In *Border Crossings* Henry Giroux cautions against treating culture as "a warehouse filled with the goods of antiquity, waiting patiently to be distributed anew to each generation" (1992, 185). In presenting the cultural moves made by IDPs in their full complexity, this work shows how displacement offers a fertile space within which cultural production and reproduction are mapped out in a society in flux. In Sudanese squatter settlements, culture and politics are interconnected fields of negotiation. These emergent practices and identities are major acts of transformation, illuminating the dynamism, contingency, and malleability of selfhood for purposes of restoring cohesion and balance. Cultural traditions as emblems of meaning making cannot be isolated from the implementation of other visions of community and mutual aid, such as rotating credit associations, *kashifs,* or donations during times of need among the urban poor. The dynamic interaction of these various relationships is critical for grasping the politics of tradition and its re-creation in situations of marginality and vulnerability. In *Black Atlantic Religion,* J. Lorand Matory raises a fundamental question: "Why [do] certain rubrics and visions of community appear to prevail over others at a given moment in a given place?" He answers, "Any given imagination of community will favor strategic interests over others" (2005, 89). Sudanese IDPs find ways for understanding these interests, alliances, contestations, and strategies for the future, all filtered through their forced migratory experiences, developing new notions of mobility, citizenship, and nation building at the microlevel of a shantytown.

Forming and nourishing networks not only helps in expressing bereavement to others with similar experiences but facilitates the formation of long-lasting ties that link IDPs to their hosts. These connections are a vital aspect of how IDPs remake home. Prolonged residence in the shantytowns has generated multiple forms of identification. Daily interactions tend to de-emphasize both distinctions between Arabs and Africans and distinctions among southerners from backgrounds marked by intolerance of ethnic difference and even interethnic violence. The confluence of interests and mutual concerns in situations of extreme deprivation and dramatic political upheaval means that, despite paradoxes and contradictions, IDPs work with their differences rather than remaining as fractured as they were on arrival.

While day-to-day interactions and social networks offer displaced women the tools with which to work against marginality, we must identify as straightforwardly and clearly as possible the specificity of the social worlds of Izzbba residents. V.R., a twenty-three-year-old from Bahr-el-Ghazal who works as an HIV/AIDS prevention officer at the Sudan Council of Churches, confirms that learning Arabic is not only a necessary and self-evident step in this setting but a strategy that elders had constantly emphasized as crucial to "learning about the home you found yourself in right now." V.R. is an active member in her small local parish, where IDPs from Equatoria and Bahr-el-Ghazal congregate for worship, celebratory rituals, and other social gatherings. The predominance of the Arabic language in these services has been one of the most prominent characteristics of worship there. She emphasizes that IDPs have made lives in Khartoum and seek to be recognized as citizens whether or not they choose repatriation to the South. The sentiments that attest to the impressive metamorphosis of the squatter settlement into home show how identities and relationships have been transformed by local peacemaking and progressive politics.

In Izzbba, ties come to bind the urban poor together, irrespective of cultural difference, as women invent new forms of belonging and imbue them with special importance. Yearnings for peace and the implementation of everyday mediations make Sudanese shantytowns zones of relative tranquility compared to similar localities elsewhere. Rather than simply revealing the destructive impact of forced migration on cultural traditions, the words and actions of displaced women illuminate the mitigation of marginality through improvisation and adaptability in response to the challenges of daily life. The material deprivation and political disempowerment of displaced southern Sudanese women in the capital city are the direct outcome of differential power structures and institutionalized hierarchies. In Izzbba, IDPs forge transformative practices that address the central conundrums of a society in transition. In urban spaces where the disfranchisement of others from North, South, East, and West is visible for everyone to see, war-displaced people become adept in making distinctions between government policies and practices and the values and actions of ordinary people.

Given the current sociopolitical circumstances and the fluidity of IDPs' ideas of home and place, this ethnography shifts debates about IDPs' lives from reiterating their basic needs to understanding the specific actions women undertake to locate resources, construct communities of their own, circumvent subordination, and reinvent lives shattered by one of the bloodiest wars in African history. Michael Ignatieff is correct to argue that "the domain of politics ought to be the satisfaction of people's expressed desires, rather than an enactment of some vision of what their needs might be" (1984, 135). This orientation invites us to elucidate the social dynamics that assist IDPs and to overcome reductive ways of explaining refugees' and IDP identities' as irremediably sundered. Julie Peteet perceptively observes that "multiple contexts are involved in the production of a refugee camp, and they themselves generate ever mutating contexts in their local, regional and global environments" (2005, 94). So too, despite low morale and considerable concern that the possibility of the New Sudan may have been buried with John Garang, IDPs do not regard the future as foreclosed. In daily life in Izzbba, pessimism is a challenge but by no means a fate. A non-Sudanese who comes from a postcolonial nation deeply scarred by warfare and ethnoreligious conflict offered this advice when interviewed on Al Jazeera TV: "One has to ride more than one horse at a time and believe in the immense possibilities of dialogue." Self and space in Izzbba undergo careful reconfiguration; both identity and home are dramatically altered, with significances that expand beyond the shantytown.

As places of residence, squatter settlements are locations where citizenship is remapped and everyday social relations enact tolerant, inclusive notions of community and nation unfathomable within the narrow horizons of political elites. This observation is not a one-way street traveled solely by southerners. Northerners and Darfurians on various occasions have cited one another's suffering as legitimate cause for change and are as favorably disposed to southerners' remaining in the capital as are southerners themselves. The confluence of interests and mutual concerns in situations of deprivation and political upheaval shows how these communities come together in the first place and how despite conflicts they work to ameliorate the persistent violation of their social, civil, and political rights. The lessons learned from the narratives recounted here can be employed as urgently as possible by policy makers and parliamentarians, community leaders, human rights NGOs, academics, and all concerned citizens who seek to usher in a new kind of politics in a country that seems to have lost its way.

Like numerous squatter settlements, Izzbba is becoming a site of innovation where multiple genres of accommodation and contestation are integral parts of everyday life. Like all theaters, they are places where spectacle, fertile imagination, and practical creativity generate eloquent forms of expression and where narratives and dialogues facilitate conflict mediation. Apprehension about the government's Arabization and Islamization project, which is propagated through mass media and political rhetoric, is widely shared. However, IDPs do not confuse government campaigns with what other Arabized Sudanese people think. Displaced women's voices interrogate the pervasive representation of "the South" as a singularly monolithic entity and "the North" as an embodiment of an Arab supremacist ideology. The peaceful coexistence of the displaced and their impoverished hosts offers commanding testimony to these understandings. Elsewhere (Abusharaf 2002), I have argued that the reinvention of Sudanese identities in diaspora communities is a potentially liberating site for honing visions of citizenship in a state under siege. Holding fast to hope despite their consciousness of daunting obstacles, Sudanese people as a whole and southerners in particular are searching for the tranquility that allows life to proceed normally, whether appreciating an ethnoculturally diverse beauty contest or viewing the return of a large herd of elephants to Opekoloe after a long disappearance as a wondrous sign of peace.[10]

APPENDIX A

Primary Informants

Names or initials are listed in order of first appearance in the text.

INTRODUCTION

Angelina Bortolo Odengala
> Balanda, from Deim Zubeir neighborhood in Wau, Bahr El-Ghazal; Christian; housekeeper at Catholic parish in Khartoum.

Christina Dudu
> Active in Sudan Council of Churches, formerly employed in its primary health care department; graduated in 1991 from College of Natural Resources of Juba University in Khartoum; owns tailoring shop in Khartoum.

L.K.
> From Niyala in Darfur, Western Sudan; moved to Khartoum in 1996 to look for work; has some family members nearby; only two of her nine children have survived; converted to Christianity after displacement.

CHAPTER ONE

Rose Lisok Paulino
> A southerner, but raised in the North, fluent in Arabic; graduated from Ahfad University for Women; worked in rural development projects with EU support; recently founded Eve, a women's organization based in Khartoum.

J.Y.
> Fujulu; Christian; displaced from Juba, Equatoria, in 1984, arrived in Khartoum at thirteen in 1993.

T.P.
> Christian Kuku from Kajo Kaji, Equatoria; in Khartoum since 1984; moved away from relatives to join her husband; lost eldest child.

CHAPTER TWO

C.W.
> Dinka; fled war in 1983; widowed; lives in Soba Aradi; Christian; formerly worked for St. Phillip's Church, which runs a school and clinic in the camp; speaks fluent Arabic but is a critic of Arabization.

Philister Baya

> From Mundri, Western Equatoria; brought up in exile in Uganda and completed primary and secondary education there, received diplomas in secretarial studies from Kianda College in Nairobi in 1978 and in development administration from South Devon College, UK, in 1984; now assistant director for administration of Ivory Bank; women's rights activist. Family repatriated to former home in Southern Sudan after 1972 agreement; joined Southern Region civil service in Juba circa 1978; displaced again to Khartoum in 1987 when Mundri, her hometown, changed hands; after fighting between the army and SPLA in Rokon killed many civilians, including her father, sister, and cousin, she brought surviving family members to join her in Khartoum; worked in the Council for the South until it was dissolved in 1991.

S.P.L.

> From Juba; had been a cleaner for the Ministry of Education; was forced to leave husband and household behind but was later reunited with husband; arrived in Khartoum in 2000; converted to Christianity after displacement.

Priscilla Joseph

> From Bahr El-Ghazal; educated in Khartoum; M.D., practiced as physician in Khartoum before entering politics; MP in Government of National Unity, now serving as director for the Women's Rights Project; member of the Peace and Justice Committee of the Sudan Council of Churches; one of twelve executive committee members of the Southern Women's Group for Peace.

Karak Maylik Nyok

> Upper Nile Dinka from Liri, in the Nuba Mountains, South Kordofan; displaced by war in 1986 to Kadogli, then separated from family to continue her education in Khartoum; lived in slums, shantytowns, and camps; was married; recruited and trained by International Rescue Committee as literacy teacher; founded FACT, a CBO that serves displaced women.

Kezia Layinwa Nicodemus ("Mama" Kezia)

> From Maridi, Equatoria; refugee in Nairobi, then came to Khartoum; was a teacher, where she acquired the nickname "Mama"; serves without salary as commissioner of Women, Gender, and Child Welfare for SPLM; active in Women Waging Peace.

A.L.

> Kuku; displaced from Kajo Kaji, near Nimule in Equatoria, to Khartoum in 1997; converted to Islam after displacement.

T.P.M.

> Displaced from Equatoria to Khartoum twenty years ago.

D.K.

> Fujulu displaced from Juba; Christian; midwife, or traditional birth attendant.

K.J.

Displaced from Bahr El-Ghazal; now twenty-five.

T.J.

Dinka; displaced in 1999; now twenty-nine.

C.J.

Koko; displaced from Kajo Kaji; to Khartoum in 1986; now fifty-five.

Joshua Diu

Male principal of remedial secondary school in Jabbrra, Khartoum.

E.K.

Forty-five-year-old Kuku Christian from Bahr El-Jebel displaced to Khartoum in 1995.

G.H.M

Dinka; in Khartoum since 1983; now thirty.

V.R.

Twenty-three-year-old Dinka woman residing in Soba Aradi.

M.A.

Displaced from Yei, Bahr El-Jebel, in 1992; now thirty-four.

C.D.

Kuku; Christian; moved from Juba to Khartoum in 2000 because of the war; previously a typist; thirty-three.

S.M.

Non-Muslim woman who arrived in Khartoum in 1996.

M.M.

Lokoya Christian from Juba; husband had been a bookkeeper; children were in missionary schools; arrived in Khartoum in 1996, with her husband who was a student; left relatives and property behind; finds life in Khartoum difficult financially and culturally.

N.L.M.

Has been separated from her husband since she left Kopoeta, Equatoria, with her son in 1989; now sixty.

CHAPTER THREE

Vivian

Twenty-three-year-old Izzbba resident.

W.B.

Shilluk woman from Malkal living in Izzbba.

O.E.O.

Christian Acholi who moved to Khartoum from Torit-Tusa, Equatoria, in 1993.

B.L.

Fujulu; was circumcised as part of conversion to Islam.

L.N.

Christian from Bari; moved from Juba to Khartoum with husband in 1999; now divorced.

F.M.

Christian from Juba; circumcised in preparation for marriage to Muslim northerner.

M.J.

Christian from Bahr El-Ghazal; moved to Kosti, then Juba; nurse employed in the camp; was circumcised after childbirth; now divorced.

S.S.

Displaced from Nuba Mountains; to Khartoum 1994; Christian; sister circumcised.

R.A.

Twenty-eight-year-old Dinka woman displaced from Bor, Upper Nile/ Jongli, in 1990; uncircumcised.

H.L.

Christian Bari from Juba, arrived in Khartoum with her northern Muslim husband in 1990; uncircumcised.

T.M.

Forty-seven-year old Dinka man; social worker in Khartoum.

CHAPTER FOUR

Awut Deng Acuil

Member of SPLM delegation at peace talks sponsored by International Governmental Authority; cofounder of Sudanese Catholic Bishops Regional Conference, Sudanese Women's Association in Nairobi, and Sudanese Women's Voice for Peace; established Pankar Peace and Good Governance Grassroots Initiative; served as secretary of information for the West Bank Peace Council in Bahr El-Ghazal region; active in Woman Waging Peace.

Suzanne Samson Jambo

NGO coordinator for New Sudanese Indigenous Network, comprising forty-two Southern Sudanese nongovernmental organizations; holds professional degrees in law and applied social sciences; principal investigator and author of *Overcoming Gender Conflict and Bias: The Case of New Sudan Women and Girls* (2001).

Agnes Nyoka

Refugee in Nairobi; coordinator of Sudanese Women's Empowerment for Peace; participated in Ethiopia-Sudan Development Marketplace and Knowledge Forum in February 2003 representing the Sudanese Women's Mission for Peace; also affiliated with the Sudanese Women's Christian Mission for Peace.

Achol Cyer Rehan

Director of Women's Associations of Gogrial County and chair of this group in Bahr El-Ghazal; organized programs to reconcile Nuer and Dinka; worked with support from Gloria Hammond, M.D., and minister in Roxbury, Massachusetts, U.S.A., and "My Sister's Keeper"; served as liaison between soldiers' camps and local women's peace groups.

Mary Hillary Wani
> Peace activist; Dinka origin; works with International Rescue Committee in Sudan helping groups of displaced women form self-managed savings and credit funds; educated at Juba University, M.S. in Development Planning from University of Khartoum.

Sondra Sudi Opeka
> Grew up in Khartoum, from prominent political family, feminist peace activist; now based in Nairobi.

J.Y.
> Fuluju Christian displaced from Yei in 1991.

S.D.
> Bari-speaking Christian displaced from Kapoeta in Western Equatoria.

EPILOGUE

A.D.
> Ethnic Balanda living in Khartoum.

Anonymous
> Azande woman, about fifty years old, living in Mandela camp in Khartoum and working as a domestic.

V.R.
> Twenty-three-year-old from Bahr-el-Ghazal who works as an HIV/AIDS prevention officer for the Sudan Council of Churches.

Camps and Shantytowns in Greater Khartoum, Sudan

Angola
> Shantytown settled by IDPs from Kordofan; partially demolished in 1994; no relation to the African nation of the same name.

Dar El Salaam
> Government-run camp to the north of the capital, near Omdurman; very large, as IDPs from other camps have been moved there; name means "house of peace" in Arabic.

El-Baraka
> Shantytown demolished by government, across the river from Haj Yousif.

El Fateh
> Government-run camps in the desert, constructed in 2005.

Jebel Awlia
> Government-run camp southeast of the capital; houses mostly IDPs from the South and the Nuba Mountains, as well as some IDPs evicted from Mayo; residents here were evicted after much of the land was turned over to private agricultural development.

Mandela
> Squatter settlement near Mayo; houses mostly Dinka people from the Nuba Mountains in South Kordofan; named after Nelson Mandela.

Marzug
> Shantytown.

Mayo
> Government-run camp south of the capital close to Mandela; houses IDPs from the South and the Nuba Mountains (Darfurians who took refuge there in 2004 were forcibly evicted after protest meeting); some IDPs have purchased or been allocated land nearby; Mayo is a common family name in Southern Sudan.

Ras El-Shaittan
> Shantytown.

Shikan
> Shantytown from which IDPs were relocated to El Fateh in August 2005.

Soba Aradi
> Shantytown near Salaama; houses IDPs from Darfur, as well as the South and Nuba Mountains.

Takamul

>Shantytown demolished by government; near Haj Yousif, also demolished by government in 1998.

Wad El-Bashir

>Government-run camp to the northeast of the capital, just southwest of Omdurman, near Dar El Salaam; an equal number of displaced persons live in squatter settlements adjacent to this camp.

Zaglona

>Shantytown demolished by government after a year.

Profile of Women in Izzbba

Based on 2001 survey of 71 shantytown residents.

ETHNIC ORIGIN	%
Nuba	23.6
Fur	16.1
Arab	15.1
Dinka	14.1
Shilluk	9.5
Nuer	5.5
Bari	4.5
Fonj	4.0
Acholi	3.0
Moro	1.0
Zande	1.0
Latuka	1.0
Firteet	1.0
Non-Sudanese	0.5

Ethnic groups represented in Izzbba include Acholi, Anyuak, Azande, Baka, Balanda, Bari, Berta, Bongo, Bor, Didinga, Dinka, Kakwa, Karamojo, Koma, Kwkwu, Lango, Lotuho, Lotuka, Luwo, Madi, Mangbetu, Moru, Mundu, Murle, Nuer, Shilluk, Sere, Turkana, and Uduk.

AGE GROUP	%
15–25	21.7
26–35	27.5
Older than 35	50.8

MARITAL STATUS	%
Married	86.3
Widowed	9.1
Divorced	4.6

RELIGION	%
Christian	93.0
Muslim	7.0

Note: Some persons who affiliate with one of these world religions also hold Noble Spiritual Beliefs.

EDUCATION	%
None	21.2
Primary	38.0
Secondary	22.5
Postsecondary	18.3

MAIN REASON FOR MIGRATION	%
War	56.7
Employment	10.0
Family	25.0
Education	8.3

RELATIONSHIPS WITH DISPLACED KIN AND NEW NEIGHBORS	%
Some kin live nearby	79.3
Family composition changed because of displacement	93.0
Interact with northerners	62.9

NOTES

All documents identified by SAD number are from the Sudan Special Archives in the Palace Green Library, Durham University, United Kingdom. Most collections contain the official and personal papers of members of the British administration in the Sudan and include writings by several authors. *Sudan Notes & Records,* a periodical, began in 1918 as an informal exchange of ethnographic observations among British district officials; later on, Sudanese also contributed. It ended with Sudan's independence in 1965.

INTRODUCTION

1. For information on squatter settlements and government-run camps, see appendix B. For demographic data on the residents of the shantytown I call Izzbba, see appendix C.

2. This ethnography has benefited tremendously from my previous work (1984–1986) as a program officer of the Sudan Development Corporation with displaced Darfurians who fled the environmental disasters in the region during the mid-1980s. This longer-term, broader context is important for understanding the nature of displacement in Sudan and the varied responses of displaced persons to their predicaments.

3. This pseudonym was chosen at random from a pool of common Sudanese place-names in order to conceal the identity of the shantytown.

4. For brief biographies of primary informants, see appendix A.

5. On the multifarious history of feminist ethnography, see Visweswaran (1997).

6. Refugees who cross internationally recognized boundaries garner more attention because they disrupt the fragile economies and threaten the political stability of neighboring nation-states. Comparatively little is said about the much more numerous IDPs caught in a complex emergency, despite their trials and travails and the frightening neglect of their most basic of needs. Even more glaring is the glossing-over of the experiences of displaced women as gendered bodies besieged by war. Not only is rape an instrument of war, but women whose families and villages have been destroyed and are fleeing through unfamiliar territory are especially vulnerable to sexual violation. When women's victimization is acknowledged, all too often commentators condescendingly presume that they are without reflexive self-consciousness or social and political perspectives of their own. Attention has largely been confined to needs-assessment reports, which in some instances give general profiles of IDPs' socioeconomic characteristics, such as sex distribution, ethnic composition, marital status, nutrition, social services, and educational attainment.

7. On the importance of understanding feminism in historical and anthropological perspective, see Moore (2001).

8. See "Report on Peace in the Sudan" by Inclusive Security: Women Waging Peace, from the Women Are Making a Difference conference held in November 2004 in Washington, D.C., with support from the Hunt Alternatives Fund.

CHAPTER ONE

1. The total number of IDPs from the civil war in the South exceeds four million; at least two million reside in Greater Khartoum, another million live elsewhere in the North, and a million remain in the South. IDPs from the war in Darfur in the West are not included in these totals; neither are those displaced from or within the East. People have also been displaced within Central Sudan; many remain in "transitional areas," including Abyei, Blue Nile, and South Kordofan. The resettlement program has not yet enabled significant numbers of IDPs to return to the South.

2. Before 1984, drought and famine displaced many people, but, as UN reports demonstrate, government policies deliberately produced displacement rather than responding to drought and famine in ways that promoted stability. See Abu Sin (1991, 1995), De Waal (2005), UNICEF (1998), and UN (2000).

3. The Sudan is one of the most internally diverse countries on the continent. According to ethnolinguists, the Sudan has more than one hundred distinct peoples and between 350 and 400 groups defined by language and dialect. For an Arabic work detailing this diversity, see Adam (1997); books in English include Ali (1995, 2002), Mazrui (1986), and Wuol (2003). Contrary to the racialized images propagated by many American media, they do not sort neatly into an "Arab" North and an "African" South. Northerners and southerners are distinguishable primarily through their language, culture, and religious practices.

4. Malwal (1993) clearly lays out the root causes of the civil war. For the argument that southern resistance to the Islamic state is based on economic as well as religious factors, see Johnson (2003, 79–81).

5. Political elites frame notions of citizenship and national belonging in ways that not all northerners share; outside the capital, local kin-based, ethnolinguistic, and cultural identities often prevail over politicized notions of national identity.

6. On the relative neglect of IDPs compared to refugees, see Bariagaber (1999) and Deng (1993). Cohen and Deng's coauthored book, *The Forsaken People* (1998a), and their coedited volume, *Masses in Flight* (1998b), both include case studies of internal displacement in Sudan.

7. The South is home to a myriad of ethnolinguistic groups, including Niolitics, such as the Dinka, the Nuer, and the Shilluk; Nilo-hamites, such as the Latuka; and Sudanic, such as the Moru, the Jur, and the Azande. While these diverse groups have occasionally come into conflict among themselves (within as well as between ethnolinguistic groups) over power and access to resources, they have been united in the Sudan People's Liberation Movement and Army. Indigenous faith traditions, called Noble Spiritual Beliefs (classified as animist by anthropologists of religion), predominate, but European missionaries have been active in the South since the early twentieth century. Some southerners are active Christians, while many more are formally Christian but practice indigenous traditions as well. On the fluidity and multiplicity of religious affiliations in Sudan, see Hammoudi (1993).

8. When Sadiq al Mahdi and the coalition government led by Mirghani attempted to revive and extend the Addis Ababa Agreement in 1998, they were overthrown by Bashir, affiliated with the National Islamic Front, who was determined to impose Islamic law on the non-Muslim South and achieve a military victory over the SPLA.

9. For an analysis of the CPA as a model agreement protecting human rights in a multicultural society, see HRW (2006). Five years before the CPA, the Pan-African Union convened a conference of Sudanese civil society organizations to envision the future of a postconflict Sudan; see Abdel Salam and De Waal (2001).

10. Raids continued over the next several days. On 25 May, armed police and soldiers with machine guns ringed the camp to keep anyone from leaving while the police searched for weapons and arrested those suspected of resistance. By late June, between one and two hundred IDPs from Soba Aradi had been detained. At least one (Abdallah Daw Al-Bait Ahmed) died in custody, perhaps as a result of torture. In October the UN rapporteur said she had visited 904 detainees from Soba Aradi in various jails and another 77 in prison near Khartoum. The *Khartoum Monitor* was shut down for reporting these events, and the lawyer who defended the Soba Aradi detainees was himself detained. However, the attempt to evict these IDPs was unsuccessful, and in July 2005 a consultative committee ended forcible evictions and set up an orderly process for relocation after notification of residents.

11. The government's policy is to "clear" shantytowns and sell the land to wealthy developers, but it does not work well, because elites rarely want to live or invest in such marginal neighborhoods. Abdou Malqalim Simone (1994) explains that the deliberate neglect of the shantytowns results from the state's focus on developing profitable investments, especially exclusive real estate bought by foreigners. Sometimes small plots are made available for purchase, but most IDPs lack the necessary capital or credit.

12. The concept of the "New Sudan" was first proposed by the Sudanese Communist Party in 1947 to articulate the vision of a democratic, pluralistic, egalitarian society. The term was later adopted by John Garang without acknowledging its radical roots.

13. There was also rioting against northern-identified merchants and government forces in Juba, a town in the South controlled by the Government of Sudan.

14. Posted by AFP on www.sudan.net/news/posted/12185.html.

15. In the backlash after the riots that followed Garang's death, forcible evictions from shantytowns around Khartoum resumed. In August 2005 the security forces evicted the residents of Shikan and moved them to one of the El Fateh camps in the desert.

16. "Khartoum Residents Say They Can Live Together in Peace but Prepare for a Return of Violence," posted on AFP August 23, 2005. See also Khalid Mustafa Madani, "Black Monday: The Political and Economic Dimensions of Sudan's Urban Riots," *Middle East Research & Information Report (MERIP) Online.* Posted August 9, 2005, on http://www.merip.org/mero/mero080905.html (accessed June 20, 2008).

17. This taunt literally means that Arab Sudanese are illegitimate; it refers to their parentage, not just their character.

18. There is ample evidence of non-Arab, non-Muslim influences in Northern Sudanese cultural life and religious practices. In *Africans of Two Worlds* (1972), Francis Deng argues that in some groups, pre-Islamic languages, dance and song styles, and attitudes toward the role of women in the economic and social life of their communities have survived.

19. Tom Stacey, "The Army That Fights on a Diet of Crocodile." *Daily Telegraph Magazine* (London), no. 186, 26 April 1968. SAD G//S/036/1008.

20. Anya-Nya. 1971. "What Numeiri Did." SAD G//S992. April.

21. See Beshir (1965), Abdel Rahim (1969), and Daly (1991). The Nyamwezi are a people in inland Tanzania who successfully, but very briefly, resisted Arab slave-trading incursions from the coast during the nineteenth century—although they did so with guns they bought from Arab traders. Tabora was founded by Arab traders in 1852 and captured by the Germans in 1891. Ujiji, also known as Kavela, was a fishing and trading center on the shores of Lake Tanganyika that was settled by Arab and Swahili-speaking traders around 1850 and used as a slave holding pen where coffles and caravans were assembled. (Stanley and Livingston met there.) Chief Mirambo closed Arab trade routes into the Nyamwezi Kingdom from 1860 until his death in 1884, but the Nyamwezi failed to fend off the Germans. In sum, the Arabs can certainly claim to have been colonizers before the Europeans, but both Arabs and Africans lost to the Germans in short order.

22. The Southern Sudan Association Limited. Press release from the editor of *The Grass Curtain,* August 27, 1970, Massacre of Refugees on July 23, 1970. Report from eye-witnesses and surviving victims now in Aba, Congo Hospital. SAD Doc. no. 642/12/1.

23. "Arab Massacre of Christians in Southern Sudan," *Church Times,* September 4, 1970, issue no. 5, 612. SAD.

24. Anya-Nya. "What Numeiri Did." April 1971. SAD G//S992.

25. Ibid.

26. Ali (2005) and De Waal (2003) offer powerful critiques of the "Civilizational Project."

27. For detailed discussion and linguistic evidence of this process of "creolization," see Qasim (1989) and (2002) (in Arabic.)

28. M. W. Parr, Official Papers, 1971. SAD 827/2/1-130, G//746/671. The Condominium Government was created by an agreement between Britain and Egypt, in force from 1899 to 1955, that left most of the military and civil government of the Sudan to the British. After Egyptian independence in 1922, the status of Sudan remained unsettled until the British replaced Egyptian troops with indirect rule. This strategy of utilizing local elites as rulers and complying with what the British saw as "traditional customs" shaped the governor of Equatoria's deference toward local languages. But here Parr is responding to the charge that British policy exacerbated regional differences within Sudan rather than helping to forge a unified nation. While British policy did protect indigenous cultures of the South, it also concentrated economic development in the North and the Nile Valley.

29. M. W. Parr, Official Papers, 1971. SAD no. 827/2/10.

30. Missionary societies active in Southern Sudan included the Italian Roman Catholic Verona Fathers and the Anglican Missionary Society, the American United Mission, and the New Zealand United Mission, all three of which were Protestant (Beshir 1965, 31).

31. SAD no. 865/13/44.

32. Missionary teaching that emphasized the evils of Muslim slave traders overlooked the collaboration of some southern groups, such as the Shilluk, and of Christian merchants in the slave trade. Christianity became part of the distinct identity of some southern groups.

33. Eisenbruch, a medical anthropologist specializing in mental health in cross-cultural contexts, has worked with war refugees from Southeast Asia, especially Cambodians, while holding academic posts in the United Kingdom, Australia, and Canada, as well as Phnom Penh.

34. The mixture of tenses here expresses trauma; the separation is an event in the past that continues to disrupt her present.

CHAPTER TWO

1. The poet himself experienced a conspicuous form of exile within his own community, not only by virtue of his unmatched genius but also by his captivity; Jammaa lived and died as a mental patient in a Khartoum asylum.

2. Out of respect for the women's privacy, I did not ask specifically about sexual assault but allowed women to tell their stories of flight in their own way. No one spontaneously mentioned having been raped, but they referred to this crime obliquely, or as something they heard about having happened to others. UN reports indicate that rape and abduction of women and girls fleeing conflict are as frequent in Sudan as in other civil wars; see UNHCR (1995). On the search for justice in postconflict situations, see Duggan and Abusharaf (2005).

3. These "tribal" courts in the capital bear a striking resemblance to indirect rule under British colonialism.

4. If the place of an interview is not indicated, it was conducted with someone in Izzbba; other locations are specified.

5. The Fur are from Darfur, located in the West.

6. Ellen Johnson Sirleaf was elected president of Liberia in 2005. Sirleaf's expertise in rural development comes in part through her work as an economist with the World Bank.

7. In the Sudan, government policies that neglected rural development led to famine after drought struck in the early 1980s; social as well as natural causes pushed the first wave of IDPs into Khartoum. See De Waal (2005).

8. Karak, who was a child at the time, conflated the tension between the Nuba, who had long resided in Liri, and the Dinka minority, who had arrived more recently, with the civil war. The SPLA attacked Liri because they thought that the Nuba were rebelling against them; they did not target the Dinka specifically.

9. Although Karak depicts her uncle's move to Juba as involuntary, it is possible that he decided to return as soon as he could.

10. Haj Yousif is a shantytown on the edge of a slum area; IDPs live in close proximity to poor people from Khartoum.

11. A bursary is a scholarship covering school fees, uniforms, and books. Karak appears to have received a small stipend or aid package as well, which may have come from the International Rescue Committee.

12. The International Rescue Committee serves displaced persons in camps and conflict areas. In northern Sudan, the IRC works in partnership with four national NGOs and eighty-some community-based organizations (CBOs). This group is distinguished by its focus on democratic control of aid efforts and its development of grassroots organizations among the displaced. Its Web site highlights FACT, along with the Women's Development Group, as among its major partners.

13. Displaced children are vulnerable to abduction. They might be forced into military service, menial labor, or sexual exploitation, which takes various forms as forced marriage, prostitution, and trafficking in girls. The notion that violent men take blood from vulnerable children is a terrible rumor, but a telling metaphor nonetheless.

14. The Government of Sudan used these Russian-made airplanes to bomb rebel-held areas.

15. Mama Kezia and her family were refugees in Nairobi, Kenya; her older children were probably able to gain refugee status in the United States and the United Kingdom because they were living in Nairobi.

16. For an international definition of cultural rights, see UNESCO (1970).

17. By "customary marriage," the priest means marriage contracted by the husband and wife without the advice and consent of their parents and the participation of the extended family and community. These liaisons may be concealed, since no witnesses are required. Although customary marriages are legal, they can easily be dissolved.

18. Dawa Islamia gives Christian clergymen financial incentives to convert to Islam. Some clerical converts may be simple opportunists, but others are motivated by the desire to serve the people where they are.

19. Some observers also contend that the forms of oppression that occur in conditions of massive violence and under the current regime in the Sudan include enslavement, especially of women; see Bales (1999) and Jok (2001).

20. The movement to impose Islamic law began under Nimeiri with the September Laws of 1983.

21. The *tobe,* a traditional northern alternative to the *hijab,* is a diaphanous fabric that shrouds the body but does not restrict movement.

22. The decoration of the body with henna, called *khidab* in Arabic, is found throughout Arab culture; its use signifies a happy marriage, and women in mourning forgo it.

23. The practice of facial scarification, while ancient in origin, cannot be definitively identified as Arab or indigenous. In Southern Sudan, it has functioned as a way of marking ethnic boundaries. In cities, this custom is dying out, and strangers sometimes find scarred faces off-putting. See Hassan (1989).

CHAPTER THREE

1. Local customs determine which kind of genital surgery girls undergo. In clitoridectomy, or sunna, a part of or the entire clitoris may be removed. A second kind of operation is excision, in which the clitoris and part or all of the *labia minora,* the inner lips of the vagina, are cut away. Clitoridectomy and excision are practiced on the West Coast of Africa, in Chad and the Central African Republic, and in Kenya and Tanzania. The most drastic form of genital surgery is infibulation, called pharaonic circumcision, in which the clitoris and *labia majora,* the outer lips of the vagina, are stitched together to cover the urethral and vaginal entrances. The goal is to make the genital area a blank patch of skin. A new opening is created for the passage of urine and menstrual blood and for sexual intercourse. Infibulation is practiced in Sudan, Mali, Somalia, and parts of Ethiopia and northern Nigeria. For accounts of African women's attempts to end theses practices, see Abusharaf (2006b).

2. Female circumcision is a sensitive subject not only because it is controversial but

also because it involves discussion of intimate bodily matters. The topic was not raised with every woman who was surveyed or interviewed in Izzbba. Some women expressed their personal opinions about female circumcision freely, while others did so indirectly, referring to what they had heard about it from other women.

3. D. Newbold, November 3, 1938, in Evans Administrative Papers. SAD G//S no. 787.

4. From Khartoum, one travels about fifty miles northward, crossing the Blue Nile Bridge, to reach historic Halfiat Elmoolouk and then Douroshab Township. Home to some three thousand residents, it is a semi-urban community comprised of ethnically diverse residents. Yet reciprocity, mutual interdependence, and equanimity mark social life, where kinlike links and a deep sense of collective identity are constructed and fostered. With research funding from Research, Action, and Information Network for the Bodily Integrity of Women (RAINBOW), in 1998 I was able to interview individual women in order to understand how they emerged as the primary brokers in the cultural reproduction of ritualized surgeries.

5. I conducted these interviews in Arabic and have translated the women's narratives myself. The speakers are identified only by their first initials to protect their privacy. For additional narratives and detailed analysis of women's rationales for circumcision, see Abusharaf (2001).

6. This concept of ritual purification is Islamic, but it is based on ancient Jewish law and incorporates a variety of rituals indigenous to non-Muslim groups as well. For example, seclusion of women at menarche and postpartum is common in the South; Zande women use the smoke bath after childbirth.

7. Some women choose to be re-infibulated prior to marriage in order to restore the appearance of virginity and chastity.

8. Some opponents of this set of practices object to terms like circumcision, which imply religious sanction or emphasize ritual purification. They use "female genital mutilation" (FGM) to underscore the violation of women's bodily integrity involved.

9. SNCTP is part of the international effort to end female circumcision. After a gathering of African women's organizations in Dakar, Senegal, in 1984, the Inter-African Committee Against Traditional Practices Affecting the Health of Women and Children was formed; since then affiliates in twenty-three African countries have been working to end the practice. In 1994 the International Conference on Population and Development in Cairo adopted the first international document to specifically address female genital mutilation, calling it a "basic human rights violation" that should be prohibited.

10. Andrew Hammond, "Sudan Peace May Help End Female Circumcision." Reuters, August 21, 2002.

11. On the Arab origins of the smoke bath, see Osman (1999). Smoke-bath rituals also existed among the Azande but were not idiomatically linked to sexuality. Major R. G. C. Brock noted that among some segments of the Azande, use of a smoke bath was reported following childbirth. There was no special ceremony at the birth of a child. After four days the infant's cord was cut. Immediately after this was done, a fire of green leaves was made at the threshold of the house where the child was born, and its mother with the child in her arms sat in the smoke for about half an hour. This was supposed to make the child strong. See R. G. C. Brock, *Sudan Notes & Records* 1, no. 1 (1918): 241–63.

CHAPTER FOUR

1. "Congresswoman Johnson Holds Capitol Hill Briefing with Sudanese Women on the Human Costs of Conflict and War." October 13, 2004, posted on http://www.house .gov/list/press/tx30_johnson/CapHillBriefingSudaneseWomen.html (accessed June 20, 2008).

EPILOGUE

1. Smaller beauty contests had previously been held among refugees in Nairobi and Kampala. An annual "Miss South Sudan" pageant is also held in North America, in locations ranging from Kansas City, Missouri, to Washington, D.C. Competition between contestants from different ethnic groups has been an issue in these pageants. Although contestants do not appear in traditional dress, their ethnic origins are well known, and the objectivity of the judges has sometimes been questioned. In response, the organizers have said that the aim of the pageant is to promote unity and pride among all Southern Sudanese in the Diaspora and to demonstrate the value of working together. In the North American pageant, debates over standards of beauty turn on the degree to which contestants exhibit a "natural" Southern Sudanese appearance, with curvy figures, lustrous dark skin, and luxuriant hair, or use cosmetics and hairstyles that are popular among black Americans who are not African immigrants and that, in the eyes of some Africans, reflect a regrettable adaptation to white-oriented standards of beauty promoted by the mass media. Modest dress is mandatory; contestants do not appear in bathing suits, as they do in other American pageants. To ensure that moral standards are upheld and that parents will permit their daughters to participate, unmarried mothers are barred from competition. See press releases posted on the website of the official mission of the Government of Southern Sudan (GoSS) in Washington, D.C.; the website of the sponsoring organization, http://www.missouthsudan.com; and articles on the 2007 and 2007 pageants: Nick Miroff, "Hopes for a Brighter Image of Sudan: Beauty Pageant Contenders Travel From Across the United States, Canada, and Australia," *Washington Post,* Sunday, June 18, 2006, C04, and "Miss South Sudan Beauty Pageant 2007. Instilling South Sudanese Values Through Beauty Pageant," posted on the website of New Sudan Vision, an independent online newspaper that bridges the Sudan and the Diaspora, www.newsudanvision.com. (All sites accessed August 30, 2008.)

2. The winner of the title "Miss Malaika" (Miss Angel) was Deborah Meer William from Fangak County in Jonglei State, who appeared in Nuer dress. She was praised for her intelligence, her ability to speak English, Arabic, Nuer, and Kiswahili, and her "natural" appearance. The pageant's organizers explicitly forbade contestants to use skin lightening creams. They explained to reporters that skin lightening had been popular among southern women in Juba when the town was occupied by the armed forces of the Government of Sudan; now southerners could celebrate their natural beauty without appealing to others' standards. See James Gadet Dak, "Jonglei State wins Miss Malaika 2007 in South Sudan," *Sudan Tribune,* posted December 4, 2007, and Stephanie McCrummer, "Strutting Toward Another World: Contestants in Southern Sudan's First Beauty Pageant Grew Up Dodging War," *Washington Post Foreign Service,* November 30, 2007, A16. (All sites accessed August 30, 2008.)

3. "Sudan's Bashir charged with Darfur war genocide," July 14, 2008, posted on guardian.co.uk.

4. Woodrow Wilson International Center for Scholars, Africa Program: Building for the Future in Southern Sudan, Forum with Rebecca Garang. February 1, 2006.

5. Sudanese women's priorities and recommendations to the Oslo Donors' Conference in Sudan (April 11–12, 2005) include major actions to grant governance and rule of law, protection from sexual abuse and other forms of gender-based violence, strengthening the ability of women to report on sex crimes, furthering capacity building, formulating a "pro-poor" policy of poverty eradication, involving women ex-combatants in processes of disarmament, ensuring the allocation of resources for livelihood, the security sector, health, and education, and reducing prevalent discriminatory policies and practices. The Oslo recommendations were produced by the Women's Rights and Leadership in Post-Conflict Sudan symposium held under the auspices of the Norwegian government, Norwegian Institute of International Affairs, and UNIFEM.

6. Initially, when the CPA was signed, local, national, and international organizations rushed to speculate about southerners' desire to return. Projections suggested that the overwhelming majority (80 percent) of IDPs expressed a willingness to repatriate. These projections were based on two distinct considerations: (1) the decision to return is inhibited by the lack of security and the slow pace of postconflict development; (2) neither insecurity nor lack of development will halt the desire of southerners to return. Returnees were categorized into South-North IDPs, South-South IDPs, and refugees, and their numbers were estimated at 1,431,000 (UN 2005, 4–6). For a clear view of the conditions necessary for the repatriation of IDPs, see International Red Cross (2005). For more recent assessments of the slow progress of repatriation to Southern Sudan, see the UN News Service, especially the bulletin of March 28, 2008, available at http://www .globalsecurity.org/military/library/news/2008/03/mil.080328-unnews01.htm.

7. Several agreements about Darfur have been signed. The latest talks adjourned because some of the warring factions of the Sudanese Liberation Movement (a group entirely distinct from the SPLM) refrained from participation in the peace effort. However, the Abuja Agreement called for cessation of hostilities, power sharing, wealth sharing, emergency aid and development, and security arrangements, among other measures very similar to the CPA. For details, see the Commission on the situation in the Darfur region, report of the chairperson, African Union Peace and Security Council 28th meeting, April 28, 2005, Addis Ababa.

8. For many, displacement meant suppression of southern languages. For detailed accounts, see the *Linguistic Bibliography of Southern Sudan* compiled by Bernhard Struck and the "List of Vernacular Literatures," both in the official report on the Languages Conference held in Rejaf, Southern Sudan, in April 1928 and chronicled in *Sudan Notes & Records* 2 (1928): 217–26.

9. For detailed analysis of these rituals, see essays on the ethnography of Southern Sudan that have appeared in *Sudan Notes & Records* since 1918.

10. Alfred de Montesquiou, "Sudan Elephants' Return a Sign of Peace," Associated Press, November 2, 2007. Posted on the *Washington Times,* Africa News.

REFERENCES

Abdel Mageid, Ahmed. 2001. "Overview and Assessment of Efforts against Female Genital Mutilation in the Sudan." Khartoum: UNICEF-SCO.

Abdel Rahim, Mudathir. 1969. *Imperialism and Nationalism in the Sudan.* Oxford: Oxford University Press.

Abdel Rahman, Amna. 1995. "Research Proposal for Training Midwives in Displaced Camps in Khartoum." Khartoum: Sudan National Committee on Traditional Practices Affecting the Health of Women and Children (SNCTP).

Abdel Salam, A. H., and Alex De Waal, eds. 2001. *The Phoenix State: Civil Society and the Future of Sudan.* Lawrenceville, NJ: Red Sea Press.

Abul Fadl, Mona. 1998. "Revisiting the Woman Question: An Islamic Perspective." *Chicago Theological Seminary Register* 83: 28–64.

Abu Lughod, Lila. 1990. "Can There Be a Feminist Ethnography?" *Women and Performance* 5 (1): 7–27.

Abusharaf, Rogaia Mustafa. 2001. "Virtuous Cuts: Female Genital Excision in an African Ontology." *Differences* 12 (1): 112–40. Reprinted in *Going Public: Feminism and the Shifting Boundaries of Public and Private,* ed. Joan Wallach Scott and Debra Keates, 201–25. Urbana: University of Illinois Press, 2004.

———. 2002. *Wanderings: Sudanese Migrants and Exiles in North America.* Ithaca, NY: Cornell University Press.

———. 2002–2003. "Local Knowledge and Ritual Reproduction in a Village Society." *Radical Philosophy Review* 5 (1–2): 126–40.

———. 2003. "When War Affects Decisions." *John F. Kennedy School of Government Bulletin* (Spring): 15.

———. 2004a. "Life in Khartoum: Forced Migration and Cultural Change among Displaced Women." Rosemary Rogers Working Papers Series no. 30. Cambridge, MA: MIT Center for International Studies.

———. 2004b. "Narrating Feminism: The Woman Question in the Thinking of an African Radical." *Differences* 5 (2): 152–71.

———. 2004c. "'The Shadow of a Man Is *Not* Better Than the Shadow of a Wall': The Uses of Anthropology in Understanding Women's Human Rights and Struggles in the Sudan." *Oriental Anthropologist* 4(1): 1–19.

———. 2005a. "Smoke Bath: Renegotiating Self and the World in a Sudanese Shantytown." *Anthropology and Humanism* 30 (1): 1–22.

———. 2005b. "Sudanese Women Waging Peace." *Forced Migration Review* 24: 44–46.

———. 2006a. "'We Have Supped So Deep in Horrors': Understanding Colonialist Emotionality and British Responses to Female Circumcision in Northern Sudan." *History and Anthropology* 17 (3): 209–28.

———, ed. 2006b. *Female Circumcision: Multicultural Perspectives.* Philadelphia: University of Pennsylvania Press.

Abu Sin, Mohamed El Hadi. 1991. *Disaster Prevention and Management in Sudan.* Khartoum: Khartoum University Press.

———. 1995. "Environmental Causes and Implications of Population Displacement in Sudan." In *War and Drought in the Sudan: Essays on Population Displacement,* ed. Eltigani E. El Tigani, 11–23. Gainesville: University Press of Florida.

Abu Sin, Mohamed El Hadi, and H. R. J. Davies. 1991. *The Future of Sudan's Capital Region: A Study in Development and Change.* Khartoum: Khartoum University Press.

Adam, Ahmed A. 1997. *Sudan's Tribes* [in Arabic]. Khartoum: Sharikat Mattabi' El-Sudan lil Ommla Al-Mahduda.

Agger, Inger. 1992. *The Blue Room: Trauma and Testimony among Refugee Women.* London: Zed Books.

Ahmed, Abdel Ghaffar Muhammad, and Sharif Harir. 1978. "Sudanese Cultural Diversity in the Context of Afro/Middle Eastern Relations." Sociology and Anthropology, University of Khartoum. February.

Ali, Hayder Ibrahim, ed. 1995. *Cultural Diversity and Nation-Building in Sudan* [in Arabic]. Cairo: Center for Sudanese Studies.

———, ed. 2002. *Ethnic Difference and Democracy in the Sudan* [in Arabic]. Cairo: Center for Sudanese Studies.

———. 2005. *The Failure of the Civilizational Project* [in Arabic]. Cairo: Center for Sudanese Studies.

Alston, Philip, special rapporteur on extrajudicial, summary or arbitrary executions of the United Nations Commission on Human Rights, and Walter Kälin, representative of the United Nations Secretary-General on the human rights of IDPs. 2005. "UN Human Rights Experts Deplore Recent Killings During Relocations of Displaced Persons in Sudanese Capital." Statement posted May 20 on http://www.brookings.edu/speeches/2005.0520sudan_kalin.aspx?rssid=united&20nations (accessed August 20, 2008).

Al-Turabi, Hassan, with Alain Chevalérias. 1997. *Islam, the World's Future: Conversations with Alain Chevalérias* [in French]. Paris: Zattés.

Appiah, Kwame Anthony. 1992. *In My Father's House: Africa in the Philosophy of Culture.* Oxford: Oxford University Press.

Arendt, Hannah. 1958. *The Human Condition.* Chicago: University of Chicago Press.

Bales, Kevin. 1999. *Disposable People: New Slavery in the Global Economy.* Berkeley: University of California Press.

Bariagaber, Assefaw. 1999. "States, International Organizations, and the Refugee: Reflections on the Complexity of Managing the Refugee Crisis in the Horn of Africa." *Journal of Modern African Studies* 37 (4): 591–619.

Bateson, Mary Catherine. 1989. *Composing a Life.* New York: Grove Press.

Battaglia, Debborah. 2000. "Towards an Ethics of the Open Subject: Writing Culture in Good Conscience." In *Anthropological Theory Today,* ed. Henrietta Moore, 114–51. Cambridge: Polity Press.

Baya, Philister. 1999. "War in Southern Sudan: Southern Women's Viewpoint." In *The Tragedy of Reality: Southern Sudanese Women Appeal for Peace,* ed. Magda Elsanousi, 95–107. Khartoum: Sudan Open Learning Organization.

Bell, Beverly. 2001. *Walking on Fire: Haitian Women's Stories of Survival and Resistance.* Ithaca, NY: Cornell University Press.

Bernard, H. Russell. 1973. "Urgent Anthropology: Further Comment on Urgent Problems." *Current Anthropology* 14 (3): 330.

Beshir, Mohammed O. 1965. *The Southern Sudan: Background to Conflict.* New York: Praeger.

Bhabha, Homi K. 1994. *The Location of Culture.* New York: Routledge.

Bourdieu, Pierre. 2004. "Gender and Symbolic Violence." In *Violence in War and Peace,* ed. Nancy Scheper-Hughes and Philippe Bourgeois, 339–42. Malden, MA: Blackwell Publishing.

Bourgeois, Phillippe. 1997. "Confronting the Ethics of Ethnography: Lessons from Fieldwork in Central America." In *Decolonizing Anthropology,* ed. Faye Harrison, 111–27. Washington, DC: American Anthropological Association.

Brookings Institution. 2002. Seminar on Internal Displacement in Southern Sudan. Rumbek, November 25.

Cohen, Roberta, and Francis M. Deng. 1998a. *The Forsaken People: Case Studies of the Internally Displaced.* Washington, DC: Brookings Institution.

———, eds. 1998b. *Masses in Flight: The Global Crisis of Internal Displacement.* Washington, DC: Brookings Institution.

Cooke, Miriam. 1996. *Women and the War Story.* Berkeley: University of California Press.

Daly, Martin. 1991. *Imperial Sudan.* Cambridge: Cambridge University Press.

Das, Veena. 1997. "Language and the Body: Transactions in the Construction of Pain." In *Social Suffering,* by Arthur Kleinman, Veena Das, and Margaret Lock, 67–92. Berkeley: University of California Press.

de Beauvoir, Simone. 1952. *The Second Sex.* New York: Vintage.

Deng, Francis M. 1972. *Africans of Two Worlds: The Dinka in Afro-Arab Sudan.* New Haven. CT: Yale University Press.

———. 1978. *The Dinka of Sudan.* Prospect Heights, IL: Waveland Press.

———. 1993. *Protecting the Dispossessed: A Challenge for the International Community.* Washington, DC: Brookings Institution.

———. 1995. *War of Visions: Conflicts of Identities in the Sudan.* Washington, DC: Brookings Institution.

de Swann, Abram. 2001. *Human Societies.* Cambridge: Policy Press.

De Waal, Alex, ed. 2003. *Islamism and Its Enemies in the Horn of Africa.* Bloomington: Indiana University Press.

———. 2005. *Famine That Kills.* Rev. ed. Oxford: Oxford University Press.

di Leonardo, Micaela, ed. 1991. *Gender at the Crossroads of Knowledge: Feminist Anthropology in the Postmodern Era.* Berkeley: University of California Press.

Douglas, Mary. 1966. *Purity and Danger: An Analysis of the Concepts of Pollution and Taboo.* New York: Praeger.

Dudu, Christina. 1999. "Southern Sudanese Displaced Women: Losses and Gains." In *The Tragedy of Reality: Southern Sudanese Women Appeal for Peace,* ed. Magda Elsanousi, 48–58. Khartoum: Sudan Open Learning Organization.

Duggan, Colleen, and Adila Mustafa Abusharaf. 2005. "Reparation of Sexual Violence in Democratic Transitions: The Search for Gender Justice." In *The Handbook of Reparations,* ed. Pablo De Greiff, 623–50. Oxford: Oxford University Press.

Eastmond, Marita. 1993. "Reconstructing Life: Chilean Women and the Dilemmas of Exile." In *Migrant Women: Crossing Boundaries and Changing Identities,* ed. Gina Bujis, 33–55. Oxford: Berg.

Eisenbruch, Maurice. 1991. "From Post-Traumatic Stress Disorder to Cultural Bereavement: Diagnosis of Southeast Asian Refugees." *Social Sciences & Medicine* 3: 673–80.

El-Bashir, Hamid. 1994. "Women and the Agony of Culture." Khartoum: Report on the Sudanese National Committee on Traditional Practices Affecting the Health of Women and Children (SNCTP).

El-Hassan, Yahya. 2000. "Sudanese Women as War Victims." *Pan African News Agency (PANA).* March 6.

El-Sherif, Yousif. 2004. *Sudan and the People of Sudan: Secrets of Politics, Mysteries of Society* [in Arabic]. Cairo: Dar El-Shruq Press.

Ember, Carol R., and Melvin Ember. 1973. *Anthropology.* Englewood Cliffs, NJ: Prentice-Hall.

———. 2004. *Encyclopedia of Medical Anthropology.* New York: Kluwer Academic/Plenum Publishers.

Erchak, Gerald M. 1992. *The Anthropology of Self and Behavior.* New Brunswick, NJ: Rutgers University Press.

Erikson, Kai. 1976. *Everything in Its Path: Destruction of Community in the Buffalo Creek Flood.* New York: Simon & Schuster.

Evans-Pritchard, Edward E. 1940. *The Nuer.* Oxford: Clarendon Press.

———. 1974. *Man and Woman among the Azande.* New York: Free Press.

Faris, James. 1989. *Southeast Nuba Social Relations.* Aachen, Germany: Alano Verl Monographica, 7.

Fentress, James, and Chris Wickham. 1992. *Social Memory.* Oxford: Blackwell Publishing.

Fitzgerald, Mary Anne. 2002. *Throwing the Stick Forward: The Impact of War on Southern Sudanese Women.* Nairobi, Kenya: UNIFEM Publications.

Fry, Douglas. 2005. *The Human Potential for Peace: An Anthropological Challenge to Assumptions about War and Violence.* Oxford: Oxford University Press.

Geertz, Clifford. 1995. *After the Fact.* Cambridge, MA: Harvard University Press.

Gilbert, Alan, and Joseph Gugler. 1984. *Cities, Poverty, and Development: Urbanization in the Third World.* Oxford: Oxford University Press.

Gingerich, Tara, and Jennifer Leaning. 2004. "The Use of Rape as a Weapon of War in Darfur, Sudan." October. U.S. Agency for International Development. Prepared under the auspices of the Harvard School of Public Health and the Francois-Xavier Bagnoud Center for Health and Human Rights, available at http://physiciansforhumanrights.org/library/report-2004-oct-darfurrape.html (accessed August 18, 2008).

Giroux, Henry A. 1992. *Border Crossings: Cultural Workers and the Politics of Education.* London: Routledge.

Gluckman, Max. 1997. "Ritual." In *Magic, Witchcraft, and Religion,* ed. Arthur C. Lehmann and James E. Myers, 40–45. Mountain View, CA: Mayfield Press.

Goldstein, Donna M. 2003. *Laughter Out of Place: Race, Class, Violence, and Sexuality in a Rio Shantytown*. Berkeley: University of California Press.

Gould, Carol. 1981. *Marx's Social Ontology*. Cambridge, MA: MIT Press.

Graham, Mark, and Shahram Khosravi. 1997. "Home Where You Make It: Repatriation and Diaspora Culture among Iranians in Sweden." *Journal of Refugee Studies* 10: 115–33.

Greenhouse, Carol J., Elizabeth Mertz, and Kay B. Warren, eds. 2002. *Ethnography in Unstable Places: Everyday Lives in Contexts of Dramatic Political Change*. Durham, NC: Duke University Press.

Gutkind, Peter C. W. 1974. *Urban Anthropology: Perspectives on "Third World" Urbanization and Urbanism*. New York: Barnes and Noble.

Habib, A. 1995. "Effects of Displacement on Southern Women's Health and Food Habits." *Ahfad Journal* 12 (2): 30–52.

Hackett, Beatrice Nied. 1996. *Pray God and Keep Walking: Stories of Women Refugees*. London: McFarland.

Halperin, David. 1995. *Saint Foucault: Towards a Gay Hagiography*. New York: Oxford University Press.

Hammoudi, Abdella. 1993. *The Victim and Its Masks: An Essay on Sacrifice and Masquerade in the Maghreb*. Chicago: University of Chicago Press.

Harrison, Faye. 1997. "Ethnography as Politics." In *Decolonizing Anthropology*, ed. Faye Harrison, 88–110. Washington, DC: American Anthropological Association.

Harvest for Sudan: A Women's Peace Initiative. 2000. Nairobi: African Women in Crisis Umbrella Program and the Carter Center.

Hassan, Yousif Fadul. 1989. *Facial Scarification: Its Origins and Functions in Riverine Sudan* [in Arabic]. Khartoum: Khartoum University Press.

Hobsbawm, Eric, and Terence Ranger, eds. 1992. *The Invention of Tradition*. Cambridge: Cambridge University Press.

Human Rights Watch (HRW). 2003. "The Wunlit Nuer-Dinka Reconciliation Process, 1999." Posted in November on www.hrw.org/reports/2003/sudan1103/13.htm (accessed June 20, 2008).

———. 2006. "The CPA and Security in Southern Sudan." Posted in March on www .hrw.org/backgrounder/africa/sudan0306/7.htm (accessed June 20, 2008).

Hunt, Swanee. 2004. *This Was Not Our War: Bosnian Women Reclaiming the Peace*. Durham, NC: Duke University Press.

Hutchinson, Sharon. 1996. *Nuer Dilemmas: Coping with Money, War, and the State*. Berkeley: University of California Press.

Ignatieff, Michael. 1984. *The Needs of Strangers*. New York: Picador U.S.A.

———. 1994. *Blood and Belonging*. New York: Farrar Straus & Giroux.

Iliffe, John. 1987. *The African Poor: A History*. New York: Cambridge University Press.

Inclusive Security: Women Waging Peace. 2004. "Report on Peace in the Sudan." Women Are Making a Difference conference. Washington, DC: Hunt Alternatives Fund.

Indra, Doreen, ed. 1998. *Engendering Forced Migration*. New York: Berghahn.

International Red Cross. 2005. "Freedom from Fear: Promoting Human Security for the Return and Reintegration of Displaced Persons in Sudan." Report sponsored by UNICEF, UNHCR, and Harvard School of Public Health.

Jambo, Suzanne Samson. 2001. *Overcoming Gender Conflict and Bias: The Case of New Sudan Women and Girls.* Nairobi, Kenya: New Sudan Women Federation and the Netherlands Organization for International Development.

James, Wendy. 1972. "The Politics of Rain Control among the Uduk." In *Essays in Sudan Ethnography,* ed. Ian Cunnison and Wendy James, 31–58. London: C. Hurst.

Johnson, Douglas. 2003. *The Root Causes of Sudan's Civil Wars.* Oxford: James Currey.

Jok, Jok Madut. 2001. *War and Slavery in Sudan.* Philadelphia: University of Pennsylvania Press.

Jones, Bruce D., and Charles Cater. 2001. "From Chaos to Coherence? Toward a Regime for Protecting Civilians in War." In *Civilians in War,* ed. Simon Chesterman, 237–63. Boulder, CO: Lynn Reinner.

Joseph, Priscilla. 2001. "Effects of War on Women and Children." Khartoum: Sudanese Women Peace Forum.

Kenyon, Susan. 2004. *Five Women of Sennar: Culture and Change in Central Sudan.* Prospect Heights, IL: Waveland Press.

Khalid, Mansour. 2000. *Southern Sudan in the Arab Imaginary.* London: Dar El Turath.

———. 2003. *War and Peace in Sudan: The Tale of Two Countries.* London: Kegan Paul.

Khamis, Joice Michael. 2002. "Women and Peace Building in Sudan." Senior thesis, School of Rural Extension, Education and Development, Ahfad University for Women, Omdurman, Sudan.

Klass, Morton. 1991. *Singing with Sai Baba: The Politics of Revitalization in Trinidad.* Prospect Heights, IL: Waveland Press.

Kleinman, Arthur, Veena Das, and Margaret Lock. 1997. *Social Suffering.* Berkeley: University of California Press.

Korn, David. 1999. *Exodus Within Borders: An Introduction to the Crisis of Internal Displacement.* Washington, DC: Brookings Institution Press.

Kukathas, Chandran. 1992a. "Are There Any Cultural Rights?" *Political Theory* 20 (1): 105–39.

———. 1992b. "Cultural Rights Again: A Rejoinder to Kymlicka." *Political Theory* 20 (4): 674–80.

———. 1998. "Liberalism and Multiculturalism: The Politics of Indifference." *Political Theory* 25 (5): 686–99.

Lomnitz, Larissa Adler. 1977. *Networks and Marginality: Life in a Mexican Shantytown.* Trans. Cinna Lomnitz. New York: Academic Press.

Loveless, Jeremy. 1999. *Displaced Populations in Khartoum: A Study of Social and Economic Conditions.* Report for Save the Children Denmark. Ohain, Belgium: Channel Research.

MacKinnon, Catharine. 1998. "Rape, Genocide, and Women's Human Rights." In *Violence against Women: Philosophical Perspectives,* ed. Stanley G. French, Wanda Teays, and Laura M. Purdy, 43–56. Ithaca, NY: Cornell University Press.

Malwal, B. 1993. "Sources of Conflict in the Sudan." Paper presented at the United States Institute of Peace, Washington, DC.

Matory, J. Lorand. 2005. *Black Atlantic Religion: Tradition, Transnationalism, and Matriarchy in the Afro-Brazilian Candomblé.* Princeton, NJ: Princeton University Press.

Mazrui, Ali. 1968. "The Multiple Marginality of the Sudan." In *Sudan in Africa,* ed. Yusef Fadi Hassan, 240–55. Khartoum: Khartoum University Press.

————. 1986. *The Africans: A Triple Heritage*. Boston: Little, Brown.

Minow, Martha. 1998. *Between Vengeance and Forgiveness: Facing History after Genocide and Mass Violence*. Boston: Beacon Press.

Mohamed, Suleiman Mohamed. 2000. *The Sudan: Wars over Resources and Identity* [in Arabic]. Cambridge: Cambridge Academic Press.

Moore, Henrietta, ed. 2001. *Anthropological Theory Today*. Cambridge: Polity Press.

Morawska, Eva. 2000. "Intended and Unintended Consequences of Forced Migrations: A Neglected Aspect of East Europe's Twentieth Century History." *International Migration Review* 34 (4): 1049–87.

Morris, Tim. 2007. "Slow Return of Displaced Southern Sudanese." *Forced Migration Review* 28 (July): 38–39.

Morsey, Soheir A. 1993. *Gender, Sickness, and Healing in Rural Egypt: Ethnography in Historical Context*. Boulder, CO: Westview Press.

Nordstrom, Carolyn. 1997. *A Different Kind of War Story*. Philadelphia: University of Pennsylvania Press.

Ong, Aihwa. 1995. "Women Out of China: Traveling Tales and Traveling Theories in Postcolonial Feminism." In *Women Writing Culture,* ed. Ruth Behar and Deborah A. Gordon, 350–72. Berkeley: University of California Press.

Osman, Ibrahim El-Qurashi. 1999. *Sudanese Customs of Arab Origins* [in Arabic]. Riyadh, Saudi Arabia: King Fahad National Library.

Parkins, D. J. 1999. "Mementoes as Transnational Objects in Human Displacement." *Journal of Material Culture* 4, no. 3 (November): 303–20.

Peteet, Julie. 2005. *Landscapes of Hope and Despair: Palestinian Refugee Camps*. Philadelphia: University of Pennsylvania Press.

Preston, Peter W. 1997. *Political/Cultural Identity: Citizens and Nations in a Global Era*. London: Sage Publications.

Qasim, Oane El-Sherif. 1989. *Arabism and Islam in Sudan* [in Arabic]. Beirut, Lebanon: Dar Elgeel Press.

————. 2002. *Dictionary of Colloquial Arabic* [in Arabic]. Khartoum: El-Dar El-Sudania Lil Kutub.

Rappaport, Nigel, and Joanna Overing. 2000. *Social and Cultural Anthropology: The Key Concepts*. London: Routledge.

Rawls, John. 1971. *A Theory of Justice*. Cambridge, MA: Harvard University Press.

Resnik, Julia. 2003. "Sites of Memory of the Holocaust: Shaping National Memory in the Education System in Israel." *Nations & Nationalism* 9 (2): 297–319.

Riak, Pauline. 1995. *Harvest for Sudan: A Women's Peace Initiative*. Draft report of proceedings. Nairobi, Kenya: United Nations Development Fund for Women, African Women in Crisis Umbrella Program, and Global 2000 of the Carter Center.

Richards, Alexandra. 2000. "Women and the Culture of Peace." Speech given on January 20, posted on www.womenlawyers.org.au (accessed September 7, 2006).

Rift Valley Institute. 2006. Sudan Field Course Bulletin. Nairobi, Kenya: RVI.

Ruiz, Hiram A. 1998. "The Sudan: Cradle of Displacement." In *The Forsaken People,* ed. Roberta Cohen and Francis M. Deng, 139–74. Washington, DC: Brookings Institution.

Ryle, John. 2005. "To Conserve You Must Transform." Paper presented at the Modern Government and Traditional Structures in Southern Sudan meeting. Neuchâtel, Switzerland, April 14–16.

Sandbrook, Richard. 1982. *The Politics of Basic Needs: Urban Aspects of Assaulting Poverty in Africa*. Toronto: University of Toronto Press.

Schneider, Cathy Lisa. 1995. *Shantytown Protest in Pinochet's Chile*. Philadelphia: Temple University Press.

Sen, Amartya. 1999. *Development as Freedom*. New York: Knopf.

Sered, Susan. 2000. *What Makes Women Sick? Maternity, Modesty, and Militarism in Israeli Society*. Hanover, NH: University Press of New England.

Simone, Abdou Malqalim. 1994. *In Whose Image? Political Islam and Urban Practices in Sudan*. Chicago: University of Chicago Press.

Sirleaf, Ellen Johnson. 1993. "From Disaster to Development." In *A Framework for Survival*, ed. Kevin M. Cahill, 299–307. New York: Council on Foreign Relations and Basic Books.

Skramstad, Heidi. 1990. "The Fluid Meanings of Female Circumcision in the Multiethnic Context in Gambia: Distribution and Linkages to Sexuality." Working Paper. Bergen, Norway: Michelsen Institute.

Smart, Barry. 1988. *Michel Foucault*. London: Routledge.

Slymovics, Susan. 1998. *The Object of Memory: Arab and Jew Narrate the Palestinian Village*. Philadelphia: University of Pennsylvania Press.

Strathern, Marilyn. 1988. *The Gender of the Gift*. Berkeley: University of California Press.

Sudan Almanac. 1961. Khartoum: Government of Sudan.

Sudan Council of Churches, Unit of Advocacy and Communication. 1996. "Effects of Public Order Law on the Poor and Displaced in Greater Khartoum." Draft report. Khartoum.

Sudan Demographic and Health Survey (SDHS), Sudan Public Health Service. 1995. Baltimore, MD: Institute for Resource Development and Macro International.

Sudan Organization Against Torture (SOAT). 2005. "Human Rights Alert and Further Update: Soba Aradi." London: SOAT, July 11.

Sutherland, Ann. 1976. *The Gypsies: The Hidden Americans*. Long Grove, IL: Waveland Press.

Tostensen, Arne, Inge Tvedten, and Mariken Vaa, eds. 2001. *Associational Life in African Cities: Popular Responses to the Urban Crisis*. Stockholm: Nordiska Afrikainstitutet.

UNESCO. 1970. *Cultural Rights as Human Rights*. Paris: UNESCO.

United Nations. 2000. Humanitarian Operations Report. Khartoum.

United Nations High Commissioner for Refugees (UNHCR). 1995. *Sexual Violence against Women: Guidelines for Prevention and Response*. Geneva: UNHCR.

——— 2005. South Sudan Operation. Posted December 17, 2005, on http://www.unhcr.org/southsudan.html (accessed August 18, 2008).

United Nations Commission on Human Rights (UNHRC). 1998a. Resolution 1998/50. April 17.

———. 1998b. "Guiding Principles on Internal Displacement." UN Doc. E/CN./4/1998/53/Add.2. April 17.

UNICEF. 1995. "Situational Analysis of Children and Women in the Sudan." Working draft. Khartoum: UNICEF.

———. 1998. "Operation Lifeline Sudan, Northern Sector." Khartoum: UNICEF.

———. 2001. *Situation of Women and Children in the Sudan*. Khartoum: UNICEF.

U.S. Committee for Refugees and Immigrants. 1999. "Follow the Women and the Cows: Personal Stories of Sudan's Uprooted People." Washington, DC.

U.S. Committee for Refugees and Immigrants. 2002. "World Refugee Survey." Washington, DC.

Visweswaran, Kamala. 1997. "Histories of Feminist Ethnography." *Annual Review of Anthropology* 26: 591–621.

Waller, Marguerite, and Jennifer Rycenga. 2001. *Frontline Feminisms: Women, War, and Resistance.* New York: Routledge.

Wani, Mary Hillary. 1999. "Escaping War and Famine in the South." In *The Tragedy of Reality: Southern Sudanese Women Appeal for Peace,* ed. Magda Elsanousi, 31–41. Khartoum: Sudan Open Learning Organization.

———. 2001. "Women's Agenda for Peace." Paper presented at the Sudanese Women's Peace Forum. Grand Villa, Khartoum, October 29.

West, Cornel. 1993. "Theory, Pragmatisms, and Politics." In West, *Keeping faith: Philosophy and Race in America,* 89–106. New York: Routledge.

Williams, Brackette F. 1991. *Stains on My Name, War in My Veins: Guyana and the Politics of Cultural Struggle.* Durham, NC: Duke University Press.

Willis, Justin. 2004. "The Cradle and the Core." Posted at http://www.dur.ac.uk/justin .willis/fadlhasan.htm (accessed June 20, 2008).

Women Action Group (WAG). 1997. Workshop: "The Differences Which Unite Us." February-March. Information packet; conference proceedings.

Wood, Graham, and Jake Phelan. 2006. "Uncertain Return to Southern Sudan." *Forced Migration Review* 25: 49–50.

Wuol Macek, John. 2002. "Rights and Role of Women in Traditional Society in Southern Sudan." Published by the author.

———. 2003. "The Nilotic People of Southern Sudan." Published by the author.

INDEX